Construction
of Architecture

Construction of Architecture:

From Design to Built

Ralph W. Liebing, RA, CSI, CPCA, CBO

John Wiley & Sons, Inc.

Library of Congress Cataloging-in-Publication Data:

Liebing, Ralph W., 1935-
Construction of architecture : from design to built / Ralph W. Liebing.
    p. cm.
Includes bibliographical references and index.
ISBN 978-0-471-78355-8 (cloth)
1. Building. 2. Construction contracts. 3. Architectural contracts. I. Title.
TH146.L54 2007
690—dc22

                                        2007028892

Printed in the United States of America

10 9 8 7 6 5 4 3 2 1

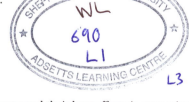

To my wife, Arlene, my daughter, Alissa, and my
son-in-law, Bob—for their continual love,
understanding, tolerance, and encouragement.

To my students past and present, for their interest
in hearing and reading what I have to share.

To new readers, offering what I hope is a
unique opportunity for understanding projects
from a new perspective.

To my dear buddy and friend, Emerson, a French Bulldog
who always manages to calm me down and keep me
humble—and loves me even at my worst.

CONTENTS

Preface   ix

Acknowledgments   xi

Prologue   xiii

1. Introduction and Context _____ 1

2. Project Inception and Determination _____ 29

3. Resolution and Design _____ 65

4. Selection, Incorporation, and Documentation __ 83

5. The Documents and Code Compliance _____ 123

6. Bidding, Award, and Contract _____ 141

7. Constructing, Erecting, and Installing _____ 171

8. Refinement and Enhancement _____ 215

9. Completion and Occupancy _____ 225

10. Post Occupancy _____ 229

Appendix: Trade Associations   237

Glossary   251

Index   289

PREFACE

Most people, including many architectural, engineering and construction management students, tend to think of architecture as something that somehow "merely appears." They do not yet have a feel for or understanding of the long process involved in the design and construction of an architectural project, nor the progression of events and work necessary.

Whether in an old neighborhood being refurbished, or in a fresh new, undeveloped site, the "piece of architecture" appears! This is understandable for the layperson but is more of a shortcoming for students. While perhaps steeped in theory and design principles in their academic process, students also need to understand the process of taking or converting a very fine design concept from a paper exercise to a finished, full-size, occupiable and usable building.

The process of delivering the finished project is simply called "construction." Those attuned wholly to the aesthetics and theory of architecture may well disdain this process, and look down upon it with less than understanding and respect. But if the truth be known, no architecture would exist without construction!

The basic issue is that no matter what one's position in the professions or in the project work, there is a fundamental and unavoidable requirement to understand the whole of the process of delivering a project. One can be totally dedicated to one phase of the project, but understanding of all phases is imperative to successful execution of work in that one phase. But understanding and appreciating the totality of a project is virtually impossible to do, looking from just the one end, the inception.

Construction and architectural projects are *not* a series of isolated events, each executed by separate groups of individuals, doing as they see fit. There is a need for coordination, cooperation, collectivism, and a drive to produce the project in the best fashion possible. Design professionals play a significant role in all this, as they produce the directions, instructions, graphics, and expertise addressing what is to be built, why, and how.

This is not to divert attention from the contractors, constructors, managers, trade workers, et cetera, who function in construction, but rather to point out that design is as much a tutorial on how the project is to be built, as it is a depiction of what is to be built. The overall design scheme (concept) is a function of, and a product of the designer—be they architect or engineer. Here the effort is to provide the composite of elements that best will contain, convert, provide for, and establish the many tangles and requirements of the owner's program: that specific document wherein the owner expresses exactly what is desired of the finished project. All owners want fully functional projects—lots of space, current problems resolved, costs within a reasonable budget, et cetera. And few, if any, want an ugly, errant, out-of-place piece of architecture.

So there is an essential and directed effort to first of all design the project, receive owner approval, and then to faithfully, assiduously, and finitely construct the project, in full size, as depicted at some reduced scale on a drawing. Simple? Yes, if you understand that construction is needed, and how that process progresses. Hence, the thrust of this book is to overview the whole sequence of the project.

This effort is activity oriented, depicting the chronological progression of work on the project, from inception to completion. It is not an in-depth dissertation on materials, systems, types of construction, and so forth. Such discussion would involve volumes of explanation due to the number of variations and combinations that are used. An appendix to this book lists trade associations that provide resources and information for various systems and materials. These associations have innumerable members who individually produce the massive array of products available for construction.

There are thousands of resources for various portions of construction of architecture, from design principles and theory to individual attributes of materials, systems, and equipment. The assortment chosen for each project is unique, to meet the requirements and desired results. What is often overlooked is the step-by-step progression of activities and tasks required to gather pertinent information, create and develop an appropriate design concept, develop accurate and wide-ranging communication documents (drawings and specifications), and install the pieces of construction.

No matter the pieces, there needs to be a fundamental understanding of the project process and progression from inception to occupancy.

Ralph W. Liebing
Cincinnati, Ohio

ACKNOWLEDGMENTS

My deep and sincere gratitude to J. Robert ("Bob") Welling for his tremendous contribution of the photographs of construction details to this effort. As both an architect in his own right and my son-in-law, his patience and skill are much appreciated, and hopefully will assist the readers in their appreciation of the points illustrated.

Thanks, too, to Jupiter Images for their assistance in providing photos of wide-ranging and widely dispersed projects completed over a number of years. This historical information and these illustrations serve to also highlight the breadth and uniqueness of projects all well classified as "architecture," but all having been through the progression of construction.

Thanks also to generalcontractor.com and constructionphotographs.com ("Photo courtesy of constructionphotographs.com") for their photos showing the various construction tasks and work. These are a great depiction of the actual construction work and help readers better see and understand the work.

Last, but certainly not least, I am grateful for the risk Paul Drougas of John Wiley & Sons took in giving me a contract for this work, and for his confidence in my approach to the topic and my ability to provide readers with correct and meaningful information. And I am grateful for his tremendous patience and that of Lauren LaFrance and Donna Conte, all of whom put up with my quirks and misconceptions. They made this book from the roughness of my manuscript—no small task.

PROLOGUE

The following is so poignant to this effort that it must be included as the focus for the book. It is a message to all readers, no matter their profession, perspective, philosophy, or position.

This is from one of a series of papers written by William W. Caudill, FAIA—architect, educator, philosopher, and visionary—whose wonderful insight still pervades the profession.

This I Believe
Caudill-Rowlett-Scott Team: Procedures
21 April 1970 WWC

Each has its time.

When I was a young practitioner, drawings were precious to us. We were taught to love drawings—beautiful working drawings, sexy renderings, and impressive full-size details—more than buildings.

Today, the young practitioners are taught to love methods and procedures—system approach, computerized programming, and design methodology—more than buildings.

In both cases, buildings take second place, then and now. The buildings do not get the love and tender care which they should get to possess architecture so necessary for satisfying human needs.

Ever so often, we need to remind ourselves—young and old practitioners—that both drawings and methods are simply necessary evils to obtain functional, beautiful buildings.

To get "from here to there," one must go through certain periods and places. The important thing is not these periods and places but the THERE.

When there is no THERE, then our mission has failed regardless of how we have traveled or where we have been.

The THERE is architecture—that aura that surrounds fine buildings and their spaces.

William W. Caudill, FAIA

Mr. Caudill addresses a very important issue, and one that needs to be included here. While his remarks are aimed at design professionals, the unaddressed void he includes is the period of construction. Certainly, his "THERE" is the common point and goal of both design and construction professionals. However, the commonality of goal does involve different perspectives and processes.

Mr. Caudill, in addressing design professionals, sets the project itself as the THERE that comes only by propriety in all processes leading up to the start of construction. The caring and love that saturates the design and documentation needs to be carried forth so the final THERE is indicative of the initial solution.

Mr. Caudill highlights exactly and distinctly the relationship of design personnel to construction personnel—and of design to construction to architecture. Construction is the "fit" between initial solution and final THERE! The projects produced vary widely in scope, complexity, form, shape, size, coloration, function, construction methodology, detail, and material. But each design scheme or concept is specific to the client and the purpose of the project. This accounts for the precision, enforcement, caring, and demands that design professionals place on constructors, to ensure faithful reproduction of the design concept in the final THERE!

Oddly enough, one can perceive that the commonality is really separated as it functions. Design professionals are concerned about the basic design form: the interplay of forms, planes, and shapes: the impact and image of the project and the functional inner working of the project; the style of architecture used as its motif; and the overall impression that the project should project.

Constructors are concerned about how specific portions of the work will or must be executed. They take a more pragmatic approach. Their skilled, hands-on work is seated in the concept of doing one's best in the area of the project work, similar to creating a single piece of a jigsaw puzzle (but one crucial to completing the puzzle properly).

For example, the designer sees "brick wall" for some element of the project. The constructor sees brick wall in the sense of what type of brick; how many; type of wall required; technique required for laying the brick; reinforcing and tie to structure; scaffolding and jump-up boards; logistics of getting material to the site and to the individual workstations; whether or not special effort to provide a fire rating is required; and so forth.

The design professional will make a more sweeping assessment and will view the finished wall in the sense of, "Does it provide the image and contribute to the design concept as I perceived it?" "Does it do what I wanted done?" "Is the coloration what I intended?" "Is the massing as I anticipated?" with little thought to how it was constructed.

It should be noted that individuals in the construction industry are overtaken, moved, and filled with pride by their participation in, and contribution to, the sheer impact and excellence of the project they work on, and come to understand and appreciate more acutely their contribution to a masterful example of building.

So it is obvious that both parties seek a good final solution but for much different reasons. That is, theirs is a commonality reached via different routes. This is the most distinctive interface between design, construction, and architecture. It shows the initial concept, its construction, and the resulting architecture produced by their mutual but different efforts.

This relationship and context is the preeminent and most crucial element at play in the design and production of architecture. Construction may be considered, without stigma, to be the vehicle that makes architecture become real, usable, occupiable, and influential.

It is impossible to overstate the importance of this linkage/relationship/progression being fully, clearly, and completely understood by *all parties* to every project.

CHAPTER

1

INTRODUCTION AND CONTEXT

THE BASIC RELATIONSHIP

The fundamental relationship of construction to architecture is that construction uses its adaptive, flexible, and knowledgeable management and its highly skilled trade workers to faithfully construct the design professional's design concept—true to the owner's program, creative and aesthetically pleasing in nature, properly functioning, based on sound design and engineering principles—into well-crafted architecture, nothing deficient, nothing lacking.

Construction has a direct, unique relationship to architecture. But it takes some initial exploration to uncover and understand the essence of that relationship and its inner working within every project sequence. It is not something that appears and disappears; it is not specific to some projects and not others; it is rather a constant relationship that has various complexions, elements, and proportions.

DEFINITIONS

Construction can be defined in a straightforward, composite but easily understood manner, for example:

> *Construction*: The act or process of building or erecting something, especially a large structure such as a house, school, store, office building, road, or bridge; the process of developing a work project

according to a systematic plan and by a definite program of carefully scheduled tasks, forming, ordering, and uniting materials by incremental means into a composite whole.

To this description of construction, we can juxtapose the following definition of the other aspect, architecture (from Cyril M. Harris's *Dictionary of Architecture and Construction*):

Architecture: "The art and science of designing and building structures, or large groups of structures, in keeping with aesthetic and functional criteria."

It is quite striking that architecture is defined in terms of "building" and "science" (which includes engineering and technology). This shows the inherent dependency on construction as an integral part of producing architecture. Architecture needs construction, it appears, but not vice versa. But still there is a need to establish more about architecture overall, and in that aspect that is not construction.

Even in its definition, architecture is a rather murky and complex concept, difficult to grasp, and with several aspects that touch many things. Reality says that architecture is simply that which has been built. Within that are innumerable classifications and types of projects, and differing styles of architecture. Architecture is not a cohesive concept, nor a fixed body of work.

There are, of course, "paper architecture," rhetorical architecture, virtual architecture, and utilitarian architecture. These all have their particular use and place, but they should not be perceived to be the reality of architecture to any extent.

"Paper architecture" is the flat depiction of a project, perhaps in three-dimensional perspective, with a wealth of accoutrements and enhancements. But in the end there is a limit to the emotion of the piece, falling far short of experiencing the project in real time and hands-on. It is a dream, if you will, as flat as Queen Anne architecture (a festooned front façade on a mundane building hidden from view and behind it), and only as real as stage and movie background sets producing illusions but not reality.

"Rhetorical architecture" involves a belabored explanation of how the piece was conceived and/or built. It is a verbal explanation of the project delving into the intangibles, principles, and other hidden attributes that may have influenced the design and appearance but do not impact use and occupancy in any obvious ways.

"Virtual architecture" is that which resides within a computer and its wondrous software and modeling. Ever-evolving at a very rapid pace, this "architecture" is really design images in electronic form, manipulated through use of the software, to allow one's eye to travel within, walk through, and experience the sense of the spaces and the surrounding structure. It is a great design tool that allows for change without a change order or eraser, and permits volumes of mutations to the design concept before settling on the final selection.

"Utilitarian architecture" is an array of projects, primarily engineering in nature and function, often rather austere, but nonetheless a form of architecture. (For an example of utilitarian architecture, see Figure 1-1.) Included here are industrial plants and factories, warehouses, communications centers, government buildings, boiler houses, wastewater treatment facilities, aircraft hangers, depots, stations, dams, navigational locks, and other often large and complex projects. In many instances, there have been very fine design statements made in these projects: very sleek, glassy industrial plants, boiler houses with picture windows to show off the multicolored (and squeaky-clean) equipment, et cetera. Perhaps stigmatized by the application of the terms "industrial" or "utilitarian," these projects nonetheless represent a form of architecture not to be discounted.

ELEMENTS OF ARCHITECTURE

Architecture involves a great many things, chief among which are the artistic and aesthetic phases of building construction. Architecture is concerned with the principles of design betterment (balance, scale,

Figure 1-1 Example of utilitarian architecture: projects directed more toward their function than toward design and construction making an architectural impact or statement. *Jeff Kramer.*

massing, proportion, rhythm, and unity). From the first preliminary idea to the approved design concept, the architect must be aware that careful and complete documentation of the project is necessary to enable its construction and to bring it to completion. The architect must be able to convert and express the intangible attributes of the design concept in a real, physical manner—that is, the project must be built with specific materials and techniques of construction and installation to accurately bring forth the design concept. What originates as a concept, through a process of documentation and construction, evolves and expands to become a full-size, real "thing."

The finished project can be a joy to the eye, but that wonderment of a building is composed of a tremendous amount of detail, parts, systems, and subsystems, all linked within the construction effort. Each element must be thought through to support and maintain the design concept and in no way detract from it. Once the design concept is created, it lives as an abstract, an intangible, a delicate balance of taste and function. The parts of this living concept are real and tangible.

CONTRACTOR'S POSITION

A compelling issue, not often addressed, is that of providing the contractor with some sense of understanding and buy-in into the design concept. Even the general contractor, who is positioned to have the best and most complete overview of the project, may lack insight into the creation and development of the design concept: why things were designed and incorporated as they were and what they contribute to the overall project scheme. Most contractors are actually more like subcontractors, in that they perform a particular portion of the project work almost in isolation.

It is most helpful if contractors can be brought to understand the project's design concept and how their skill and expertise is necessary to the project's success—not only to complete it properly, but in its continuing usefulness and appearance. Normally, though, a contractor does not have the luxury or benefit of insight into the design concept unless there is a negotiated contract whereby the contractor is brought on board early by the owner—preselected before completion of the contract documents. Or a construction manager (CM) may be contracted to provide design phase services, in the form of insight and advice on construction methods and materials. In neither case does the work of the contracting elements necessarily intrude on or disrupt the design process; their function is to provide added insight and information that, if used, will result in a project that is more refined and coordinated to the benefit of all. It is really the owner who is the final decision maker as to how much and what information is incorporated into the project.

PROJECT DEVELOPMENT

Each project progresses through the architect's office in a set manner, in a series of planned stages—some imposed by contract, some to ensure the best job possible. However, producing the working drawings consumes nearly half of the architect's fee (the payment from the client to the architect). Obviously, if the professional devotes that much of the fee to this one phase, it gives strong credence to the conclusion that the drawings are most valuable in the construction of the facility. In fact, they are vital to producing the correct work in every aspect of the project. Thousand of decisions are made during the working drawing phase, and hundreds of thousands of items may be involved.

> A recent [2002] study designed to uncover how architects make product decisions yielded a particularly interesting fact: architects, on average, must select 1,500 products and make over 17,000 decisions on what is best for the project and the owner. That's 17,000 answers to 17,000 important questions. How big? How high? What color? What shape? What style? Moreover, what products will give the owner exactly what they have paid the architects to design? The list of questions about what products to incorporate in a project can be overwhelming for architects and their clients.
>
> from Dan Ouellette, "Selling Stone Products to Architects," *Stone World*, May 2003

Many architects treat this phase of the work in an offhanded manner; others try to ignore it completely; but it must happen (there is no shortcut). There is no easy way to convert the project from the original concept into a real structure without incorporating feet and inches and producing all the minute details of the working drawings.

RECENT CHANGES

The circumstances of architectural practice today are quite different from those of a few decades ago, and certainly different from the turn of the last century. In the long view, practice at the start of the twentieth century placed the architect in almost an elitist role, not by design or determination, but by the mere status assigned to the profession by the general public. Most laypeople were not exposed to architects in their lives. There was nothing they could relate to that brought understanding to them regarding how architects worked, influenced their lives, and made their surroundings better.

The profession at that time was consumed by the need for near perfection, since the greater number of items in any building had to be individually designed and custom-made. Few items were stocked or made on production lines that produced an inventory of items ready for use. The profession was immersed in the need to document the project thoroughly and accurately, in almost an instructive manner. This involved teaching the manufacturers and fabricators how to fashion the parts, and teaching the trade workers on the job site how to put the building together so it would reflect the overall design concept.

For many reasons, the running of the years brought innovations in the construction and design industries. Construction followed the changing and progressive path of most industries throughout the years of this past century. It paralleled the development and changes that are so evident every day and in every aspect of life.

The profession maintained its cutting-edge mentality, with a core of professionals always breaking new ground, followed by others (usually more conservative, not necessarily less talented) who adapted, adjusted, moved to, and modified the work. Design styles changed, but so did the manner of documentation. Just as communication of all sorts has found marvelous new phases, equipment, and techniques through the years, so too have the construction industry and the architectural profession.

Modern 3-D computer modeling allows one to traverse a project, moving electronically through a project that exists only electronically. A very fine design device, which substantiates good features and exposes the bad, computer modeling nonetheless cannot meet the need for transposition to the real thing. That change is usually outside the ability of someone who is not trained or attuned to the virtual. Even the best and frequent use of computer games and programs does not necessarily acclimate the layperson to appreciate, via computer, what the final (real) project will be, how it will feel, and how it can be used.

Much is made of architecture as it is designed and built with avant-garde direction by what are called "signature architects" (or the emerging term "starchitects"). These projects are new, wondrous, revolutionary, cutting-edge design concepts of the most fertile minds of a relatively small group of daring architects worldwide, supported by a very limited number of clients. They are the results of a mindset to produce a new expression or "statement" about design or structure, or perhaps simply a new approach to a known type of building. (See Figure 1-2) These projects are small in number but widely published, highly touted, discussed, celebrated, and sometimes maligned. In contrast, there is a *prodigious*

Figure 1-2 Example of cutting-edge projects, at the other end of the architectural spectrum from utilitarian works. Walt Disney Concert Hall. *Alpen/Walker Images.*

array of projects—thousands—designed with high skill and innovative design concepts, and worked through talented hands, which please their clients, function extremely well, and are constructed for the long term. They are the vast and overwhelming body of work in architecture.

It touches our lives every day, in ways we may not perceive, whether in urban, suburban, or rural venues, not only in the aesthetics of the buildings surrounding them, but also in the spaces created by those buildings and the functions of both the buildings and the spaces—in schools, colleges, and universities; stores, shops, and malls; hospitals; churches; multifamily housing; some single-family housing; industrial and manufacturing facilities, and so on; sprawling or small; high-rise, multistory, or single story; highly active or subdued in function; complex or simple and straightforward.

For example, look at the wide variety of high-rise office buildings. While each functions well as office space, they look quite different. These projects receive a disproportionate amount of publicity, examination, discussion, analysis, rigorous comment pro and con—and often wide and lasting acclaim. They are the topic of seeming endless discussion that tries to justify the whole project and each primary part. They are celebrated by the profession of architecture; analyzed, criticized, and held as examples in schools of architecture; and held in wonder or high disregard by the general public, which knows only what it sees and not the nuances of good design and architecture.

Each of these projects is brought to fruition through the efforts of many who perform quite varied ancillary services and tasks, both in de-

Figures 1-3 to 1-5 A marked contrast in sizes, forms, style, designs, and construction among a selection of buildings, all with the same basic function—offices.
Figure 1-3 Empire State Building. *Corbis Digital Stock.*

Figure 1-4 Trans-American Building. *Photo Disc/Getty Images.*

Figure 1-5 New Swiss Re building in London; affectionately known as the "Gherkin." *Alberto Otero Garcia.*

Figure 1-6 The sequence from design to built or completed project.

sign and in realization of the completed project. This is a sequence of tasks and events that creates and produces the finished project. It is, for want of a better word, the grunt work that transforms the creative design concept into the final reality: the process of "how it got that way." (See Figure 1-6.)

Architecture, then, is the result or the product of several sequences and efforts; the combination of many talents and skills; the real manifestation of a mental concept.

One point that needs clarification is this:

Architecture is not exclusively equated to only the cutting-edge,
innovative, eye-catching, unique projects. It exists and
is continually produced over a far more vast array
of images and configurations, in far-flung locations.

There is an overwhelming body of work produced by talented and dedicated architects who please their clients in less imposing and less publicized ways. Even the most visible signature architects have as a good portion of their total body of work, far less ostentatious projects (which help pay the bills and fill the time of staff between "big" jobs). It is not uncommon for a signature office to design warehouses concurrently with, or in the intervals between, more glitzy and prestigious projects. The world over, the profession of architecture is practiced with continual results that protect and enhance communities and improve the lives of the occupants and users of the projects. The vast majority of the time, the general population is totally unaware of the work done by the architect and the daily impact it has on their lives, in so many ways and locations.

So, for the sake of discussion, let us set the premise that "architecture is the complete array of buildings and structures that have been, are being, or will be built, for human occupancy and use." We purposely avoid any discussion about styles, concepts, values, appropriateness, good-or-bad evaluations, or marginalization of projects. Our task is to relate how each of the projects has progressed from inception to completion—not *what* is built and not *why* certain designs, materials, and systems are used, but *how* projects are produced, from perceived needs to mental processes and images to "bricks and mortar"—that is, standing building stock.

THE AXIOM

Architecture is the manifestation of design
achieved through construction.

This is the fundamental and perhaps too simplistic (but true) axiom regarding the process that produces the world's architecture. This axiom holds in all climates, all cultures, all styles, all levels of expertise, and all levels of need. The intent is to address this axiom and to provide explanation of the several parts, how they interact, and how they feed one another, until the project is completed, occupied, and used. The process moves from the idea, through deciding what exactly to provide or construct, and then to producing the documentation for construction. Last but certainly not least is the cooperative process of construction: contractor and designer working to produce the project that the owner is anticipating.

> Construction, for the most part, is nonjudgmental concerning architecture. Its task is the pragmatic conversion of a concept to a usable entity, whose design, style, and appearance have already been set by others.

Note that this axiom does not analyze a work as good, bad, or indifferent architecture—it merely states the path followed to produce architecture satisfactory to the client, to the profit of the contractor and the profit and reputation of the design professionals. No matter the type or style of the structure, it still produces these byproducts and conveys these benefits to the various parties. Every project follows this path and produces its own set of results for each party involved. The ideal situation is that in which the needs of all parties are fully met by the finished project.

Some purists would indicate their strong displeasure and disdain at any work being referred to as architecture that falls short of their prescribed definition or perceptions. But the world is not so restrictive or simple. Architecture worldwide is a broad, expressive panorama of varied talents, all directed toward the singular goal of providing a project consistent with the needs and desires of the client. Certainly, some clients are more open to new ideas and images—to the more creative and imaginative and to the fact that their project may become more widely known for its image and status than its function. But many other clients seek practical solutions through an architectural effort quite different in intent—they seek problem solving, increased capacity, and other more practical results.

The final design concept and physical appearance of a project is an expression of the mutual desire and intent of the client and the architect. While the architect is engaged to work as an agent of the Owner, this is not a matter of subservience. Rather, the architect takes the programming that was mutually produced by the parties and interprets and adjusts it into a coherent design. Sometimes the client guides or even demands to direct the design effort. But more times than not, the client allows the architect to create one or more concepts. This is the direct impetus for innovative design, unique appearance, fashioning of materials, orientation, and distinctive image in each and every project—none replicating another (except where more mundane prototypical work is involved). Owners choose the one design concept/solution that is to their liking, and the rest of the project work is directed toward producing the project as depicted on the approved concept drawings (preliminary design drawings).

In view of the fact that the same type of talent, knowledge, and skill are required to produce the entire range of projects, the architectural process must vary with the desires of the client and the results anticipated. This in no way demeans the direction and work of any individual architect. Rather, it speaks to the specific challenge of each and every project and the flexibility required to resolve the issues and produce a meaningful design for the client. It also indicates that project parameters vary and change, over a very wide range—and differing project goals reflect the need to please and satisfy the client. But there is one leveling process that all projects must negotiate—the process of construction.

At some point, no matter the type of project, the status and talent of the architect, or the drama of its design, every project must traverse the construction sequence. Here the project—design and all—is turned over to the constructors for their execution of the requisite hands-on work. The route to producing architecture of any style, type, or level of design accomplishment is a collaboration of tasks, work items, and application of varied skills—some dangerous; some roughly hewn, backbreaking, and rudimentary; others dirty, greasy, oily, or awkward; still others labor-intensive, using human power in place of sophisticated machinery or technology. Projects cycle in stages where, at times, one wonders if the final project will ever match the original design concept—but most projects do.

In the construction process, the design professional is not relegated to the position of bystander, but there are various levels of participation. Therefore, it is necessary that professionals know, understand, and fully appreciate the extent of the project and the process of construction. There is need to be flexible, decisive, strong, instructional, and educational; a good manager; and to achieve the correct interface between client and contractor.

So, the next question is, how does the design concept of the designer for a new piece of architecture become a reality?

CONSTRUCTION

Looking through the various definitions of architecture there is usually mention of two aspects or elements—art and science/engineering/technology. Any architectural curriculum that does not include both is really not addressing the whole of the profession and its work. Regrettably, the continual diminution of time available in the academic process inhibits the ability to address both aspects of architecture. Even when breaking the definition into attributes, there is some specific wording and need not only for design of the project, but also for its erection. This in itself calls for an expansion of the design concept into construction terms and graphics, and the addition of personnel whose expertise involves intimate functional knowledge of construction systems, materials, the depiction and detailing of the same in various locations, and the full array of documentation required to construct the project.

Certainly the process beyond design involves a great many tasks and personnel. This includes the engineering disciplines, which are necessary to incorporate their expertise to augment the architectural work, and to bring everything from stability (structural engineering) to comfort (HVAC and electrical engineering) to the project. These disciplines, too, must go through a period of analysis and design, which parallels and conjoins the architectural elements. They all are installed and activated within the proper context in the project through the various tasks involved with construction.

TOTALITY OF WORK

There is no doubt that, by any definition, architecture has two aspects—art and science/engineering/technology. In that context, architects would seem well advised to know about both. This is not to say that individual architects need to be experts in both, nor equally versed in both. It is to say, however, that both are necessary to create and realize architecture.

An architect may choose to become solely a designer, devoted only to the task of conceptualizing and creating designs and resolving owners' needs and demands, within a functional and attractive complex. But designers become far better with knowledge of building technology, engineering, and construction, so that they at least understand what more is required to present a finished and usable edifice to the client. To create an elitist attitude to the point of dispelling any linkage between design and construction is totally false and misleading.

The linkage between the two aspects is so essential, crucial, and important that it is virtually impossible to think of attempting separation. The most grandiose of designs lies fallow, unrealized, and in a questionable state if it is never constructed. A good example of this is the Illinois Tower, which Frank Lloyd Wright designed in the 1960s (see Figure 1-7). Although it was never built, it was Wright's contention that this project could be used to construct a building one mile high. He knew that many, many technological advances would be required; innovative concepts for access and evacuation would be necessary, among many others.

It is interesting to compare Wright's design with the reality of the World Trade Center towers (see Figure 1-8). How would the construction of the two projects compare? And more importantly, how would the mile-high building operate within the findings and analysis, done and in progress, about the WTC and its demise? Physically wildly demanding on the construction crews (working a mile high), the mere construction, let alone the numerous other considerations and accoutrements, would be daunting. And how would the health, safety, and welfare of the occupants and users be addressed?

In this exercise, it is quite evident that realization of a design concept is an important part of architecture and should be explored, taught,

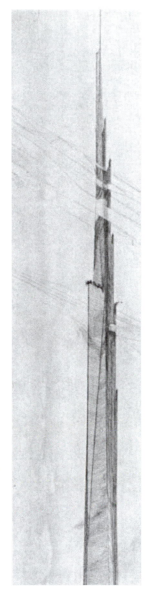

Figure 1-7 "Mile High" Illinois Tower, proposed and designed by Frank Lloyd Wright (never built) as an expression of both his vision and innovative spirit.

Figure 1-8 Although tragically destroyed, the design and construction of the World Trade Center towers is well documented and an excellent case study from which much can be learned. *PhotoDisc, Inc.*

integrated with, and become an intrinsic part of the project. Truly design and construction must be bonded together to ensure that each is pursued in the correct context and within proper bounds. One does not dominate the other. Rather, they must be cohabitants working back and forth in lockstep, to faithfully produce the wonders, nuances, and features of the design through the work of construction, using newly created forms, processes, and procedures where required. The design makes demands; the construction must produce the solutions to support and replicate the design.

> Concept and implementation must be seamlessly related if the built work is to be architecture and not just a building.
> —*J. Patrick Rand, FAIA, Distinguished Professor of Architecture, School of Architecture, North Carolina State University*

> . . . the act of architecture is not finished when the design is done, but when the building is built. However, most students see, and are taught, that a design is the end product.
> —*Gerald G. Weisbach, FAIA, Architect/Attorney, San Francisco, CA*

Construction is a team activity almost from the very start. Various players and combinations of players contribute to the team effort, some on a continual basis, some coming and going at various junctures. All are necessary to the success of any project.

This is perhaps best said by William Dudley Hunt, Jr., FAIA, who wrote in his book *Encyclopedia of American Architecture*:

> The construction team is the loosely knit, diverse group of individuals and organizations that performs the many functions necessary to bring buildings into being. Often thought of as only consisting of those who design buildings, and those who construct them, the building (construction) team is actually much more complex . . . *all* elements, including owners, are essential in transforming a need for a building from an idea to a completed structure.

Hunt distinctly observes and understands that buildings and other construction projects involve the resolution of many issues, result from many efforts and much personal expertise. Clearly, he indicates that no one person can execute any project plan in every aspect. And, clearly, he notes that while the collective definitions of buildings or building stock may be "architecture," that very name is a combination of two vital elements—art, and either engineering, science, or technology (all roughly equivalent)—yet another specific indication of "team."

It is quite evident that the concept of team is preeminent in the creation and production of architecture. Traditionally, and still now, the architect is the leader of the team, knowing more about the total project than anyone else. There has been some undercutting and diminution of this concept by the introduction of other tasks and professions. But it remains that the architect forms a team of consultants with varying engineering skills to produce the project. The many and multifaceted requirements of the owner/client require attention and resolution as part of the charge to the professionals and the success of the project. More and more, technology is so imposing and so convoluted that special and dedicated attention to certain phases of the project is absolutely essential. While the architect can set the overall design concept, it is essential that the architect form a team of the various engineering disciplines to incorporate the necessary additional designs of the many supporting systems in the project. Obviously, it is beneficial to all if this team consists of a group of highly compatible people who work well together and are expert in their respective fields. There is not time or room for contention within this group—it must be focused, coordinated, cooperative, and well directed.

The concept of team is crucial to the success of the project not only in the final product but also in the entire process, and in the correct interface between all portions, systems, and functions of the project. This concept pervades the project and really needs to be nurtured to ensure that all participants contribute—on time, with their best information and creativity, and in a fully cooperative manner. This is not a competitive situation, but one of total and full inclusion, cooperation, contribution, understanding, compromise, adjustment, and unity of purpose.

To support the concept of team in the execution of construction projects, the following excerpt is offered. This is taken from the 2004 report, "Collaboration, Integrated Information, and the Project Lifecycle in Building Design, Construction and Operation—WP-1202." This report was produced by the Architectural/Engineering (AE) Productivity Committee of the Construction Users Roundtable (CURT) (www.CURT.org).

"The goal of everyone in the industry should be better, faster, more capable project delivery created by fully integrated, collaborative teams. Owners must be the ones to drive this change, by leading the creation of collaborative, cross-functional teams composed of design, construction, and facility management professionals."

Toward that end the committee makes four recommendations and articulates a vision of the future:

"1. *Owner Leadership*: Owners, as the integrating influence in the building process, must engage in and demand that collaborative teams openly share information and use appropriate technology.
2. *Integrated Project Structure*: The building process cannot be optimized without full collaboration among all members of the design/build/own project.
3. *Open Information Sharing*: Project collaboration must be characterized by open, timely, and reliable information sharing.
4. *Virtual Building Information Models*: Effectively designed and deployed information technology will support full collaboration and information sharing and will lead to a more effective design/build/manage process."

A FULLY COLLABORATIVE TEAM EFFORT

Can it be that architecture exists only in the wonderfully creative minds of the designers, whose mental capacities, when triggered by project circumstances, then focus, hone, and crystallize random factors and considerations into a cohesive design concept—which is then translated onto paper or an electronic screen—but then does not appear again until the project is finished?

GENESIS OF ARCHITECTURE

Architecture is indeed founded in the minds of the designer, who has marvelous insight into and control of design theory, design principles, a sense of space, and the ability for the creation of forms that combine the foregoing into a tasteful, attractive, and functional entity. Unfortunately, architectural design can all too easily be dismissed as fantasy, and unreasonable. But the function of design and designers is to provide new directions and perspectives—new schemes to solving problems. It is here that style becomes an adjective—where "what it will be" is a concern, along with how it will last, et cetera.

Here, rhetoric is both rampant and to some degree valid—better here to describe how or what is being done, than to try to explain later what was done (in a sense to justify or legitimize it).

The architecture then goes dormant and almost literally disappears. There is an on-going process in place to transform hazy concept into functional reality—to transform ideas, small-scale drawings (renderings), and models into hard and fast, full-scale work. What is called fantasy becomes reality through the ingenuity and innovation of skilled managers and trade workers who craft the design into a finished and functioning project. Despite what may be said or thought about design, it can and does become architecture, on a daily basis.

THE BLEND

The key to a successful project is the appropriate blending of design, construction, and management. No one of these should be given an inordinate role in the project—each needs the other in order to succeed. Each obviously has its place on every project site, but the preeminent issue is that the three elements be combined in an ongoing manner that produces the project through a communal or team effort.

This cannot be stressed enough. It is the absolutely correct way to approach a project, and every aspect of it, from the most insignificant and mundane to the most ostentatious and impressive. Fundamentally this is a matter of respect, which is either brought to the job site by the various personalities involved or is somehow developed. (It is impossible, though, to legislate or require that respect be shown to all others.) It may be that the project leader, whoever that may be, shows respect to others, and has developed such a method of operation that everyone is touched by the aura of that person and seeks to both please and work with that leader.

There are many situations similar to this, whereby the mere presence of a person can influence the attitudes and actions of others. Obviously, many actors carry an element of this, where they create such a mood that they move the audience to the emotion they seek. The same is a very helpful approach on the construction job site—not for mere emotion but to move all participants in a cohesive and single-minded direction. Perhaps the best word is "inspirational." A "can-do" spirit, carefully and professionally applied, moves even the most reticent of participants. This is not the traditional "rah-rah!" approach, but rather a confident and knowledgeable spirit that best utilizes others in their particular way, for the best combined result. Perhaps the key is a flexible attitude in all parties, and a willingness to adjust to conditions and personalities—to give and take, not for selfish motives, but for a better presentation, work effort, and project.

There is a widespread, almost industry-wide distrust between designers and constructors. This is a most unfortunate, wholly unhealthy atmosphere that pervades many projects, at least to some degree. In some, it is so distracting that meetings become major, ferocious, disruptive arguments, and so confrontational that physical restraint must be used by one party on another.

In striving to protect their own self-interest, each group seems to feel that the other is intent on compromising its efforts. Certainly, no one believes that members of either group enters a project with a predisposition to create havoc, cause problems, harass, or take the other to nasty litigation. But this seems to be an unconscious belief.

Designers are agents of the owners and are hired to work the parameters of the project to the best interest of their client. They produce documents that set out a formal array of construction information and directions, within a legal framework that acts to retain proper status for all parties (including the contractors). There should be no intent to undercut or compromise the construction effort—this would be wholly foolhardy in that such actions directly inhibit proper and correct production of the project as the owner desires.

Contractors may feel burdened by how the project is designed, the documents, and the expectations put forth as to cost and timing. But all of this should be agreed to at the onset to meet the desires and needs of the client.

Designers, on the other hand, often regard contractors as those who can unfairly manipulate the project work or provide less than value in many aspects of the work (cheaper materials, less skilled labor at inflated prices, etc.). In addition, designers may see contractors as those who play on the normal range of shortcomings in any set of documents. By meticulously finding and taking advantage of all such loopholes (or so the perception goes), the contractor can create an added profit. Such shortcomings should have, in the designers' eyes, been found and exposed before the formal contract was signed, so they could have been resolved in a better manner.

In short, designers all too often view contractors as pseudo-predators who sacrifice and compromise the project for their own self-interest and profit (not providing full value for dollar given). So long as this atmosphere exists (this perception is always there in one degree or another) and until both parties gain a good measure of confidence in each other and their actions, vying for position will be part of everyday work. Too many projects have become excruciating experiences with resulting animosity that lingers long after completion. So there is a distinct need for better understanding, on both sides, of the whole design-construction process.

The better understanding that young professionals have of construction processes and tasks, how field operations work, how individual materials and systems are fabricated and installed, and the direction and skill of the trade worker, the better the process of project production. And the reverse of this is also true. The contractor needs to respect the design process and the work done, as much as the designer needs to be respectful of the contractor.

THE NEED

Perhaps the first and highest need is for the complete understanding that construction is *necessarily* a team effort between design and construction, and totally noncompetitive. Aside from the actual physical building work, construction is a very complex interplay between quite varying perspectives and directions.

First, it is necessary that all parties put aside prejudice and other demeaning attitudes and accept the fact that the others are as necessary to the success of the project as they are. Design professionals bring a subjective aspect to the work. In any design situation there are many solutions to any problem. Part of this process is to come as close as possible to the needs and desires of the owner. This narrows the choice of solutions, to some degree, but still the professionals are needed to focus in on the one solution that solves the owner's basic problems. Design is a factor in developing concepts through thought processes that are not necessarily contained in written or graphic form. It is bringing many quite varied concepts and real things together to produce the new project (see Figure 1-9).

Figure 1-9 Design professionals bring a subjective aspect to their work, which brings creativity and innovation to projects to enhance their basic premise. *PhotoDisc/Getty Images.*

The contractors, in turn, bring a pragmatic approach to the project, along with their hands-on expertise. Fundamentally, the contractors have the ability to do anything required to execute the project. This is a tremendous advantage in creating a successful project. Often design concepts are so complex and so new that they challenge even the best of contractors. But contractors are quite adept at finding ways to manipulate their processes and meet those challenges. It is noteworthy, though, that design professionals are heavily (but not exclusively) creative and design oriented, while contractors are mostly pragmatic and less concerned with creativity, design, aesthetics, and other intangible project attributes. In essence, the prospects are limitless. Between the design professionals and the contractors, and given enough time, anything that can be conceived, designed, and documented can be built (so long as the client/owner has enough money to pay for the project and enough desire to own it).

However, in the work of both professionals and contractors, the ability to create and execute the work comes at a price—literally. Many projects are modified from their initial configurations simply because the execution of the concepts is so costly that the owner's budget cannot provide all the necessary funding. It is here that the construction managers and project managers in the various offices play a role in closing the circle of the project, finding the best blend of design concept, execution, and funding. With proper construction background, training, and experience, managers offer a special insight into the project work. Often they are able to offer alternative methods of construction, other materials, or design modifications that retain the essence of the original concept but in a more affordable form.

The marvel of construction is that within the contractual authority and responsibility for the "means and methods of construction" (per AIA Document A201, General Conditions of the Contract for Construction) is the ability to ascertain, determine, or establish a way to build and achieve every configuration, opening, attribute, profile, edge, image, detail, and construction required by the design concept.

While this ability parallels the knowledge of the design professional, it often surpasses that know-how and achieves well beyond anticipated ends. This, of course, may come with added cost and often added time for the effort. Still, the marvel of producing virtually anything that is part of a design is a credit to the ingenuity and expertise of the construction forces—administrative, supervisory, professional, and skilled.

BASIC RESPECT

It is fairly obvious that dominance is not the key issue—it is not a manner of who can make demands on others, or who can influence the owner to the greatest degree, or who can force their will on others. It is rather a matter of respecting the work of others, working to meet the issues in a cooperative manner, and providing the owner with the project as close to the approved design concept as possible, within budgetary bounds.

Unfortunately, ego, anger, or past bad experiences too often influence the attitudes and actions of some of the parties. When these negatives come into play there is a project scenario that does not serve anyone very well. One's ego can be fed by being a part of a highly successful project—so why force an attitude on others that inhibits their work?

In the construction industry today, there are dynamics at work whereby construction projects are being executed in new, different, and often innovative ways. Things have and are changing quite dramatically. Sometimes, these changes are the root cause of new irritations, or they regenerate old wounds. Project work for the most part is constant, even though it changes somewhat from one project to another. It is the personnel and their relative roles that change for one reason or another.

DISPELLING THE ISSUE

The point often lost or ignored is that the deepest desire of the design professional is to produce a project as nearly perfect as possible for the client. To do this means to create a design concept that fits the owner's program and then to document that concept in a manner that conveys all the information required for faithful construction, in clear, complete and unequivocal terms. There should be nothing frivolous involved, nothing thrown in for no legitimate reason. And there certainly should be no intent, attempt, desire, or time to set out documents and terms that purposely impose on, attack, or seek to be adversarial to contractors. There should be no intent to penalize contractors or to do anything in a manner that will reduce their effectiveness or reduce their profitability (but some will still quibble over the level of profit).

The drawings are so commonly accepted and understood that they are seen as the primary and in some cases the only valid documents. But the truth is that the associated specifications are equally important, as they are purposely created to contain the information that simply cannot be displayed graphically. It may be that the volume of words is imposing and appears threatening, but this is not the intent of the design professional. Granted, there may be provisions for work to be done in a manner different from the norm, requiring adjustments in the contractor's procedure, but this is done for a reason. There is no inclination or desire to be adversarial in the documentation. They may appear to be strong, strange, and strident, but the goal is achieving the finest of projects for the client.

When contractors are merely given the task of doing such work, the practical side kicks in and may bring them to question why. If met by a strident answer, sparks can fly and the contractors may well feel put-upon when asked to try to do something new and different, outside the straight line of their expertise, and at their cost. While a contractor buy-in earlier in the process may help, that is rather difficult to achieve in the Design/Bid/Build (D/B/B) program, since the contractors are involved only after the design is fully developed and documented (what is, is what is required). Any buy-in is best restricted to methods and timing, since the basic design concept is already agreed upon by owner and design professional, and virtually firm. But input to better and/or quicker execution of the concept work is a valid place for the contractor to buy in, to become a more involved partner in the project.

Fast-forward now to the day when the project is sparkling clean, meticulously appointed, shiny, festooned perhaps in some colorful dressing, and ready for speeches, platitudes, and a ribbon-cutting. Here, marvelously, stands a new piece of architecture. True to a style; true to detailing, coloring, product selection, proportion; a good new example of design direction, a time period, or a designer's body of work.

But what occurred between these two idealistic, rather charming and inspirational events? Well, actually two periods of time or processes: documentation (of the design concept) and the actual work of construction. In the former is the work of transforming a design concept—an idea, a solution—into hard and fast construction information. A new lexicon is required, and what may have been hazy detail, unresolved and indistinct, now becomes distinct, directive, and instructional. To overcome the sense of being overwhelmed by a maze of tasks and information and of daunting intricacy, the process and progression needs to be understood. This is best done by working one's way through the entire process, at least at a basic level.

First, there is need for mutual agreement and understanding what exactly what we are talking about when we say "progression."

> *Progression*: A successive sequence or series of continuous and connected work, events, or tasks in which each is related to its predecessor so as to produce a proclivity for action or a process of incremental movement toward an established goal.

In this definition, we have combined several aspects of progression into a single definition that addresses construction and architecture. Here there are really three separate processes within the progression addressed in this book (see Figure 1-10).

The design professional and the owner are active in the first (lefthand) portion as the project is formulated and documented. The contractor may have some very limited knowledge and direct participation, as may construction managers. However, this portion is traditionally the purview of the ownership as it is made to express its desires and requirements for the project or program and to oversee in general terms the creation of the design concept and its subsequent documentation.

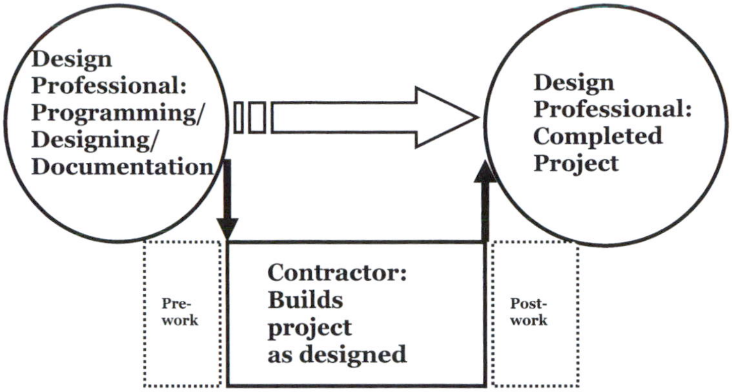

Later, at the end of the project upon completion (the righthand portion), the design professional is again the preeminent party as the project closes down and the owner takes occupancy. From this point the design professional is the active outside party in further assessments, studies, reports, analyses, et cetera. The contractor may have a limited participation in the form of callbacks, et cetera, as noted.

The contractor and allied forces (subcontractor, suppliers, manufacturers, etc.) work between the extremes of project formulation and project completion (see Figure 1-11). Their work is executing the actual, hands-on construction work and creating the reality of the design concept.

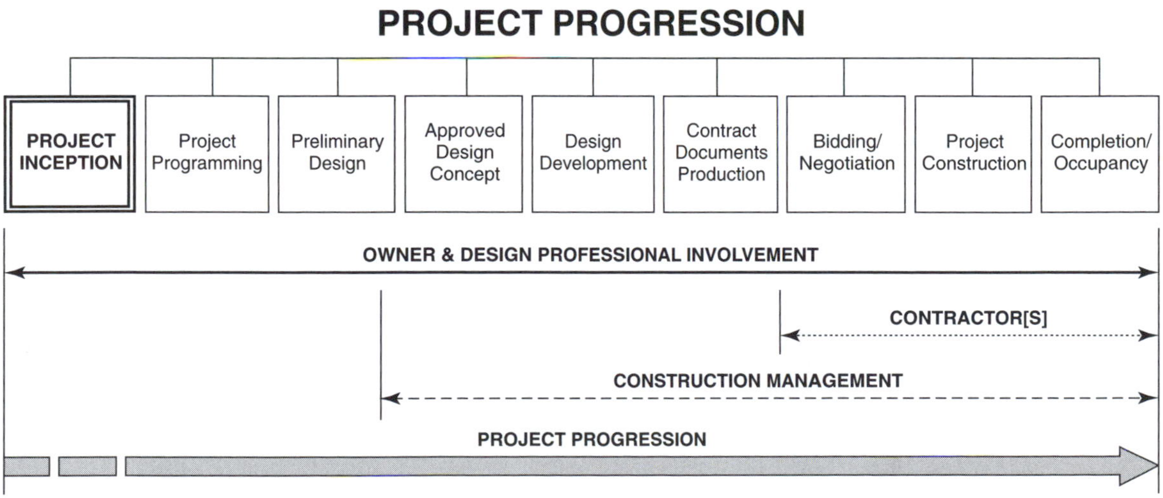

Figure 1-10 The participation of the design professional and the construction force. Note that the primary work of the professional is at the inception through documentation phases, and then at the completion of the project. Construction is the function that takes the documentation and builds the project, and makes it ready for owner occupancy and use.

PROJECT PROGRESSION

Figure 1-11 The overall scheme of the progression of a project.

This is perhaps the truer progression (as we defined it above) since the work must be done in a regulated format. The contractor's field superintendent is the person who, perhaps, has the best and deepest grasp of the progression required by the project and the work schedule. This person is acutely aware of the desired end result—a profitable project for the contractor, and a satisfied customer in the owner. Doing rework, or tearing work out due to its being out of sequence, is intolerable. It is simply to be not only avoided but "planned out" of any work progression or schedule to be used.

This work of planning out the work tasks, their relationship (what depends on other work, etc.), and the sequencing of personnel requires a skilled hand and great depth of knowledge of the construction process. And it is not just recent construction that has forced this new operation management.

In April 1930, construction of the Empire State Building began in New York City. This was a masterful project, innovatively done, in a time far before modern construction methods, materials, and technology (see Figure 1-12). This building was built in but twenty months and was the product of amazing innovation by the contractor, to sequence and facilitate the work process to allow for rapid and relatively easy construction. This is an excellent project that is well worth study due to the combination of the era of the project, the crude (compared

Figure 1-12 The Empire State Building was built in the record time (for its era) of 20 months. The contractors accomplished this through the creation of new procedures and details of construction designed specifically for the type of project and the schedule. *Lewis Wickes Hine, National Archives.*

to today's) equipment, techniques, methods, and technology available, and the insight of the contracting firm. (See *Building the Empire State*, by Carol Willis and Donald Friedman, published by Norton in 1998, which is based on actual field notes and journals written during construction.)

If necessity was ever the mother of invention, this was its premier example. There was terrific pressure to finish the building as soon as possible for both competitive and status reasons. Due to the Great Depression, workers were easily available, worked for minimal wages, and worked in such a manner that they literally put themselves out of work (by working so efficiently that they finished the project quickly and so rendered themselves unemployed in very bad economic times). The contractor was forced to create new methods for working higher than ever before, without benefit of traditional work equipment and processes, and in the heart of busy New York City. There were no tower cranes—only small jibs that were steam powered. Some supplies were delivered by horse-drawn wagons. How do you lay brick up to 100 stories high, from the outside of the building? Indeed, how do you build the entire complex of the exterior walls, from the inside? The challenges were monumental, but they had to be first accounted for to complete the building, and then fitted into the progression of work in their correct place at the correct times.

UNDERSTANDING THE PROGRESSION

The progression in every case, no matter the size, type, or complexity of the project, is a logical format of tasks—some performed in tandem, some concurrently, some in isolation. It is a matter of stepped procedures that follow a prescribed path appropriate to the project—a series of events that interface and build one upon the other until the project is finished. It is devoid of new work being installed at the wrong time—that is, before other required work is placed to support or form a place for the new work. The logic of this progression is within the contractor's purview and falls under the responsibilities of the contractor for construction means and methods. It is the planning, routing, and execution of work that moves design concept to finished project.

Construction and architecture are conjoined and inseparable. Each needs the other to accomplish their mutual goal. This is seen most easily in the progression of a typical project (with the understanding that conditions and requirements do change between projects and necessitate modifications in the process) from project inception to project completion, occupancy and beyond.

The intent of this book is to overview the whole project progression from the very beginning to the very end (and a little beyond). Within the discussion in this book, there are some primary issues that must be kept in mind:

1. Projects vary widely in both scope and complexity, and the discussion here is a generalized view that does not begin to address a project of some fixed parameters—it merely sets out the sequence of tasks.
2. There are a multitude of tasks within any given project and the extent and details of each can be quite simple or highly imposing. Each task or construction operation is a complex combination of ideas and conclusions and a massive amount of physical labor.
3. It is impossible to finish a block of work involving a given material, such as concrete, all at one time. For example, it is counterproductive to lay concrete sidewalks along with the concrete foundation, simply because both are concrete.

In addition, there is a tremendous array of information involved which could fill other books, and in many cases already has. We urge reference to the appendix on trade associations on this book's companion Website, www.wiley.com/go/constructionofarchitecture. The latter are narrow-scope, special-interest groups and organizations that can provide highly detailed information about a narrow range of products, work, materials, or training. Consult these resources for more information about any of the tasks mentioned or indicated in this text.

A warning: it is vitally important that the reader take this book as a matrix—an outline for work on construction projects. It should not be taken as an absolute process that occurs on *every* project *exactly* as written here. But it is critically important that readers stretch their minds to envision the complete spectrum of construction projects—from the smallest to the most extensive and massive. The progression is in each of these, in modified form, perhaps, but still present; it is not tied to any single type, size, or configuration of project. It is universal but flexible and necessarily adjustable to every project.

Within the construction industry, the range of projects in magnitude and complexity is enormous. Construction is not simply single-family housing, light commercial, high-rise, multiple building projects, et cetera, but also ranges to massive airports (e.g., Denver, Colorado, and Hong Kong, to mention a couple of recent projects), to awesome hydroelectric dams and power-generating projects, navigational locks and facilities, and so on (e.g., China's Three Gorges Dam project, the Niagara-Mohawk system at Niagara Falls, New York, and projects similar to the Panama Canal). Also, it must be understood that construction is a worldwide industry where amazing projects can be located anywhere—in any time zone, country, and climate—and be of any size or capacity.

But what is also quite amazing is that the progression of each project, no matter the size, location, or complexity, is very much the same. What varies is the level of activity and effort involved, the length of time required, and the sheer magnitude of what must be accomplished. A small contractor may be deeply concerned about buying a new truck, but larger operation may be concerned about the continual purchase of large pieces of equipment for 24-hour-a-day operation, and the eventual scrapping of such equipment in an equipment graveyard (i.e., of totally worn-out units) on but one project.

EXAMPLE OF PROGRESSION FLEXIBILITY

Two identical buildings are to be built on
separate sites— one flat, the other quite hilly.
The work progressions for these projects are identical,

EXCEPT

more time, equipment, staff, operations, and effort are
required to grade and prepare the hilly site.

Table 1-1 is a short list of projects that have been built through history that challenged and stretched the talents and skills of the designers and workers. These, of course, are also part of the construction industry—the part that is rather hidden to laypeople, since they are never involved with or exposed to them. Humans tend to assimilate only what they experience, so we tend to see construction as houses, stores, offices, schools, et cetera. But there is much construction beyond these.

Research any or all of these (they all are well documented and fairly easily found) to better understand them and their construction progression.

It is quite obvious that the circumstances and demands of each project are unique and differ from those of other projects. Not only does each project have its own personality due to the imposed requirements, but also its overall context sets it apart. The renovation of an industrial plant, while maintaining production operations, is a far different project than a new building on an open site; a small low-rise building differs greatly from a hospital; a warehouse, while massive, is not nearly as complex as a school half its size; cold-weather construction varies drastically from hot-weather operations, and both may occur on a single project; high-end residential work is an altogether different problem than an industrial office building, which in turn differs from a high-rent

---

TABLE 1-1—EXAMPLES OF MASSIVE CONSTRUCTION PROJECTS IN VARIOUS HISTORIC ERAS

Pyramids at Giza (Menkaure, Khafre, and Khufu)
Parthenon
Pantheon
The Colosseum
Roman aqueducts
Pueblo Bonita
Aztec/Inca/Mayan pyramids/structures
Hagia Sophia
Notre Dame/Chartres/Cologne
Salisbury; Gothic cathedrals in Europe
Persian ziggurats
St. Paul's Cathedral
Houses of Parliament
St. Peter's Basilica, Rome
Great Wall of China
Empire State Building
Chrysler Building
Woolworth Building
Washington Monument
Westminster Abbey
Industrial plants that house aircraft construction or automobile assembly; long and convoluted production lines
Variety of high-rise buildings around the world: Taipei 101/
Sears Tower/Burj Tower (Dubai)
Aswan Dam in Egypt; Three Gorges Dam in China
Hoover and Grand Coulee dams in the United States

---

commercial office building. A single-family residence can cost upwards of $25 million, while a whole production plant can cost but $10 million. The variations are innumerable and across a wide spectrum—but each has its specific and special progression—a road map to its way of "being built."

In addition, a mere change in a wall system creates a different scenario for the project and different timing. It is both impossible and needless to list or describe each project sequence. Case studies of individual projects are available for closer, in-depth analysis.

For the sake of simplicity and since it is basically chronological, the progression discussed in this book is based on the mainstream and traditional Design/Bid/Build project delivery system. Other such systems will be discussed later, but the primary intent is to display the prevalent straight-line timing of the work progression as an educational tool. Certainly the other systems are valid and successfully used, but fundamental understanding lies in the basic simplicity of the work tasks in tandem in the D/B/B progression.

CHAPTER
2

PROJECT INCEPTION AND DETERMINATION

THE CAUSE

Over a period of time, circumstances change; new needs arise; new problems develop or old ones are compounded and defy satisfactory resolution; there is a desire for an upgrade or improvement in working conditions, and a better image; business increases and seems to be on a strong upward trend for the foreseeable future; new technology and new equipment create the prospect of increased productivity and new production and product lines; and so forth. The list also includes circumstances such as the following:

- Business demands greater production.
- Added staff are required.
- New product lines evolve.
- New production equipment is available.
- Added warehousing is needed.
- Expanded shipping capacity and facilities are needed.
- Family grows; elderly accommodations are needed.
- School population rises.
- Expanded health care service and/or facilities are required.
- Replacement facility is required (fire, storm damage, dilapidation, etc.).
- New branches and business locations are advised; relocation.
- Greater inventory and sales areas are required.
- Refurbish and renovation; upgrading.
- Expanded services.
- Combining/consolidation of facilities.

Some, if not all, of these circumstances arise in many combinations and situations—business (commercial and industrial of all types), institutional and educational organizations, single- or multi-family housing, and so on. But no matter when, where, or how they appear, they eventually will accrue to the point where some permanent solution is undeniably necessary.

In a word, these circumstances establish *NEED!*

Usually, a physical need results in a mental perception and the conclusion that some type of construction project is required. In some instances, like nursing homes, health care facilities, and bank branches, owners are required to formally address regulations and to establish their need and justify the proposed project. Sometimes this involves applying for a formal Certificate of Need showing approval of the project by lending agencies, governmental agencies, and other such regulatory agencies that have a direct interest in the success of the project. The process of resolution then begins, with the thoughtful perceptions, instincts, and pragmatic reality of owner/client/user/tenant/occupant that, simply, "Things cannot continue as they are!"

In fact, this is but the germ or root of a new construction project, in one form or another. Need does not immediately translate to construction. Certainly, construction will be required, but only after a process of analysis, conceptualization, design, and documentation. The anticipated construction is the terminal activity in a project process and progression that can be quite lengthy, and in any event is quite searching, rigorous, and detailed. There needs to be a scheme or plan for the construction to follow to reach the finale, that is, a completed building satisfactory to the owner.

PROJECT INCEPTION/INITIATION

No owner wakes up one morning and decides to do a project. Neither should there be any illusion whatever that if a spontaneous decision were made, the project would begin at once—there is as yet no concept, no parameters, no basic requirements, no design, no construction documentation, no ground-breaking, no contractor mobilization, no visible activity that indicates that a new project is in motion.

The owner has yet to progress through a long and quite arduous process of analyzing what to do, how to proceed, what goals to set, how to establish reasonable financing, and the overall parameters of the project in full detail and with firm conviction. There is much to consider, much to do, and the need for tough, sound, realistic decisions that create the matrix in which the project will function, evolve, and come forth.

The decision to engage in or pursue a construction project is one not easily made. Largely, for most owners, it is a journey into the unknown. Even those who have some previous experience with construction often find that their new project can be a most daunting, confounding, irritating, confusing, and stress-filled sequence. Having little or no knowledge of construction (other than perhaps some do-it-yourself projects in their home), the layperson finds the entire process all but completely foreign. Even astute and successful merchants and businesspeople find the process filled with new and unusual tasks, both for themselves and for the personnel they hire to perform them.

With no experience and certainly no training in design and construction, it is of utmost importance that the owner find and hire the best design professionals and contractors for the project. But again, this is not easily achieved since there is no reliable checklist that provides exacting information for the correct fit. This leaves the owner in the situation of needing to seek out candid and experienced input and advice. This is not the time to merely consult the yellow pages or throw a dart at the list of possible professionals and contractors. The history and reputation of the people to be hired are quite important to the work required by the owner, and to the overall success of the project.

It is important that those engaged as design professionals and contractors be aware of this situation and react to it correctly. This includes being sensitive to the owner's situation, keeping in communication on an on-going basis, patiently explaining materials, systems, procedures, et cetera) and being willing to share the direction and progression of work and how it fits into the project. The owner will more than likely be in a very uneasy situation and will require added information and literally an education as to what is transpiring.

The inspirations, needs, desires, perceptions, predictions, or other impetus for any project emanates from the owner. This may come in the form of outside influences, such as increased business or potential, new technology, request for added space from a tenant, opportunity to operate in a new area, reconstruction after an incident or disaster, and so on. Usually there is a period of evaluation and analysis preceding any definitive information about the actual construction. Consideration is given to what the needs are, where and how much financing can be developed, how repayment can be achieved and sustained, and other impacts on the current operation when (or if) some new construction is undertaken. Obviously, this is not a decision made easily, quickly, or frivolously.

At the end of this process, the owner will have a good but very generalized idea of what is needed in the project—its size, image, function, perhaps some construction thoughts (materials, framing, etc.), capacity,

The **Owner** is the individual or organization (of any business or contractual configuration) who is the instigator/initiator and ultimate buyer and possessor of the project. By virtue of the latter, the owner is totally responsible for the financing of the project, prior to, during, and subsequent to construction. The owner is also the person or firm who has identified or developed the need(s) that could be resolved by a construction project (for a new building, addition, and/or renovation of an existing facility). Usually the project owner is also the landowner who has direct and proper control of the site on which the project is to be located. In some cases, the building owner merely leases the land, but has the legal authority from the landowner to build the project. In any event, the owner (or jointly, owners) is the entity who holds bottom-line responsibility for compliance of the project with all applicable codes and regulations. This onus comes as part of ownership but is often an aspect not apparent to the owner. It is a legal responsibility that the owner needs to know about (or should be told about).

The local government, in issuing a building permit, will place the issue of compliance on the owner, since this is the person who will own, maintain, use, pay taxes on, and be in total responsible charge of the property. This person or representative of the organization will have a major impact on the concept and execution of the project, in every aspect, from start to finish. That includes the impact of the project on the community, initially, and on an ongoing basis. This involves a good dedication of time over the term of the project, although not necessarily a daily involvement. Often project decisions will rest with this person (or ultimately the organization), who must assess the decision(s) against the owner's concept or intention.

The owner becomes, or is referred to as, a **client** when involved in the hiring of, and relationship with, legal, design, construction management, constructor, or other professionals. The words *owner* and *client* are often used interchangeably. Usually this is also applicable to the actual user of the project, such as the lessee or tenant of a single space in a shopping mall, or the owner/user/occupant of a single, isolated building or complex.

The (**land**) **developer**, in the main, is a speculator who purchases a tract of vacant land, installs (quite often) the infrastructure and utilities, creates lots or sites (as owner or separate entity), and then offers such sites for further development through building construction. For example, a developer will purchase a tract of land, clear and grade it as necessary, install streets and utilities, and create a subdivision or commercial park. The individual lots/sites that are created are considered to be "undeveloped sites," which can then be sold to others for construction of their facilities. In many cases, the developer will offer an expanded service package by offering the sites on a build-to-suit basis, in which the developer hires professionals to design and build a facility for the purchaser. The completed building and the land are either sold and turned over to the purchaser, or are leased out by the developer.

User is a term with multiple meanings in the construction industry. The term usually refers to the person or organization legally defined as lessee or tenant, who uses at least a portion of a project but is not the owner of the entire complex. It also defines the individual occupants or employees of the facility, who live or work within the building; it may include the public in general, who may visit or do business there.

Occupants are persons who are in or approach a nontransient status. The term is applied most frequently to those who live or work in a facility. This contrasts with those who occasionally visit, or users who conduct business for relatively short periods of time. Often "occupant" is expanded to include guests in hotels or motels, and similar types of usage. The term is applied by many building and other codes to denote those who can be expected to be in or around buildings that the regulations control and safeguard.

A **lessee** is a person or organization who gains the right of access to, and use of, a property/facility through a relatively long-term agreement, that is, a lease, usually set forth in terms of years of use, and which usually outlines parameters for use, maintenance, and so forth, including periodic fee payments. Although now used for apartment and condominium units, the lease was primarily a commercial instrument for many years, because of the complexity of language, the rights conveyed, and other legal parameters. This instrument conveys no aspects of ownership, and hence involves less responsibility for property development, maintenance, compliance, et cetera.

The **lessor**, of course, is the person or organization (or agent for either) who is usually the owner of the property/facility offered for use by others (lessees) on a long-term basis (i.e., through a formal lease). The lessor is the entity that receives the fee payments required by the lease, and provides services and/or utilities as provided in the lease agreement. The lessor is legally responsible for the property, particularly if that person is also the owner.

A **renter** is one who gains access to and use of property, through payment of a rental fee. Although similar in concept to a lease, a rental agreement (if written) is on a less formal basis than a lease. Primarily, it involves a shorter-term process (rent a tool on a daily or weekly basis, rent a motel room for a weekend, etc.) than a lease. Oddly enough, a renter is often regarded differently than a lessee in some regulations, since their presence in a facility involves far less familiarity, and hence they are could be placed in greater peril in an emergency situation.

The **lender**, **banker**, **financier**, **financial institution**, **mortgage company**, and **insurance company** are an array of individuals and organizations that specialize in supplying money for the construction of projects. These may be banks, savings and loan institutions, mortgage companies, insurance companies, or private investors. Such financing can be done through interim financing (called commonly a construction loan), where payments are made at specific points throughout the progress of the construction, and at completion are converted to and paid off as a mortgage. Also financing could be by a straightforward mortgage that makes one payment when the project is complete (common in home-building). Money for project work as it progresses is supplied in advance by the builder or contractor who borrows it for that purpose or uses available funds for which the new owner makes repayment. In some cases contracts for supplies and subcontract work are written so payment will be made when the owner pays the contractor. Courts frequently frown on this practice. However, the flow of money for the project is a constant consideration. Since no one participant wants to be forced into an untenable situation, there are constant efforts to transfer financing to others. It is not uncommon for financing to be a major cost in the construction process. No matter what the source may be, there will be an added cost in interest (payment for the time the money is used until it is repaid).

The owner's representative is a person on the staff of the owner or is hired separately to act in the owner's absence and to offer the owner's perspective in all matters. Usually this is a person with a design and construction background, who easily understands the project work and can contribute the owner's perspective in a meaningful manner. Depending on the desires of the owner, this person may or may not control or direct design and/or construction. Usually this person is directed to evaluate and participate in the process and to assess compliance with the contract documents. The primary function is one of liaison and of being a direct, easily accessible communications link to the owner. A separately hired person may be called clerk-of-the-works (see below), and be on the design professional's payroll (with full cost reimbursed by owner). If the person is a staffer of the owner, there may be other duties assigned within that organization. Usually though, the owner seeks more of a clerk-of-the-works presence which is available daily, in lieu of the staffer who is on a part-time, prescribed schedule for meetings, observations, etc. In any format, the person acts in regard to the owner much as the project representative does in regard to the design professional.

maintenance, and so forth. More than likely, though, the owner will not be fully versed on current construction, unless she/he has been engaged in other projects recently. Owners of businesses are completely involved in their own business, not in the planning and construction business; they need clear, straightforward help, advice, guidance, options and alternatives, pragmatism, direction, understanding, education in construction/planning, and simple good sense. Quite often the owner is aided in drawing conclusions or making decisions by the design professional. Unable to resolve a situation without assistance, the owner/client may need to hear a solution or a series of options/alternatives from the professional, in order to crystallize and direct his/her thinking. This process is one of the major and most positive aspects of project programming. Also, the owner will seek (or should be advised to seek) legal counsel for contractual and other legal matters.

SELECTION OF DESIGN PROFESSIONAL

Who comes first? Most businesspeople will have an ongoing relationship with an attorney, for obvious reasons; even well-run, sound businesses have intermittent but recurring need for legal assistance. But with construction and especially design professionals, the needs and relationships are quite different—they may well be single-incident occurrences. True, owners may have smaller construction projects sporadically, when they hire contractors directly for small, confined, or isolated work projects for which no overall design work is required. But major construction projects are not frequent efforts. Hence, the owner is left with little experience, if any, and few resources for consultation in regard to engaging design professionals.

The term **design professional** is a collective term/title that refers to a person (or firm) who has the education, training, experience, and other qualifications to meet the prevailing state laws that offer registration (a form of licensing) of professionals—more specifically, of architects and engineers. Registration usually involves passing an extensive written examination after the receipt of a college degree; also, a period of experience is required in all states of the United States (other foreign jurisdictions have similar requirements), prior to final registration. This person can take responsible charge of a project by applying the required registration seal and personal signature to contract documents, as required by the law. Once registered, the design professional may be required to take continuing education for registration renewal. Generally, the term indicates persons who have all of the necessary legal credentials to engage in their profession.

An **architect** is a design professional whose primary role is the compilation and analysis of information and the creation of a detailed design for the project, to meet the specific needs and desires of the client. Best hired very early in the project, the architect's services involve work on the project during each phase, including, but not limited to, initial programming, site feasibility/selection, development of the design concept, and overall control and administration of the documentation and construction of a project. Acting as the client's agent, this involves collecting information regarding the owner's needs and desires for the project, and the conversion of that information into data and drawings that are usable by the contractors who build the project.

The architect is often characterized as "part engineer, part artist" educated and skilled in good engineering (in a somewhat limited manner—but aware of the various engineering systems, etc.), with the added aspect of artistic considerations (i.e., aesthetics—making the project attractive in appearance, in addition to being correctly and substantially constructed). This design work is far more subjective in nature than the more calculated, quantitative work of an engineer. Few design formulas or other set procedures are available for design work, so the architect relies on acquired knowledge and skill in intangibles, subtleties, relationships of forms, and other generally established attributes of good design. Some architects are dually trained and perform final engineering designs as well as the architectural work. Still others are trained as both attorney and architect. The registered architect can function in many capacities including code official, educator, corporate project manager, construction manager, and so on. The architect usually does not practice in a specific narrow specialty, such as structural engineering or surgery (in the medical profession).

(Professional) engineers are persons who are registered, similar to architects, according to state law for work, participation, and practice, in one or more of the many fields of engineering (numerous areas of engineering are not construction oriented). Professional engineers cover a wide range of activities, but in this discussion it is intended to indicate those persons educated, trained, tested, and experienced in one or more aspects of engineering related to construction and building design. Civil, geotechnical, structural, electrical, consulting/mechanical (plumbing and HVAC work), acoustical, et cetera, are engineering disciplines used in building design. The work can be extremely involved, quite complex, and high-profile, from building foundation design to withstanding seismic conditions to process and production equipment design and installations. The work is highly mathematical in nature, where analysis and calculation lead to conclusion and selection of members, designs, equipment, and systems appropriate to the required task(s). In construction, either the engineered systems are incorporated into the overall building design or the building is designed to specifically enclose their function.

A **principal** is an individual, usually a registered design professional, who is one of the primary owners and functionaries in a firm of design professionals. This person or several persons have the final responsible charge of the work produced by the firm. This person's expertise may be in architecture or engineering, closely allied to the main orientation of the firm; the firm may be architectural/engineering or engineering/

architectural. Depending on how the organization is structured, a principal is concerned with both the technical aspects of the work produced and the running of the business operations of the firm, but in that may function in a narrower area—marketing, document production, or contract administration, for example. Other principals in the firm function in allied but different areas of the practice for a coordinated, overall program. In small firms, the principal may of necessity function in many roles, as the work and business demands.

The term **partner** denotes a party to a business operation in which fiscal and technical aspects are shared between persons in a legal partnership. In many instances there is full equity between partners; in others, there can be a differential based on the amount of capital investment of each party (and the amount gained from the firm's profits) and the level of responsibility assumed. **Junior partners** often are brought into the firm as a means of rewarding and elevating competent, experienced employees, and as a means to smoothly perpetuate the firm. Basically, a partnership is a formal legal arrangement where the parties share fiscal, technical, and administrative responsibilities; they exercise their particular expertise to the mutual benefit of all the partners and for the success of the organization overall.

The title of **associate** is a means of identifying (1) second-level responsible members of the firm, (2) those in a higher administrative position, who can speak on behalf of the firm, and (3) those who have added technical expertise and are capable of leading a design team in one or more aspects of work. Often a person is promoted from the ranks and is given added authority in the firm's operations, with or without a capital investment. It is another form of promotion to retain and reward those experienced employees of high skill and ability, with potential for even higher advancement (to partner, or perhaps even principal), at a later date. Usually associates are supervised by a principal, partner, or other owner, but also, quite often, they supervise staff members in project production and other work phases, in the role of project architect or job captain.

Sole proprietors are single registered professionals who own and operate a business or professional practice, with no partners or others with a financial interest in the business. They may have backers, investors, or stockholders (if incorporated), but none who have an active part in the technical operations. Quite often such firms are an outgrowth of the professional acquiring work while in the employ of others—perhaps as a sideline or moonlighting projects. With enough backlog of such work, the person feels secure in opening a new firm. In most instances such firms thrive well on smaller projects, from perhaps a limited number of very active clients who produce a continuous stream of work. The firm may expand with added employees as the number of projects increases, larger projects are commissioned, or deadline demands become so imposing that additional staff is required. Also, some firms appear to be sole proprietorships (signature name architects, for example), when in fact there are unnamed or silent partners or associates.

The term **designer** can be applied as an ancillary or short title for the design professional who develops the basic overall project design concept. This involves assimilating the programming input from the owner, client, regulatory agencies, et cetera, into a preliminary or schematic design. Quite often the designer will be active only in the early stages of a project, functioning as the design input on many (or every) project entering the office.

In some states, certain buildings may be designed by designers who are not registered design professionals; this is most obvious in the home-building industry. Nonregistered persons may do design in professional offices, so long as they are supervised by a registered design professional. The designer assembles, assimilates, and accommodates all of the diverse information into a properly working and related overall scheme of operations, for the owner/user. Then the task is to create the enclosure in which this scheme will be housed, including selection of forms and shapes, materials, and to some degree construction systems. The final design is a direction to the production staff as to exactly what the client is expecting, but from a general, overall perspective, lacking the minute detail required for actual construction. Quite often the designer plays a relatively small part in the project after the design concept is finalized and approved by the owner/client, and works its way through the production and construction sequences.

The **project architect (engineer), discipline lead**, or **job captain** is the individual member of the Design Professional's staff who is in charge of, and responsible for, the technical development of the project, including contract documents, and construction. Usually this is an experienced, registered person—who may also be an associate in the firm or even a principal (depending on the size of the firm and the type of project). The project architect is responsible for taking the final approved design concept and seeing to its conversion into a fully detailed, properly specified set of technical documents. This conversion must be both faithful to the design concept and usable by the contractors. It must be in keeping with good construction and budget controls. This person assigns, directs, and supervises a team of staffers of varying skill levels who produce the documents. She/he also develops details, selects materials, coordinates with design and the specifications writer, establishes procedures and standards for the project, and provides both general and specific supervision over the production staff.

The **contractibility manager** is an individual or team leader with strong construction background who can act in a formal program as a third-party assessor in a project. This person is usually on the staff of the design or design/build firm. This function is to seek improved or more appropriate project design, production, methods, materials, procedures, procurement, costs, and so on, which can then be incorporated or used to produce a better project overall. The contractibility manager is best utilized throughout the project sequence to assess each phase of work for optimal results. This person supports the entire design/construct team by offering and utilizing high-level expertise not common to others.

CAD operator or **CAD technician** are terms currently used in lieu of the traditional "draftsman" or "drafter." They represent a more accurate designation noting a rather generic title, and the equipment utilized. The term pertains to those who work with and convert information given by the professionals. In keeping with the overall design concept, their work is incorporated into a set of working documents suitable for use during construction. The CAD operator may be an entry-level or more experienced person (even a registered professional) trained in operation of various computer software programs that aid production of contract documents. The level of responsibility of the position is based on experience, technical knowledge and expertise, and depth of contribution the individual can make to the project. The operator may also be trained in and capable of properly applying a limited amount of technical knowledge training (see Technician, below, for the appropriate training sequence). In any case, the operator requires oversight, direction, and guidance of a design professional (or perhaps even a technician) for correct application of technology, proper display of the information, and a direct meaningful contribution to the project production process. Most firms require employees in this category to have a level of technical know-how that permits them to make a direct, sound, and additive contribution. This is preferred to a mere parroting of sketches (making accurate CAD-produced drawings based on hand sketches from the project architect, or persons on other higher levels than the CAD operator, but without being able to add any significant information to the drawing).

Cooperative (co-op) students are staffers enrolled in an academic program designed so the student cycles between periods (six to twelve weeks is normal) of work and school. The work often is arranged by the school and is usually in the field of academic concentration or one closely allied (not merely working while in school). It is not unusual for academic credit to be given for this work; at the least, separate acknowledgment is made. This program allows a student to gain meaningful and valuable experience, closely related to the profession or work status ahead, while still engaged in education. The programs are held in good repute due to their graduation of experienced graduates who will easily assimilate to new employment and quickly develop as full contributors. The program was pioneered in the College of Engineering and Architecture at the University of Cincinnati in the mid-1920s,

The **specifications writer** traditionally has been a more senior person or a highly experienced person in a firm, fully dedicated to production of project manuals and specifications. More recently, the specifications writer has evolved and changed in a very marked manner. Now people with or without professional registrations, with architectural, engineering, or even nontechnical backgrounds, are becoming specification writers. The personal interest and acquired expertise of these persons has created a cadre of very dedicated staffers and private consultants who provide invaluable service to their firms, their clients, and the projects at hand.

The crucial skills are to gather and assimilate information and then fit it into the widely used format of the Construction Specifications Institute (CSI) in a grammatically correct technical style. There is no doubt that a technical background as well as construction field experience is helpful, but it is not mandatory. A drive for accuracy, completeness, detail, and wide use of resources are the profound attributes of a good writer. More often a dedicated full-time assignment, this work can be a part-time assignment in smaller firms and can be done by the project architect or others in times of low levels of work. However, this should never be perceived as easy work, as the technical and legal implications are enormous. The specifications are essential to project success.

More often than not the specifications writer maintains the firm's technical library and is the primary investigator and evaluator of new products, information from manufacturers, salespersons, and manufacturers' representatives. This work requires an experienced eye and full understanding of the legal as well as the technical construction information contained in specifications. In this way, materials and systems can be selected with confidence and not by whim. Without this type of person and activity, the firm is susceptible to faulty construction by indiscriminate and unsubstantiated selection of inadequate or untested materials that may fail or prove inappropriate. Additionally, the firm runs the risk of remaining ignorant of new products, new technologies, innovations in the construction industry, and changes both in manufacturing and manufacturers.

Project representative/contract administrator are interchangeable titles denoting the professional firm's on-site (field) representative. These persons may be full-time or part-time as required by the project, the firm's work load, and/or the client's desires. This staffer acts as close liaison between contractor(s) and the professional firm and staff. The project representative conveys information both ways, resolving problems that have no drastic impact on the design concept, observing the work in progress for compliance with contract documents, and assisting the professional firm in certifying the monthly payments to the contractor(s). The representative/administrator has no authority to supervise, direct, change, or stop the work itself. This person creates the presence of the design professional on the site to facilitate the work and solve problems, where the same depends on input from the professional. A registered or unregistered but highly experienced person, knowledgeable about construction materials, methods, procedures, operations, activities, and of course, the project itself, may be given this assignment.

The **(land) surveyor** is a person trained, qualified, and registered in the art of surveying and establishing land boundaries and establishing grade (height) elevations, variations, and profiles. Also, the surveyor calculates mathematical "closures" around land areas to verify or establish correct dimensions and ownership. From this, they can create plats (maps/drawings) that depict the field operations and show the various aspects of the land area and surface. The surveyor will research and show various utility lines, easements, and all other legal considerations concerning the property. The land area may be one lot, a parcel, a tract, or numerous adjacent tracts (as for the right-of-way of a highway). The surveyor may also serve as the layout engineer, who physically establishes the building lines and other theoretical project parameters on the project site. The layout engineer also sets permanent monuments and other surveying markers to indicate and verify property lines and other aspects of the land area, which impact the project and ongoing ownership.

In most instances, there is an array of help for an owner anticipating hiring an architect or other design professional. For example, the American Institute of Architects (AIA) and the American Council of Engineering Companies in Wisconsin has a comprehensive program and booklet called "QBS—Qualifications-Based Selection," which shows the owner how to run through a procedure that processes questions and answers approaching the hiring of design professionals (see www.qbswi.org).

While an attorney can be helpful, the attorney should not be the single driving force behind selection of the design and construction teams. Rather, the attorney can best serve as an advisor as to the process for selecting the professionals. Construction, while involved with legal considerations, is still a process unto itself and should not be convoluted or hampered by unnecessary legal entanglements. The attorney can be of some resource value to the owner, but in the end it is important for the owner to make an independent decision that has the right feel in personal terms, and rests on a background of sound experience and success on the part of the design professional.

Of course, the owner may have some previous experience with construction or may have a friend, classmate, business associate, golfing partner, church fellow, organization member, or other acquaintance who is either a design professional or has insight into the design professions. Calling upon any of these will provide the owner with added and valuable information for either the interviewing and hiring process or for specific recommendations.

The selection process, in any event, needs to be a very businesslike, carefully orchestrated exercise with probing questions and wide-ranging, open discussions, making a real effort to find linkage and commonality of purpose.

THIRTY QUESTIONS ASKED OF AN ARCHITECT IN AN INTERVIEW (PRIOR TO HIRING)

1. What do you see as important issues or considerations in our proposed project?
2. Are there any special or unique challenges to our project?
3. How will you approach this specific project?
4. How will you gather information about the needs, goals, et cetera, associated with this project?
5. What do you see as constraints for our project?
6. What do you see as the opportunities that our project presents?
7. Whom from your firm will we be dealing with directly on a day-to-day basis?
8. Is that the same person who will be designing the project? Who will be designing the project? Who will be our project manager? Who will be the principal in charge?
9. How much time can we expect the principal in charge to devote to our project?
10. Why are you especially interested in this particular project at this time?
11. How busy is your firm? How many projects are in your backlog? What kind of projects are they?
12. What sets your firm apart from others as it relates to this project? What do you consider to be special about your firm? How can we verify those special characteristics?
13. What are the steps in your design approach that will inform your activities for this project?
14. How would you characterize your design philosophy and design approach?
15. How will you organize your design approach and apply your philosophy to our benefit?
16. How do you propose to utilize the constraints and opportunities previously identified by you in your design approach?
17. What information and services do you expect the client to provide?
18. When do you expect us to provide this information or these services?

19. What is your experience and record of accomplishment with respect to achieving targeted hard construction budgets? How is the process of meeting budgetary targets handled within your firm?
20. Will you provide us with specific examples and references from the past five years that confirm your ability to meet hard construction budgets?
21. How will you establish your understanding of our expectations for this project? What will you show us along the way to explain the project? Will there be models, renderings, drawings, and sketches?
22. How will you communicate to us your expectations for our project? How can we communicate our expectations to you?
23. How do you establish your compensation?
24. What type of agreement will you suggest that we use? How do you see the process of negotiation of that agreement?
25. If the scope of the project changes, how will your compensation be adjusted for either an increase or a decrease in scope of services? What type of documentation will you provide to support any adjustments? How will we adjust the hard construction budget to account for those changes?
26. How do you propose to address the many and varied regulatory requirements of a project like ours so that the time consumed by regulatory approvals is minimized?
27. What would you suggest as your preferred method of delivery for construction?
28. What services will you be providing during construction under that method of delivery?
29. How disruptive to our routine operations should we expect the construction process to be for us? How long do you expect it to take to complete construction for this project?
30. Is there anything that we haven't covered that you wish to either share with us or ask us?

The most important and fundamental issue in hiring a design professional is their state-mandated professional registration credential. Every state has professional registration laws for architects and engineers, and some states have "seal laws" wherein buildings of certain types *must* be designed by or under the direct supervision of a registered professional. (Some categories of buildings—most commonly residential—may be designed by unregistered professionals.) Under the registration system, there is usually a code of ethics that binds design professionals in how they conduct their professional business and how they present themselves in a personal and business manner. It is most unwise to entertain the thought of hiring any unregistered professional, since numerous legal problems could arise, the least of which is direct legal enforcement against the professional. The basic concept of registration, which usually entails a requirement for a college degree, a period of experience or internship, and the successful completion of a written examination, is that the person registered has been trained and examined and is qualified to practice in the profession. This process is exactly the same as for other professionals, such as doctors and attorneys.

High-pressure and rhetorical interviews usually prove to be superficial and inconclusive. On the design professional's part, there should be a sincere and genuine interest in the project and the client's welfare. Obviously, personalities play a part, but they should not be overplayed or become the primary criterion. In residential work, it is best to avoid (even though pricing may be attractive) work by relatives or close friends—they often are harder to pressure to meet schedules and to follow the program for the project. In addition, they often add features that they feel the owner really wants, based on their more intimate knowledge about the owner rather than based on the owner's true need or expectation.

Unless the owner has a history or an ongoing relationship with the design professional, there is usually a process of selection. This can be a difficult process, since little time and exposure are involved, and quick impressions often drive the decision. Whatever method is used to form a list of potential professionals, there should be a process of one-on-one interviewing. This is the best process for the owner to ascertain the most appropriate person(s) to execute the project. Interpersonal interviewing gives the owner a feel for the professional in both a technical sense and in personal qualities (compatibility with owner's thoughts, demeanor, attitude, personality, etc.). It is important that the owner be fully comfortable with the professional(s), since their relationship will be lengthy, often quite close, and in need of harmonious consensus and understanding on many issues.

Usually the process of selection is based on the owner and may include the following factors:

- Previous experience with a design professional and the desire to use them again
- Advice from a colleague or others whose opinion is valued by the owner (a recommendation)
- Advice from other persons in the business
- Knowledge of another similar project that is attractive to the owner and presents the perceived image desired
- Interviews with a list of professionals from a professional society

- A formal competition (expensive but may produce better and more innovative designs; confined mostly to large governmental and institutional projects)

Overall, the architect still is the primary influence on a project, creating its context and its configuration by resolving its programmatic parameters and applying advisable aesthetics. In that context, the architect is usually the first professional hired for a project. Architects are attuned to doing programming and certainly the other phases of design, documentation, and implementation of the contractual obligations.

THE DESIGN TEAM

As needed for the design of various work on the project the architect will hire, under formal contract, consultants representing a series of engineering disciplines. This complete grouping (including the architect) forms the full design team that covers all requisite work for the project. The following illustration describes the consultants and shows a list of disciplines that may be utilized.

Consultants are persons or firms who specialize in a narrow aspect of a project. This is a broad range of persons who are highly skilled in a limited area of technology valuable to a project (see the listing of consultants in Table 2-1). Usually the consultant is hired by the owner directly (as an added contract) or by the design professional (with the cost included in the whole fee structure, or as an added expense). The contract is usually for a limited amount of time, a portion of the project, or to specifically deal with resolving problems within their area of expertise. In many cases, they are registered design professionals who have chosen to specialize in the one narrow field; others may come simply with ample and appropriate training and experience in their field. Good examples are structural/civil/mechanical (HVAC)/electrical engineering, acoustics, geotechnical/soils, traffic, food service, value engineering, color, A/V equipment, signal and alarm systems, et cetera.

More often than not, the efforts of the consultant are blended into the contract documents and made part of the overall design scheme (for example, the inclusion of prescribed, increased acoustical treatment as a part of the basic wall, floor, and ceiling construction). Some consultants may have their own specific drawings, specifications, and a Project Manual (plumbing, subsurface soil borings, HVAC, electrical, civil works, etc.).

Table 2-1 is a partial list of consultants that can be used by a design professional. Not all are used on every project but many are, with others being added as the need is apparent.

TABLE 2-1—LIST OF POTENTIAL CONSULTANTS

Structural engineering	Mechanical engineering
Behavioral science	Life cycle analysis
Electrical engineering	Master planning
Development building	Civil engineering
Landscape architecture	Scheduling
Food service	Interior design
Energy conservation	Fire protection engineering
Fine arts	Construction management
Value engineering	Graphics
Traffic engineering	Surveys
Acoustics	Zoning/land use/planning
Environmental	Codes and regulations
Lighting construction	Specialized regulations
Cost estimating	Models/photos
Special equipment	Package engineering
Renderings	Computers
Communication systems	Process piping
Audio-visual equipment	Real estate
Conveying systems	Facilities programming
Decoration and color	Geotechnical/soil investigation
Hardware	Security
Material handling	Research/programming
Piping engineering	Packaging engineering
Process engineering	Legal/construction law

Obviously, not all of these disciplines are required on every project. The selections are made to incorporate the specific expertise needed to contribute to the project, as required by the overall design concept and scheme of construction. Where unique and highly specialized work is required, a consultant is invaluable in establishing proper solutions in a timely and appropriate manner.

From all of these questions comes a need for more discussion, so that the client/owner and design professional become comfortable with each other. The demands of any project are rigorous and require understanding between parties to meet responsibilities of all types.

OWNER–DESIGN PROFESSIONAL RELATIONSHIP

During the process of interviewing and hiring a design professional, the owner should be given some insight into the processes that each particular office uses to produce its work products. The design professional should discuss previous projects and clients and present general credentials.

As part of the hiring process, or more specifically, immediately after the Owner-Architect Agreement is signed, the architect should schedule some discussion sessions with the client. The reason for this type of discussion is to convey better to the client the range and depth of services and documents to be provided. Too often, professionals assume a demeanor that infers that the client knows who they are, what they do, and how they do it. Merely projecting an air of professionalism is wholly inadequate to creating an insightful and lasting relationship. More and more, reality indicates that firms vary widely in how they approach their work and what sort of services and documents they provide.

This discussion is essential to acquaint the client with the specifics of the professional's work processes and the details of the work products. It also is the time to create a strong relationship to carry both parties through the project. There is need for a thorough understanding of these processes and work products on the part of the client. Although professional work products may appear the same or similar, how they are developed and produced varies widely between offices. Even experienced clients need to be updated as to how their project will be documented, and what the professional will provide the client. All of this needs to be part of a preprogramming process, so that from the very beginning of the technical work, there is unity of spirit and understanding between client and professional.

There are pervasive, widely held, and deeply rooted misperceptions among clients, in regard to design professionals and their services. Even those who have worked through other construction projects often do not fully understand the processes and production of the project documents, the professional services involved, and the need for a bonded and combined approach to the project. Professional office procedures vary as widely as the number of firms, so there is no stock or fixed process that clients can rely on to occur on their projects. Of course, clients new to construction may well have little valid insight into the processes of both design and construction—and so they need the discussions most certainly.

This is so imposing that it is essential, early on, that there be a frank and open discussion between the parties to the Owner-Architect (or Owner-Engineer) Contract as to exactly what can be expected from all parties during the progression of the project. This is necessary no matter what project delivery system is to be used.

It is part of the responsibility of the design professional to set a meeting or meetings (besides those for programming, which is a separate and distinct additional discussion) and to firmly explain the use and impact of various documents, the limits of services included in the basic fee, how other services can be included and the fee adjusted, and the process whereby all of the other phases of the project will be executed.

This is not a dictatorial mandate or an ultimatum, but rather a very calm, businesslike, professional, insightful, fair, and descriptive discussion, whereby no situation is overlooked, and virtually every situation that can be reasonably expected is discussed. If the professional is under normal AIA contractual obligations as agent for the owner, then there is need to ensure unequivocally that the client/owner is supportive of the professional in every aspect and understands how the relationship may be attacked or attempts made to unravel it. This relationship needs to be as strong as possible, certainly not to the point of collusion or conspiracy, but one where the two parties fully relate to and understand each other.

The discussion should entail, among many others, such items as these:

- The function and necessity for each of the contract documents
- The number and type of submittals that will be processed under the basic fee
- The incorporation and use of standardized General Conditions even where the owner has its own such documents (they need to mesh together and the standard version will more than likely have wider coverage than that of the owner—which is necessary)
- The function of the professional in overseeing and policing the owner-contractor agreement, and the issue of impartiality (even though the design professional is hired by the owner)
- The issue of changes during construction, and necessary related documentation
- The possible attempt of the contractor to form a wedge between owner and professional, and how that benefits only the contractor
- Discussion of the various project delivery systems, and any choices already made by the owner; how commensurate adjustments may be required in the contract documents and responsibilities
- The offering of information about full certification for sustainability (green building) as a program option for the owner—and the use of the principles and materials of green construction without full certification
- Other issues

It is also vital for the design professionals to have this information out in the open, so the relationship with the client is a knowledgeable, open, free-speaking arrangement. Where this is not in place, the professional is often relegated to a subordinate position and faces criticism and complaints from the contractor(s). Certainly, this is a gross misperception that should never be part of the construction project. Here it is unequivocally necessary that there be a unified, combined, cooperative, and coordinated effort by all three contractual parties, within their contractual obligations and between them.

Where the client understands the professional side of the project there is far less irritation, and efforts to transfer the problems of one party to another are foiled. Each must have confidence in the other, and should not be the source of disparity of any kind, even at the lowest level. It is essential to the project that there be a fully cooperative spirit, even though the client is party to two distinctly separate contracts. All parties—owner/client, design professional, and contractor—*must* approach and produce their work with each fulfilling his/her responsibilities and working in unison with the others.

DOWN SIDE OF THE RELATIONSHIP

In far too many instances, dispersions are cast on the design professional(s) by the contractors to better position themselves when problems arise, to support their claim for added payment and time, and to shed blame for quirks in the project work. This is especially true when the contractor is hired by negotiated contract, and is as close to the client as the professional—often closer. Here equity among the parties tends to disrupt a smooth-running, budget-abiding project. This is also true in several of the project delivery systems now available to clients.

The real question in these less-than-favorable situations is why the client (or owner) hires the particular design professional, only to provide no support for or understanding of that party's effort and contribution. The project is a development of the program based on information from the client. If the design concept is flawed it should be remedied prior to the awarding of the construction contract—not through in-progress undercutting, finger-pointing, reassessments, and other diversions. The documents for the project should be those that represent the project as the client desires.

The construction manager (CM), when part of the design team, may have other input, but this should be cycled through proper discussions and considerations and not through derogatory comments about the professionals and their efforts. In many instances, it is the function of the CM to suggest alternative design and construction solutions to the design professional. Here it is suggested that superior construction knowledge lies in the CM, which can be of value to the client and the design concept. But this cannot be allowed to lead to an adversarial contest of wills, but should be a cooperative assessment and consideration in the client's best interest. Even here, full support of the client should be established by the design professional from the earliest possible date.

The bid or negotiated price is based on the Contract Documents, which include Plans and Specifications submitted to the contractor.

While other valid design solutions may exist, at this time, the project that is to be built is contained in those documents.

The architectural profession has seen its influence on projects, its range of services, and the integrity of its work eroded over the last several decades. Part of this is attributable to the level of fees required merely to cover the cost of labor and office operations. Part has been the perceived lack of backbone among the professionals, to stand up and stake their turf, and defend it. A major factor has been the mindset of owners for better cost estimating and control, shorter time frames, stiffer deadlines, and reduced if not single-source responsibility. The contractors hold, in a sense, the purse strings, and thereby have the ear of the client. It simply does not make sense for the client to hire a professional to establish a project program, and then allow that program to be whittled away by those who had no hand in developing it. Often, construction managers tend to demean and discredit the expertise of the professionals. That needs to be challenged at every instance.

Design professionals simply must make a stronger and better case for themselves, up-front, and in a manner that withstand challenges from all others. Design professionals have the expertise, and should not allow those who come later to the project to disrupt either the project concept and solution or the relationship with the client. However, professionals must also be fully prepared to perform all the tasks that fall to or are assigned (by contract) to them.

As an aside, the "presentation/discussion team" that makes the early-on approach to the client and holds these discussions necessarily needs a specifications writer as a fully participating member, along with firm principals, designers, marketing personnel, et cetera.

SITE SELECTION AND FEASIBILITY

Many owners require professional services in regard to site selection and/or feasibility, and often involve the design professional as at least one voice in actual land purchase or use. Of course, a real estate expert or agent would be engaged in the search for land, any negotiations, and the actual acquisition of real estate. But for purely technical/building considerations, the various design professions are invaluable members of the site selection team.

The site can take any of a number of forms; single lot, parcel, tract, or acreage. These are roughly defined by the size of the property (from smallest to largest). Many business owners have real estate holdings anticipating some future relocation, construction, or additions, but often they need to acquire adequate land for new and future construction. The process of making such a choice is very important to the owner, so that money is not spent for a site that is too restricted, too small, or poorly located for the owner's operations.

There are wide variations in this task and the whole progression, depending on the current circumstances of the client. If land is owned outright or if there are options to purchase, the process can be refined to one of feasibility—finding out what will work to the best advantage of the client, overall. However, if there is no land readily available (i.e., owned or with an option to buy) the process is complicated by the need to find and secure adequate land to meet the intent of the project. Every aspect of the project must be considered, so the property acquired is proper for the owner's intended operation and business scenario, and is both adequate in area and satisfactory in profile to allow expeditious and suitably priced construction.

PROPERTY SURVEYS

The site selection process requires the use of two surveys. Both need the expertise of the registered land surveyor (see Figure 2-1). This first one is the line or investigative survey, which in essence is a review of records

Figure 2-1 Land surveyor at work. *PhotoDisc/Getty Images.*

and not a lot of field work. The second, the topographical survey, will be discussed later during the beginning of the design process.

It is, of course, necessary that the site selection process be based on correct and current information about the site, so the site selected is appropriate to the project and will not create future problems for the owner. Land records are part of the documentation retained by the local government. These records describe the outline boundaries and overall size of the property.

Whether the owner owns a piece of land or not, the feasibility study of any property is most important to the project. If the owner is going to purchase land, feasibility studies may be required on each parcel of land considered;

there is no other way to compare them, item for item, without ascertaining the same information for each site.

Of course, the total size of the tract should allow ample room for the project at hand and for additions in the foreseeable future. To purchase a site too small is a waste of money usually, as the next project will then require either shoehorning onto the restricted site, or the purchase of more land. And new land may not be available adjacent to the first holding. Land is, of course, expensive, and there is no advocating buying land just for the sake of buying. Rather, the owner must be farsighted enough to project additional success for the new project and the eventual need for more and more land.

Home buyers lie in a slightly different category if they are looking to a subdivision for their new house. Here the land is already divided and restricted somewhat—although in some instances a second or third lot may be available. Developers in the residential sector look to larger tracts—in the range of five acres—as an attractive offering. The new owner is afforded the opportunity to live in a rather secluded environment, perhaps shielded from neighbors and roadways. In addition, the developers can rid themselves of undesirable land that inhibits building. The new owner may well be satisfied to have a portion of the land left natural and undeveloped, as a guard against intrusive development on their immediate property lines.

In some instances, the prospective buyer may even be flown over the land to view the complete context of the tract with regard to all other important features—roads, rail access, other development, future purchases, and so forth. While perhaps extreme, this type of measure must not be discounted since it is essential that the owner make a good, sound decision, with full knowledge of the land purchased.

Follow-up

Once a tract of land is settled upon, it is of greatest importance to have that land completely established and verified. This can be done by a modified line survey through examination of the legal land records, to establish the legal boundaries of the property. It is important to know exactly how much property is involved and the shape of the tract, as well as what land lies adjacent. At this time in lieu of a topographical survey, the site should be walked in its entirety to establish the general contouring of the land, any physical improvements, natural formations, streams, and other features that impact development. Often this is difficult and expensive work, particularly where the site is heavily overgrown, contoured, and wooded. But the end result is a better understanding of what is being purchased or utilized, and how this bears on the project overall.

Once the entire context of the property is known, it is equally important to establish and seek out all of the encumbrances that are imposed on the land. Of course, some physical site features like rock outcropping, severe slopes, et cetera, are quite apparent and verified by walking the site, but there can be numerous other instances of encumbrance. Basically, the fundamental thing the owner must understand is that not all of the land may be used for development of the current or future projects.

The key element to be established is the buildable area of the tract. This is defined as the area available for development and building, after all legal and physical encumbrances are accounted for. Often, only a relatively small portion of the site is buildable (see Figure 2-2). Here, obviously, is a function of the feasibility study: if the buildable area is very small, the site may not be the best selection. The buildable area must be weighed against other aspects of the site before rejection, but it is a major factor in the decision.

Zoning regulations are one of the encumbrances. Through laws for proper land use, compatibility of uses, and quality of life, zoning regulations set out requirements for various elements of development on each lot. The primary restrictions are setbacks, or "required yards." These are established distances from each lot/property line to the place where an improvement may take place—like a building. The required yard distances vary with the type of zoning, and even between various similar uses. The landowner is not permitted to build within the setback areas, which are applied to each property line (front, back, and sides).

These required yards reduce the area of the lot in which a building may be erected—i.e., they establish the buildable area of the lot. They provide suitable distances between buildings, and they separate uses for the overall quality of the community. In some industrial zones, the owner may build to the lot lines (with some other restrictions) since the uses on adjacent lots are similarly intrusive. Single-family housing is usually prohibited in such industrial zones.

Easements can play havoc with property in that they run as required or needed. They do not necessarily follow property lines and can adversely impact the buildable area—i.e., they can reduce the area available. An easement is a legal constraint acquired or established on the property as delineated in the deed, and is defined as follows:

> *Easement*: an interest in land held by a utility, a government agency, or a person other than the property owner, which entitles the holder to a specific limited use or enjoyment (road access, access to under- or above-ground utility, public or private drainage); the holder of the easement may define or prohibit use of the easement area by the landowner.

More often than not, easements are related to infrastructure items—storm and sanitary sewers, water lines, telephone cables, high-voltage

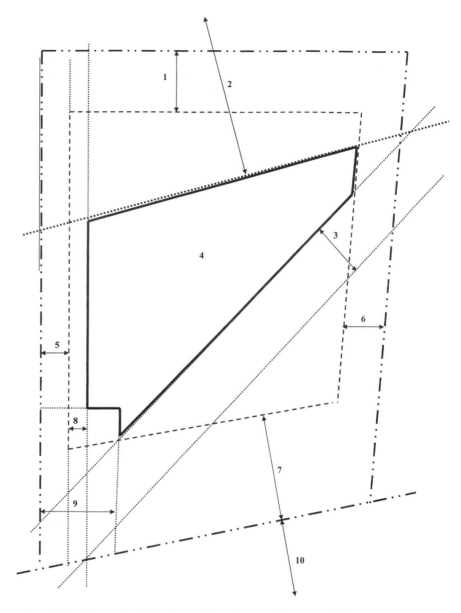

Figure 2-2 A theoretical site plan, with various regulatory restrictions and easements shown. Construction may only occur within the bold-line buildable area. The perimeter property lines are shown as —··—··—

Key to numbered items:
 1. Required rear yard setback (zoning)
 2. Utility easement for large installation (power transmission lines, etc.)
 3. Smaller utility easement (sewer, water, telephone, etc.)
 4. Buildable area (only area on lot available for construction)
 5. Required side yard setback (zoning)
 6. Required side yard setback—may vary from other sides (zoning)
 7. Required front yard setback (zoning)
 8. Small surface drainage easement
 9. Utility easement for access to site (natural gas, perhaps)
10. Dedicated road right-of-way (contains paved roadway)

transmission lines and towers, and so forth. In addition, they can be dedicated to surface drainage, access through the property to adjacent property, and similar requirements. Not every lot has associated easements, but each lot must be examined for easements and their impact on the development of the lot. They can randomly crisscross the property, as deemed necessary by the easement holder, greatly reducing the owner's flexibility in developing the property.

There are also natural features that act to impair development. Areas with thick woods and undergrowth can be dealt with, but often are quite expensive to clear and prepare for building. Underground springs; streams, both flowing and intermittent; and floodable areas add to the impact of water on the site and on the construction. In some instances, rock outcroppings and layers of rock occur very close to the building area, again adding to the cost of site preparation and development and even the cost of actual construction.

Every owner wants a flat, level site as their ideal for development. Actually there are few of these, as "dead level" is usually nonexistent, and land that approaches level is usually dished and holds water instead of draining it. Some slope is desirable to naturally drain surface and storm water from the building (never toward it). On the other hand, slopes of radical dimensions and steepness again act to impair or complicate development. Often such areas are merely left undeveloped, and used as part of the shielding or passive enhancements of the property. This reduces the cost of site development and long-term maintenance work.

Utility company records are in place and kept current to show the locations and sizes of service lines adjacent to the site. These can be tapped and connected as necessary for the project. A lack of utilities shows the owner shortcomings that perhaps are solvable but at added cost. For example, if the site is overwhelmingly attractive except for the size of the water service, and the new project when functional will use a large volume of water, the feasibility report should further investigate to see if and how the water service can be upgraded. There will be added expenses, but these may be considered minor if the many other aspects of the site are appealing.

The various elements and pieces of information must be factored into and be a part of the feasibility report and analysis for the owner and the decision on the site—to facilitate a reasonable acceptance or rejection of each site considered.

MATCHING PROJECT TO TOTAL LAND CONFIGURATION

There can be some dual tasking in that the site/land situation can proceed on one track while the project program is being developed. At some point, though, the two must be compared and adjustments made to one or both. For example, the footprint that seems appropriate may have to be adjusted due to the layout or contouring of the land. Parcels of land may be re-evaluated in view of the scope (extent) of the new facility and how the whole of the project can be accommodated and fitted onto the parcels (one-by-one consideration is required, and each must be evaluated against the others before sound final decision can be made).

A warehousing or manufacturing operation may seek a location with easy access to an interstate highway interchange, preferably one that provides both east-west as well as north-south access. Perhaps railroad access is desired; a spur then is required from the main tracks. Size and shape of the property; streams and drainage and any susceptibility to flooding; contour and vegetation of the land; availability of utilities—these all are issues that fall under the purview of the real estate agent.

Factors that impact building layout and design will involve the design professions, for example, adequate area for the planned facility as well as some increment of future expansion. Other concerns for consideration are encumbrances on the land (easements), wetlands, environmental issues, soil bearing capacity, drainage, infestation, possible flooding (even flash floods), zoning issues (that bear on footprint area, setbacks, "give backs" such as road widening, reciprocal access, height limitations, etc.). Each project and owner has a unique set of site considerations—no one wants a shopping center that is not easily accessible, or a school in an industrial district.

One can picture in the mind's eye any sort of configuration for the land to be used for construction of the project. Some, usually rather rare, are wide-open sites with or without adequate infrastructure. More than likely such a tract would be part of a developed area or subdivision, but development tends to produce a number of fairly small individual lots for construction.

An alternative is the overgrown and/or fully wooded site. A good portion of the project cost must be expended in clearing the wooded area, or at least enough of it to provide an adequately sized area for the project construction. This can be a very costly and time-consuming exercise, since the growth may be dense and will include trees and undergrowth of all varieties. In addition, there may be drainage courses, rock ledges and outcroppings, streams, and difficult contouring that inhibit easy clearing (see Figure 2-3).

Figure 2-3 Clearing a lot involves removing vegetation, undergrowth, and trees, and regrading by moving soil around as required for the project. The process was accomplished prior to excavation for installation of the foundation system. *PhotoDisc/Getty Images*.

Within each discipline a feasibility report can be formulated with guidelines and options for the client to utilize, with the Realtor ® to find the exact and proper site. Some owners choose to do this search on their own, while others already own the land to be used. In any event, the project can be inhibited or disrupted where a faulty site is selected and design professionals are not used early to uncover the nuances. Any site, obviously, can be used, but each has its own set of problems that impact any planned project. It is better to uncover and know about worst-case conditions early, rather than to proceed based on inadequate, faulty, or incorrect information and conclusions. This process can occur before or concurrently with programming, but it usually is misplaced if done after the program is established. That would reduce the number of sites that could be considered, or could force the programmed project onto a site that could not fully or properly accommodate it.

In reality, the site feasibility study needs to be extensive enough to ascertain that the proposed (and as yet undesigned and unplanned) project will fit onto the site without widespread and drastic site improvements. While it appears to be a situation of the cart before the horse, there is a need to have a preliminary idea about the size and configuration of the project. This hints at doing some of the feasibility work before programming, and some concurrent with it. Then site and project can be matched so they complement each other and fulfill the project expectations. Of course, there is high risk in designing the project and then seeking a site, or trying to fit or cramp the project onto a site that is undersized or impaired in any of many and various ways.

PROJECT DELIVERY SYSTEM

In the process of developing a project, the owner must also make decisions that affect the legal and administrative aspects of the work. Often because of the financial implications with the land purchase, et cetera, the owner will engage the overall complexion of the project. This is done quite frequently in conjunction with legal counsel. The owner, it goes without saying, is trying to maximize the project and its impact in a positive manner on her/his operations. To do this, the owner is interested in how the contractors will be handled and dealt with in the normal run of the project—and most certainly in the case of any difficulty, and in the aftermath of the work.

To maximize the positives from the project, the owner will make a decision on the project delivery system (PDS) that best fits the result required or expected. There is a host of these programs and various configurations of contracts, all open to selection by the owner. It is necessary that the owners settle on a PDS early, so the documentation of the design concept can be adjusted to meet the demands of the PDS, and best project the work to the various contractors. This consideration and work is usually carried out in conjunction with site selection and programming, or in tandem with those activities.

Hence, in addition to the program for the project, the owner must make different and somewhat separate determinations and decisions that involve the project delivery system seen as best suited for use on the project. This discussion is pertinent as part of the project's progression. However, this text is predicated on the use of just one of the systems—Design/Bid/Build, the traditional and currently most used system.

Each owner has to make this decision, as the choice of project delivery system will influence many factors regarding the project—financing, timing, relationships between parties, seat of responsibility, etc. The variety of these systems has been developed due to the desires of owners who, for varying reasons, found the D/B/B system inadequate to meeting all of their needs and desires.

Various project delivery systems have been developed in an innovative manner, rather individually, and then formalized through added use, wider distribution of information, and in some cases, through new associations supporting one or more systems. In essence, they are varied configurations of contracts and contractual obligations, aimed at maximizing the advantage to the client, and the client's desires for the project. Most are directed toward cost cutting (through saving money by paying less interest on construction loans) the setting single-course responsibility (i.e., simply making one telephone call to the responsible party for any project problem that arises). For the range of project delivery systems, see Figure 2-4.

The selection of the PDS is most important and is usually made by the owner in consultation with legal counsel, because of the more complex contractual provisions and interfaces. The design professional may or may not be involved (and may not even be selected as yet). In addition, with some systems another party is included in the project team. This usually involves a separate contract (the "third" contract besides the contracts with the design professional and the contractor, where construction management is involved).

The PDS has little if any real influence on the project program but can have a very distinct impact on the contract documents. The effect is directly tied to the specific system selected for use and may well include added work, slightly reduced work, or work in other formats as far as the final contract (working) documents are concerned. With this, the owner is best advised to make the PDS decision early on, so all parties and work coming thereafter can be made aware of the project's configuration and can adjust to it.

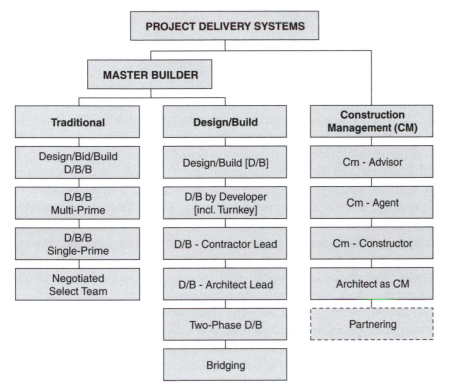

Figure 2-4 The various project delivery systems (PDS) available to the owners, who may select a system that they feel is best suited for their projects and their interests.

SITE TOPOGRAPHICAL SURVEY

Once a specific site is selected, the owner's responsibility is to provide a fully detailed and wide-ranging topographical survey of the property. If the owner already holds title to the land, at least a review and update of the information on any existing survey is necessary. The most current and reliable information is crucial to job progress and cost reduction.

The property information researched and developed for the site selection decision is usually just enough to allow the necessary analysis. Of course, it is vital to view the sites under consideration in their full context and relationship to roads, rail lines, utility resources, and so on. Also, of course, the general size, shape, and lay of the land must be considered.

The topographical survey is essential for both the design professional's use and for several of the major contractors who will work at the site. Most of the time, the owner's entire tract of land is included in the survey, but in some cases only the portion of the parcel to be used for the new construction work is included. In any event, it is most important for any landowner to have a complete and accurate survey, produced by a registered land surveyor, so there is record of the holding. Often owners will go further and acquire a Registered Land Certificate, which involves some added legal paperwork, but which in a sense guarantees the owner there will be no diminution of the land area should subsequent surveys impacting the land (i.e., on adjacent properties) bring conflict to established information.

Surveys can be costly ventures and the cost is directly in proportion to the amount of and ease of acquiring information from public records, and the ease of access and verification of the information in the field. All land areas are owned by someone, and all land areas (parcels, tracts, lots, subdivisions, etc.) are recorded with a local public government agency (usually the county recorder and auditor). Information on those records is modified by various surveys as they are completed and recorded. This is the first place to start the search for land information, and for the most part is reasonably accurate.

Surveys are complex mathematical exercises whereby certain distances in certain directions (of the compass) circumscribe the property and literally form a "closure"—the point where the mathematics meet at a specific point. In the field on the actual property there are numerous markers—stakes, steel pins, concrete monuments, metal plates, bolt heads, nails in poles, notches cut in concrete sidewalks, etc.—used by surveyors to indicate various points like property corners (where the property lines change direction). But as with any human effort, some errors do creep in, and sometimes newer work causes disruption of markers and renders them ineffective.

The survey work in an isolated, confined project area is required to be more highly surveyed. It is necessary that every aspect of the property used as the project site be included, from size and property sides, to their distance and directions, the topography of the land shown high and low arums slopes, and so on. This needs to be detailed down to the point of establishing a "clearing line" that shows where the wooded portions of the site are cleared, and the woods remain beyond and then all man-made or and natural features for drainage, buildings, (existing or partially remaining) wooded areas, rock outcropping, etc. This is a massively informative document and the information is vital to both the design and construction functions.

Additionally, it is necessary to establish the buildable area of the property, the portion of the site that is not encumbered by some regulatory requirement, like zoning, easements, et cetera. Owners often find this process quite revealing in that a good portion of their property is withheld from their use and given over to others for their use. These can be both private (in the case of some easements held by nongovernmental groups) or public (held by government agencies through their regulations).

SURVEY CHECKLIST

The following items are required on all surveys. Site/plot plans may be utilized provided they note the survey that is used as the basis and all of the following information is included. All of this information is usually required by building code agencies to ensure proper and complete documentation of the project location, and conditions impacting the proposed construction. Numerous other regulatory agencies also have a specific interest in a portion of this information.

- ☑ Title of project; name of contractor and/or owner; date; name and seal of registered land surveyor who performed or supervised the work
- ☑ Indication of County, Township, Section Number, Parcel Number, and Lot Number
- ☑ North arrow; scale indication (no smaller than 1" = 50' − 0"]
- ☑ Indication of property lines, dimensions, bearings, monuments found and/or set; sum total of land area
- ☑ Adjacent lots within 100 feet (indicate if vacant); adjacent buildings within 50 feet
- ☑ All roads, streets, alleys, including widths, type of paving, centerlines, and dedication
- ☑ Distance to nearest intersecting street
- ☑ All easements for utilities (water, gas, electric, telephone, sewer, etc.), access, drainage, etc.; holder of easement rights
- ☑ Driveways, parking aprons, access sidewalks (indicate materials)
- ☑ Proposed building[s], accessory structures, walls, fences, all with complete dimensions
- ☑ Required yard or setback lines along each segment of property lines (where required by zoning regulations or other instrument)
- ☑ All bench marks or other elevation devices; sea level elevation of each
- ☑ Topography of building site and surrounding area to be developed; grade contours at intervals of 1' − 0" change in elevation
- ☑ Existing and proposed spot grade elevations at
  - o Property corners
  - o Corners of proposed structure[s]
  - o Minimum of two [2] points on the side lot lines opposite the corners of
    - ■ The proposed structure[s]
- ☑ Elevations of all floor level of building[s]
- ☑ Sewer, manholes, house laterals, with type of sewer, size of sewer, invert elevations at manholes and house lateral connections
- ☑ All features for storm water disposal; downspouts, drain tile, yard drains, area well drains; swales and drainage courses
- ☑ All manmade and natural features on the site (walls, rock outcroppings, fences, old foundations, etc.)
- ☑ Trees to remain and those to be removed; clearing line where wooded area is to remain

Figure 2-5 A project plot/site plan developed from a survey, including specific location of the building.

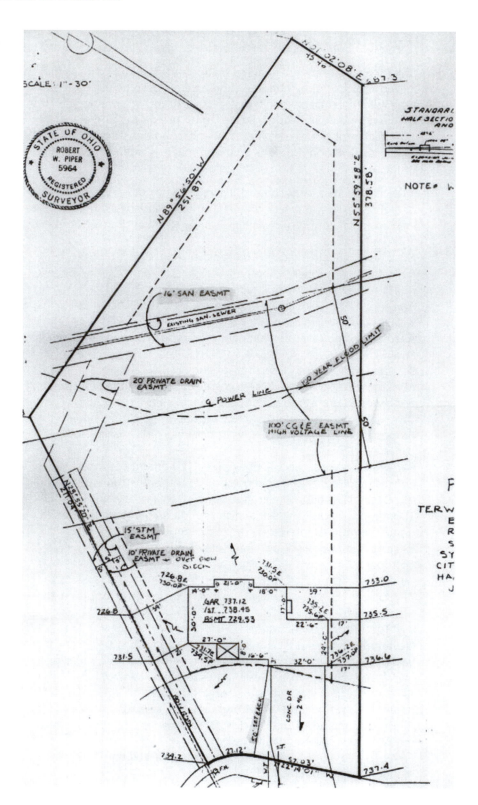

This illustration is an example of a project site plan based on a property survey. The street is located at the bottom of the drawing. Note the various zoning setback lines (dotted) and the limits of the several easements overlaid on the property. There are two buildable areas, one where the building is located (near the street) and one on the upper side beyond "16" San Easmt'—but also note that this portion of the site is located in the 100-year-flood limit (note limit line running across the site), which prohibits construction. In the end, the owner of this property has but one choice where to locate the building; only slight rotation or relocation is available within the remaining building area (see Figure 2-5).

3

RESOLUTION AND DESIGN

PREDESIGN PHASE

Programming

It is crucial that the project program be fully understood, both in how it is created and in how it functions to guide, inform, and inspire the project designer (according to Professor Edward T. White, Florida A&M University). (An old adage held that the architect should live with a family for two years prior to designing their house, to understand their life style and interrelationships.) In the simplest of terms, architectural programming is the problem-finding and problem-definition phase of the project. This is a new aspect that was not part of the listed phases of work until fairly recently.

The program should not be held or perceived as a "grocery list" of necessities or a more whimsical "wish list" of desires or nice-to-have features. The program is the result of a systematic method of inquiry carried on by those trained in such work. Many firms work exclusively in this area and have developed highly refined forms and methodologies. Fundamentally, the program is the gathering, organizing, analyzing, interpreting, and presenting of project-related information. Often there is a level of pure interrogation involved, where one question will challenge or contradict another. The quest is to get all of the information, and in a correct or proper form.

Client input and regulatory searches are the two preeminent elements of programming. This is a process of what Professor William Pena calls "problem-seeking," in which the design professional attempts to ascertain in depth, the processes, procedures, work flow, relationships, problems,

> The more time spent early on in comprehensive, incisive, and *decisive* programming, the more the tasks of designing and documenting the project are facilitated. This converts to specific, higher-quality documentation, which assists better construction. High-quality construction, in turn, produces a quality and satisfying project.

contradictions, ideas, precedents, perspectives, desires, needs, and goals of the owner for the new project. It is of utmost importance that the client understand the need for programming and the rigorous process required to produce it. There should be a full and open discussion to explain that the program must be the best possible document that the collective parties can produce, and that the better the program the better every aspect of the project will be. Shortcutting programming is a disservice to the client and certainly is highly restrictive and an inhibition to the designers of the project. The design professionals and the programmers know all of the information required, but their insight should be thoroughly explained to the client, early on (see Figure 3-1).

A series of meetings, use of formal questionnaires and interviews with owner(s) and also with major administrative and operating managers within the departments of the organization are essential to understanding the operations and fundamentals for the new project. This

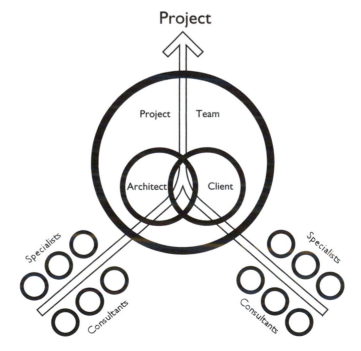

Figure 3-1 The participation of a team for the programming of a project. *From William M. Pena,* Problem Seeking, *4th edition (John Wiley & Sons).*

will be a period of probing, questioning, and rather intense and aggressive investigation (not confrontational, but in the spirit of getting all of the information in correct and proper form) to ensure that the program includes the correct operational information and the correct array of working relationships—all crucial to project success.

Much as the tailor or dressmaker takes extensive notes and measurements in order to produce a quality, custom-fit garment, so the design professional seeks all of the information that will allow the production of a quality, custom-fit building or complex. It is entirely possible to make or break a project in this early phase. It will literally be a room-by-room, space-by-space, department-by-department, and relationship-by-relationship discussion. Such problems as forgetting issues/concerns, miscalculation, misunderstanding, assumption, unilaterally filling in information, miscommunication, and lack of recording and addressing important details can lead to a faulty, unsatisfactory, errant project, disliked by the owner and possibly the source of a major dispute, if not litigation.

THE PROJECT PROGRAM

The project program is a function of the owner, guided by the architect. It must meet the following needs:

- Provides information about desires and the general concept of the project—answers the architect's questions
- Provides all information required by the architect to design the project—intimate discussion of life-style, features, design style, specific parameters (where available)
- Discusses budget and contingency funding
- Discusses possibility and method for changes

No owner wants to pay for a project that has not captured the desires or imagination of the owner, much less the proper operational and functional aspect of the owner's business. It is irrefutable that the better and more complete the programming, the better the project. This is so true (especially in an atmosphere of extreme financial matters and high costs of projects) that professional curriculums in several colleges have programming as a specific and separate study. Some even have a separate, added discipline or option; people are being specifically trained as architectural programmers.

It must also be said that clients often cannot list or articulate their needs and desires. This information must be drawn out of them through incisive questioning, in-depth analysis, probing, and correlating bits and pieces of diverse information. The ultimate goal of project programming is the production of a complete, in-depth, candid, and revealing document that expresses everything the owner expects in or from the project. In that, the client must be made aware of the need to be fully open, accurate, and fully involved in the programming—anything less will produce a false program that will lead to an inappropriate and unsatisfactory project. The client cannot vacillate or hold back any information vital to the project configuration, nor anything that is open-ended or unresolved—doing so creates an uncertain program and impairs progress and appropriate design solutions. Programming is directly akin to the itinerary for a trip—it lists important issues and directs one to distinct landmarks. It is detailed, precise, and hopefully, all-inclusive. The owner may have to be sold on this effort, but in the end the time spent will pay dividends in lower initial cost, smoother running projects, and a better fit of the project to owner needs/desires. Long-term, it provides greater efficiency and lower operating costs. Contrasted to the other costs of a project, programming is but a very minor item, which belies its true value.

Programming also involves the search into the regulations that apply to the specific project. These parameters are required, as the regulations and codes are law and must be observed through compliant construction. In many cases, formal permits are required. It is better to uncover the requirements early and incorporate their solution into the basic design, than to run across them later. In the latter case, there is frequently major disruption of the design concept to allow for proper addressing of the regulations. In reality, the codes and regulations are project requirements from the point of view of the general public. They exist because certain aspects of every project involve public access and/or occupancy, and therefore, governmental attention is required to provide a safe environment. Owners must be made to understand that meeting these provisions is part of their responsibility under the law, even though compliance may add some cost to the planned project.

When programming is actively and correctly used, it acts as a powerful lens to focus a large amount of quite divergent information regarding the project, in a logical manner and in a form that facilitates its use in developing the design concept, in the execution of project documentation, and of course, in the actual construction work.

The Program

Other than the contract between the owner and the design professional, the program is the first project document reduced to writing. The impact of this document cannot be overstated and must be fully understood. It is essential that both owner/client and design professional buy into the final document, on every level and on every item. The program may well be a rather voluminous and highly concentrated document crammed full of vital information, from mere comments and snippets to major and firm conclusions. It cannot be flawed or fraudulent in any way. Where there is a lack of total unanimity and understanding by all players of the two contractual parties, there is room for discussion, misunderstanding, and dismay. Too often clients who are allowed to accept inappropriate programs come out with finished projects that they cannot fully account for—i.e., with questions like "How did that get into our project?" Open-endedness is virtual failure in programming.

While the program is remote to the construction activities and the contractors, it is nonetheless the key element of the design concept—and that concept, when developed, is the crux, soul, and basis of the construction. It is this document that directs the project and indicates what the final project must be, functionally and operationally. There may be some indicators regarding the aesthetics and overall appearance of the project, but this is usually minimal except where the client has a very distinctive physical image that must be part of any project.

The sole reason to design anything is to create a better fit between what is and what needs to be. Hence, the act of programming is necessary for getting all the facts on the table. Complete data-gathering and analysis also facilitate the development of alternative designs, evaluation and selection of alternates, and defining alternative, more detailed analysis. In programming for schematic design, the overall organizing concept, and the concepts, this phase of the work becomes the definition of programming: organization in a design from the overall, main organizing idea to the most minute detail of the design.

Programming consists of three activities—analysis, synthesis, and evaluation—at various points in the process. The process of programming is not necessarily linear: it uses imaging, presenting, and testing to clarify the various purposes that information gathered during programming must serve. Programming's ultimate job is to uncover all of the important aspects of the design problem. It is a sweeping search to uncover or extract all the information that encompasses anything and everything that has to do with the project. But programming purposely leaves out most of the smaller detail.

Programming is a major tool in communicating both the intentions of the design team and the requirements of the user; the research is the tool for understanding the client, including needs, values, and requirements in more detail and accuracy. As the most cost-effective place in the design process, design can deal with the various constraints that are uncovered. The sequence of programming and design events involves the following:

- Strategic goals and objectives
- Legal and regulatory parameters
- Building functions and unique activities
- Space requirements for each room and associated adjacencies
- Specific requirements for each room
- Specific requirements for each building services (mechanical) system
- Site constraints and development requirements
- Design and planning considerations
- Concept solution
- Project budget
- Project schedule and delivery constraints

The program requires item-by-item analysis and contains the first parameters of the project design. Design is a very rigorous process, and one where trial-and-error and alternative solutions and approaches are rampant. It is a time when little is settled and when a tremendous amount of information must be digested, rationalized, and correctly placed. There is no formula for design, but rather each project must be approached on the basis of its unique features and requirements.

Neither does the designer or design team have a preconceived solution in mind. If they did, they would ill-serve the owner by forcing or cramming programmed needs into a fixed solution, manipulating the needs rather than the physical features of the project. The design process evolves as information is analyzed, brought together side-by side, and pieced together in correct relationships. Areas are analyzed (by function, perhaps) in a process called "balloon diagrams" (see Figure 3-2). Here, the program requirements are collected into similar locations and located in correct relationships (again, all part of the program). The balloons can be relocated, turned, flopped, or otherwise moved as various possible solutions are developed.

Clients usually are asked to sign the chosen design to indicate approval of it, and request that it be taken to documentation and on to construction.

DESIGN PHASE

Project Design

Project design is not something easily explained or understood. It is a matter of the architect, engineer, or other designer assessing the re-

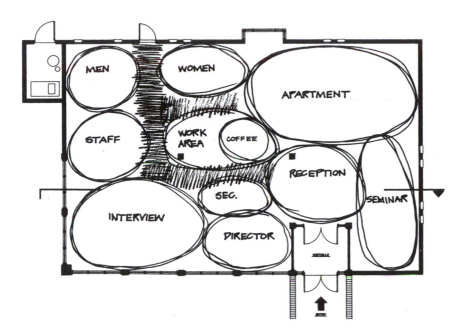

Figure 3-2 Example of a balloon diagram. *From Mark Karlen,* Space Planning Basics, *2nd Edition (John Wiley & Sons).*

quirements of the owner, establishing routings and relationship between operations, departments and personnel, and combining these into some shape or form of enclosure. That enclosure is then "designed" or created through the mental processes of the designer utilizing learned design principles—axioms and attributes that form pleasing, attractive, and yet functional shapes.

Today's design process has departed from the traditional methods of innumerable sketches and study models produced to assess various attributes of the emerging design. Today, the computer allows for virtual expression of the project. In fact, the whole of the design can be established, rotated, walked-through, examined, and modified with great ease. Elements can be changed with little effort and analysis is enhanced by the wide variety of ideas that can be explored. The process today is broader and more in-depth than ever before.

Still, basic architectural design is founded on principles from long ago. Every project must provide or account for function, strength, aesthetics, and economics. Still true today, these principles were developed in Roman times. In general terms, projects must function as required by the owner; they must be strong enough to carry the imposed loads and meet the imposition of natural elements (wind, rain, earthquake, etc.); they must be attractive and pleasing; and of course, they must meet some established economic constraint (i.e., a budget). No matter the type or style of project, these four principles prevail.

In addition, six architectural composition principles still are fundamental parts of every design. They are used in varying combinations but remain simply: proportion, scale, contrast, balance, rhythm, and unity.

These all are highly intangible and quite subjective in nature, but they appear in every project scheme to some degree. In that context, they contribute to the highly subjective aspect of the design concept. (The subjective aspects are the factors not specifically defined that cause some people to like the design and others to disdain it. They are factors in every project.)

Subjective means to evaluate, assess, and analyze something based on personal views, values, background, or thoughts (i.e., "shades of gray," so to speak), to determine if the item is to your liking or not; and not on a solid checklist, list, or set of firm points that create a scorecard pointing to right or wrong, good or bad (i.e., a definitive "black or white" determination).

The designer blends a combination of these variant considerations into the mental image first developed for the project design. They then can be explored in variation through computerized analysis, and they are resolved in what the designer perceives as the best solution for the requirements set forth.

Design is a process that is directed toward resolving four general areas contained in every project:

- Needs and desires of people—physical, intellectual, aesthetic, and emotional (comfort, function, accessibility, environment, etc.)
- Influences on architecture—natural, cultural, and technological (climate, available materials, level of construction expertise, etc.)
- Major requirements of architecture—function, strength, aesthetics, and economics (as noted above)
- Design elements of architecture—plans, forms, and composition (floor plan is the key element of the design and the success of the solution, with all other considerations emanating from the plans)

Design can be seen as following scientific processing, in that it closely follows the six steps established by Galileo for scientific exploration:

1. Define the problem.
2. Establish objectives.
3. Collect pertinent information.

4. Analyze the problem.
5. Consider possible solutions.
6. Solve the problem.

In architecture, Steps 1 through 4 are called "programming"; Steps 5 and 6 are called "design."

In addition to these structured matters, there often are much wider opportunities for greater creative expression on the part of the designer. Most clients/owners have no fixed idea or concept of what their project needs to be, should be, or even what they want it to be. They are open to suggestions. There is no one fixed, set, absolute solution or concept for any project. There are reasonable solutions that can be extrapolated from the program and molded within the creative work of the designer. Many concepts and ideas will be explored; many may lie unexplored simply because of time constraints or simply because they were not thought of.

The crux of project design is to find the design concept—the overall strategic plan for the project—that best suits the program and solves the most problems and desires of the owner. Indeed, several solutions may be possible, but even among them there is one that will come to the fore, pleasing all involved and seemingly doing the best job of meeting project requirements.

The architectural character of the project is established when all of the elements of architecture have been incorporated in the project as a whole, and in proper relation one to another. Many people believe there are intrinsic qualities in the character of buildings that cause office buildings to look like office buildings and churches to look like churches. Of course, many other people disagree. Today there is a blurring of such distinctions due to many things like costs, changes in aesthetic tastes, and proliferation of wider use of less traditional and more experimental shapes; also in such situations as churches becoming so massive that they resemble arenas or fieldhouses. The world is replete with examples of unusual buildings that have resulted from this blurring of distinctions (see Figure 3-3).

The process of design can be long, arduous, involved, most complex, and quite confounding, and it is always an experience of searching, seeking, and developing a valid concept.

Development of a Schematic (Preliminary) Design

Following, or perhaps even as part of, programming analysis, the project designer will begin to formulate an overall design scheme or concept for the project. It is not unusual for certain aspects of programming to

Figure 3-3 An example of cutting-edge architectural design. A radically different-looking building but one that apparently pleases the client/owner and satisfies required image and operating functions. *Courtesy of Jupiterimages Corporation.*

make some project features and elements immediately apparent and stand out in such a way as to point to distinct directions for the design concept. These are important indicators and are sought out during early programming sessions. They are of utmost importance to the project designers because of their more generalized importance, which can influence subsequent problem-solving and design efforts. This is crucial to the project, since it must accurately reflect the relationships and locations of the various functions of the project, both within the planned structure and surrounding it.

Those factors of the program that indicate some immediate directions do not, however, imply that there are a limited number of solutions. Every project program has a vast array of factors, parameters, and requirements that can be resolved in numerous ways. The designer will explore these, discarding those that fail to measure up overall, or otherwise fail to allow for the incorporation of more factors. A preliminary conclusion is often overturned when more information is developed during programming. This exploration is normal procedure for every project and is not a drain of time and money (the fee) allotted to the project. It is obvious that a good program forced into an inadequate or improper concept will fail—and usually quite early. So the processing of program information is steady, studious, careful, and most flexible to allow for changes, rethinking, and new directions within the initial concept or a subsequent one.

The process is one of designing and creating a concept from a nucleus of information and expanding that work by incorporating more and more programming information in regard to relationships, operating functions, areas, personnel workstations, and activities. This work is based on and verifies the programming, and will also disclose where more information is necessary. This process is roughly akin to fitting pieces of a jigsaw puzzle together: what piece fits where, and how exactly they fit to allow other connections and expansion of the picture. Things in a project are not quite so simple, in that the project pieces may require being fitted in any of several ways, while still meeting the need or function. Hence, the process involves investigation, innovation, imagination, and experimentation—all properly based on valid programming!

Numerous schemes must be developed and tried to see which fit the program (and which do not) and how well one fits as opposed to the others. This is the essence of a highly focused design process of fitting required functions and relationships (as deemed necessary by the owner's program) into the design concept developed by the designer— i.e., fitting the operations of the project into the physical form. There is never one set, unchallengeable solution. Obviously, this is the place for presenting a variety of options to the owner; selection here could influence (even drastically) what happens or must happen in other aspects of the overall scheme/plan. The final decision of the owner in consultation with the design professional should be viewed as the best solution, giving due and full consideration to *every* circumstance of the project.

Revisions, Changes, and Additions

Since design is the seeking of solutions in differing ways, no project has but one finite design. The usual process for the design of a construction project is akin to trial and error, whereby the design professionals formulate varied designs which meet the programming requirements. Configurations, orientations, and even some relationships may change, but without drastic impact on the overall function of the plan. It is the work of the design professionals to bring all the elements of the program into focus. This involves creating solutions, almost literally tearing apart and starting again. Every aspect needs to be fully explored from many different angles and perspectives. The process is a rigorous one, wherein many staffers are involved to reach what is basically a consensus solution as the primary presentation. Other solutions are also developed to show variations of the basic solution. Often elements of several solutions are combined and incorporated in the final, approved concept.

In addition, owners often will choose to utilize a construction management (CM) format or delivery system, whereby the manager is hired as an agent of the owner. Here the CM can be brought on board during the latter stages of the schematic design process. By lending insight into construction practices, materials, and systems, and with in-depth cost information, the CM can provide information that will make the design concept even better (in the eyes of the owner). By making suggestions for changes (not so much in the design concept, but in the ancillary portions regarding choice of materials and systems) and by adjusting construction requirements to provide less cost, the CM as the owner's agent influences the final approved design and the eventual reality of the finished project.

This process can also be employed where the owner negotiates a contract with a general contractor (GC), early on. Actually the GC here acts much like the CM agent would act, and provides construction data to the design process. In either situation (CM or GC), the function is one of advice, insight, and refinement, and is not a major driver in the design process. Obviously, when these parties are involved this early in the project they acquire added insight into the basis of the project; this is not information that is readily available to contractors in other delivery system formats.

In the end, it is for the owner to make the subjective decision of which design scheme or concept is preferable; the professionals usually aid the selection process by discussing various pros and cons of each plan with the owner. It is extremely rare that the first design is so satisfactory that no further preliminary work is required. In the main, several meetings and discussions are required as the professionals create, develop, and present options, take comments and instruction from the owner, and then revise, change, modify, add, or delete to adjust the scheme to the new criteria. Specially trained, skilled programmers and designers can shorten this process by being very incisive and analytic, coming close to a final preferred choice very quickly. Obviously, this is to the credit of the professionals, and it can be a source of added funding to the entire project sequence since the entire allocated fee (most firms budget each phase of their work) is not absorbed in the preliminary design phase.

DESIGN APPROVAL (BY OWNER)

Approval of Design Concept

It is not unusual for the architects to present several alternative concepts for the owner's evaluation. This, of course, involves both the elements of the project and the associated cost. The structure can be portrayed in any number of possible schemes that the owner needs to assess and understand. Not only the function but changes in the appearance are offered, which need careful consideration on all levels and in all details. There are always several perfectly acceptable configurations and solutions for any project, so the presentation of options is both prudent and necessary. The owner is best served by choosing the configuration with the best fit for all of the project program parameters. With pertinent guidance and advice from the design professional, the owner must make the final decision as to which project concept will be used.

Once the overall project scheme has been selected and proven satisfactory, it is advisable that it be formally approved by the owner in writing. (Some firms require signed drawings as evidence of the approval.) At this point, it is usually just the overall rendering(s) and the floor plan(s) that are developed, since these drawings control other aspects of the project and provide a good deal of information for other drawings, documents, and concepts. Indeed, if the plans do not work, the project again can be in jeopardy for not achieving a good final result. The floor plans give the overall extent and configuration of the project, while the renderings provide the exterior appearance, in large measure. Neither are highly detailed—this is, after all, a design "concept," or the basis on which the remainder of the project documentation will be based.

Final Approval of Design Concept

This is the first major milestone of the project. This approval must be documented, formally and in writing, even including signed drawings. This is needed so there is no hesitation as to what exactly the project is to entail. Often, guide specifications listing materials and systems are also included, to give further indication of just how the project will be constructed and how the contract will be fulfilled. The information at hand is still very preliminary and lacks minute detail, but it sets firmly the direction, requirements, and intent of the professionals in meeting the programming needs. This is truly the manifestation of the programming. Also, this marks the formal end of the schematic design portion of the project's design phase (as noted in the various documents of the AIA; see listing of work items contained in each project phase).

In addition, this is the beginning of the transition of the owner's program requirements into the language and directions to the trade workers who will utilize the contract drawings in building the project.

Subsurface Investigation

In some cases the subsurface investigation of a given site will be part of the feasibility study. This occurs primarily where the site has rather well-known soil conditions that may not be appropriate to the proposed project. It makes little sense to select a site that will unnecessarily add substantially to the project cost. The investigation in this stage of the project could be a deal breaker, if it is found that soil conditions are highly marginal to flatly adverse.

However, subsurface soils investigation is an essential part of the design of the project. In all but the smallest of projects (including most single-family residences), there is need to know what strata lie below the project. The subsurface information is necessary to proper design of the foundation system, and hence is required shortly after the design concept is approved (if not before).

Every project does, of course, engage the earth—not only the surface visible to us but a portion of the earth's crust under the project site. Excavations for projects vary in depth, but the soil existing under any project is a circumstance that simply must become a known value—a part of the criteria to which the project is designed. Of course, the project substructure/foundation system is the interface between the building project and the earth.

To ignore the soil conditions is neglectful on the part of the designers and engineers. It is ill-advised to follow this course, since those soil conditions can have a major impact on the project's construction and its costs. There is, in fact, a whole discipline of engineering devoted to soils, soil analysis, and geotechnical information. The direct viewing of the undersoils and their analysis is crucial to these persons and to their advice in regard to how and where the building should (or must) engage the best of bearing soils.

Undersurface conditions are extremely unpredictable and are not something that can be guessed at or taken for granted. In fact, even the spot analysis of a site (i.e., isolated locations of test holes) often belies the whole of the undersurface. Soils can and do vary, often widely, within the same building site. This is one area where the change in conditions is a valid addition to the project cost through the use of fixed allowances (if changes are readily anticipated), unit prices, and change orders.

It is obvious that the site cannot be excavated and then analyses made of the soil, since such a venture could prove useless if the soil is such that construction is inhibited or prohibitively expensive. This is no method of investigating unseen subsurface soils, so the method of investigation involves acquiring samples of the soil. The system most commonly used is called "soil borings." This involves driving a hollow tube, about $2^1/_2''$ in diameter and composed of two halves (see Figure 3-4). Often called "split-spoon sampling," the tube is driven to a level that may be pre-established by analysis of local geology and its mapping. This is a general limit that may be adjusted if deemed necessary.

At any rate, the tube can be driven as deeply as required. As it is driven, the soil is contained within the void of the hollow tube. When the tube is extracted, it brings with it the soil captured within the tube segments

Figure 3-4 Soil boring. *Courtesy ELE International Inc., Soiltest Products Division.*

(much like the liquid that can be retained in a soda straw by inserting it into a liquid and plugging one end with your finger as you withdraw the straw). The tube segments can be laid out on the floor and opened to expose a string of earth that shows the depth, composition, and coloration of the various soils through which the tube has passed. The sampling even shows the paving or grassy top soil at the location(s) and the various veins of soils that underlie the top surface. Here analysis can be done on the various soils to establish which is capable of bearing or carrying building loads. Some portions of the soil samples will be totally inadequate for this use. Some of the soils will be shown to be very stiff and quite strong—and fully capable of holding up a portion of the proposed building.

For larger buildings, soil borings will have been taken earlier, for analysis and use during foundation design, allowing soils engineers or engineering geologists to establish proper bearing capacities/values based on soil composition and the thickness of their layers. The bearing value set by soils engineers then indicate to the structural engineers where the foundations can be located, the building loads safely carried, and reliable stability provided for the building. Soils bearing capacities vary widely, and are usually expressed as pounds or tons per square foot (for example, 3,000 pounds/sq. ft.).

The best bearing soil is bedrock that has never been exposed to the light of day. Often bedrock lies quite a distance below the surface. But many times, depending on the project size and weight, there will be other soil types that are capable of providing adequate support. So there is no strict rule that bedrock must be found and used. In addition, soil layers are not parallel in all instances. In some places they are radically sloped or otherwise erratic, precluding easy use for bearing. In this case, it may necessary to form level pads or steps where the bottom of the foundation can rest.

Soil analysis has a direct impact on what foundation system is used and how that system is designed. This all, of course, is both essential and critical to the success of the project and the proper, functional, and safe use of the building.

DESIGN DEVELOPMENT PHASE

Design Development

This is the second portion of the design phase, and begins to bring much of the detailed information required for the project to the documents. From what has been largely written material or conceptualized drawings, the work of this phase brings specificity to the project: feet and inches, details, exact locations, and distinctive directions and instructions (in both graphic and written form). This involves selection of materials and systems, based on the detailing developed to meet the design concept. Simply put, this phase is the gathering and piecing together of data which shows exactly the construction to come. The documents developed during this process are usually done in a manner that allows them to be used as the actual contract (working drawings) for the project. This, of course, requires the incremental addition of the complete array of necessary construction information during the production phase (see listing of services provided in each portion of work).

The approved design concept is now expanded and detailed, with the addition of a vast amount of construction information and the development of the contract specifications and other project documents. These include exterior elevations, wall sections, some critical details, identification of crucial specification items, etc. As this development progresses, there will be a natural process of having to tweak other elements or aspects of the project that have gone before, even the overall scheme; there is not, though, any major revision or disruption to the approved scheme. Since so many elements must be fitted together and as new information continually comes to the project, there is a need for minor adjustments and refinements to make everything work in harmony for a good final design.

This phase of the design professional's work takes an important amount of time (usually numbered in weeks and months, depending on the size and complexity of the project). It has long been held by the AIA that this phase requires approximately 20 percent of the total fee received for the project. However, computer-assisted drafting (CAD) has made marked inroads into this timing and has in most instances reduced the percentage of the fee that must be allocated to this work. This work also has been reoriented so that it is really the beginnings of the actual contract working drawings. The drawings produced will merely be expanded during the document production phase, as myriad detail is added.

While computerization has assisted in work being produced in shorter time frames, there may still be a lingering question as to the overall and consistent quality of the drawings produced. For the most part, operators of CAD systems have limited meaningful, broad-range, and intricate construction information, which may impede the quality of their drawings. Most cannot be left alone to produce working drawings as required, but need close supervision and input. This is a most crucial consideration during design development, in that such fundamental decisions are made that in-depth knowledge and experience are mandatory prerequisites. Many offices still have project architects or more senior drafters making hand sketches that are then converted to CAD format. Even the software industry is recognizing, more and more, that in the obsessive quest for better and more sophisticated software programs, the industry has left a major gap: the resolution of the proper introduction of construction information, and the settling in of software programs and techniques. Changing things too soon and too often means that many offices do not even try to keep pace. Every introduction of a new program, despite its upgraded capacity, is upsetting to project schedules and requires new, time-consuming training.

The process of design development is a measured and necessarily cautious activity, ensuring that the correct basic project information is set down for expansion and development later. It is basic display of basic information. If there are flaws and errors here, they may well not be discovered and become so incorporated in the project documents that they survive and are erroneously built into the project. This work is incremental, as information is both added and developed. Early information must be refined into its proper context and fit into the project work. Obviously it is here that experienced and knowledgeable personnel are vitally needed, so full understanding of the information and its manipulation can be accomplished.

Part of the information development involves researching products, finding new information, and careful analysis of it. Project work relies on the work of the design professional to create and provide proper direction and instruction to the workers involved in the construction. Where correct and adequate information is set out in proper construction terms, the work will progress far more smoothly—and correctly!

4

SELECTION, INCORPORATION, AND DOCUMENTATION

CONSTRUCTIBILITY

In an era when catch phrases have become a way of life, we must acknowledge that one very imposing word is now a major part of the architecture and construction lexicon. That word is "constructibility."

Constructibility is the ability to be constructed, as ascertained by an in-depth analysis of proposed construction to assess the best way (among many available) to proceed, the most cost-effective methods and materials, and the ease with which the work can be accomplished, faithful to the design concept. Constructibility has developed into a major factor in construction and is a valid consideration from the design phase of work forward.

Simply put, is the work required to produce the project buildable (i.e., contructible)? Can it be performed relatively easily, and with advantageous cost implications? One of the major side issues is the fact that there are generally many solutions to any one problem. The matter of constructibility could well be the principal factor in the decision-making process. In the norm, constructibility review is an ongoing process but is initiated and most heavily pursued during the design phase of the project. This is done so that the documentation (and the design concept if necessary) can be adjusted to portray the correct construction scenario. In the past, the constructibility review was pursued solely as deemed appropriate by the design professionals. With the implementation and use of the construction manager (CM) project delivery system, the constructibility review was started and given over to the CM, who had the deeper construction expertise. This is not a matter of assessing or checking on the design professional, but rather is a process to suggest and review alternatives that may be appropriate, *without* adverse impact on the aesthetic design reflecting the design concept. Overall, constructibility review establishes a more refined project for the owner early in the process, primarily since the many possible solutions can be reviewed and the best solution utilized.

Trade workers and the construction industry as a whole take great pride in the fact that they collectively can build anything, given opportunity and enough money. Often there is need for innovative and unique techniques; research for new, better and more appropriate materials and systems; and cutting-edge intelligence and daring to achieve the goals required. Construction as a whole has been highly successful in this, supported by a manufacturing sector worldwide that has the wherewithal to provide everything the construction operations require.

But how does this impact an individual project, and why is it a consideration in a chapter about documentation? Constructibility combined with documentation forms the backbone of the project, and allows for its creation, development, refinement, and construction. In simple terms, the design concept must be examined to ensure that a proper program of constructible sequences can be applied to it, and from that comes the need to express those sequences in the contract documents. This information is then conveyed to the contractors and their trade workers for further analysis ("How are we going to approach this work?"), management, and actual execution of the work.

It is quite easy to fall into a trap in design and documentation, where work is depicted to satisfy a problem but is virtually impossible to build. How often and for what periods of time can workers be required to lie on their backs to install complex or intricate items overhead? (Or perhaps the real question is, can they do it at all?) Work must be accessible. No sequence of work can allow one item to cover another that is to be installed after the first work, and so forth. Is there sufficient space to use the proper tools to install the work?

"Blind work" is a continual nemesis in construction. For example, underpinning an existing wall is a common practice, yet the backside of that construction is never seen. One can only rely on proper preparation and construction in the hope that the work is both correct and properly executed, if it cannot be readily or reliably verified.

CONVERSION

The conversion of the preliminary and conceptual design information involves realignment, formatting, research, decision making, and heavy augmentation. When completed, the information must be carefully and completely transmitted via drawings and specifications to the field personnel, for both the professionals and the constructors.

This task is so fundamental that if it is not done, or if it is poorly done, the project will never be built as portrayed earlier and as now anticipated by the owner/client. Since the client is not that familiar with this process and does not fully understand it, there can be pressure for quick completion during the period of time required for this work. Often the professional must explain the work and its contribution and value, since hours will continue to be billed, and indeed, the billings may substantially increase in size, due to the added personnel and hours now being utilized. Sometimes a good number of months and even years are required, depending on the size and complexity of the project.

DOCUMENT PRODUCTION PHASE

Production of the Construction (Contract) Documents

This phase of the project work entails a major staff effort to produce a complete set of Contract Documents (see Figure 4-1):

- The Agreement or Contract for Construction between owner and contractor (usually developed separately by legal counsel, with limited input from design professionals, using standardized forms like those published by the AIA
- A full set of well-executed and well-coordinated working drawings appropriate to the project

Figure 4-1 Extent of the participation of design professionals in a project.

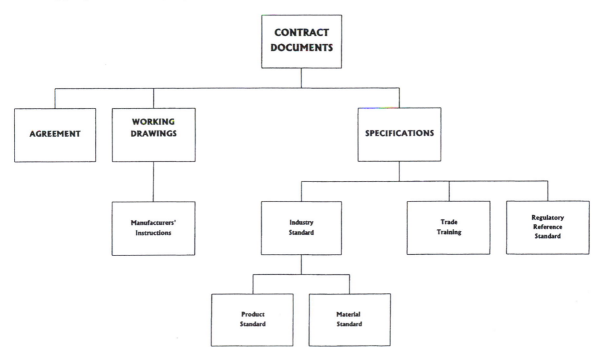

■ Associated technical specifications, with appropriate administrative provisions and forms

Because of the complexity of projects and the high cost of building, and for the safety of workers and later users, construction is heavily dependent on what is shown and what is written about the project. There is also a need to graphically show what is required. However, to provide readable drawings, there is also a need to place a tremendous amount of project-related information in written form. This has evolved into a pairing of documents—a set of drawings (graphic representations of the project) and a set, book, or manual of specifications (written material about products, systems, and procedures specific to the project). Figure 4-1 lists the categories of information that should be contained in each type of document, based on the theory that the information can best be shown in the location noted on this chart.

As outlined below, the contract documents consist of several items, legal instruments, or documents. While all are important, the two that are the most difficult to execute are (1) the contract or working drawings, and (2) the specifications. Both are necessary to convey all of the information that the contractors require in building the project. Their extent and content is wide-ranging, in-depth, and very, very detailed.

For the most part, it is necessary that these two sets of documents be supportive of each other—"complementary and supplementary" are the legal terms—since neither one can fully explain the project in itself. The illustration shows the breakdown of information for a typical project, and how some information can be shown graphically (in drawings) while others are so detailed and descriptive that it must be shown in a written form (the specifications). An analysis of the chart easily shows why the items are listed as they are; that is, it is obvious that some information is normally written or normally drawn. The essence of this decision is really, what is the best way to convey this information?

Working (Contract) Drawings

Traditionally, working drawings have been two-dimensional graphic representations of the project. To properly and completely display all of the features and construction of the project, the drawings usually include the following:

Site plans	Foundation plans
Site improvement plans	Floor plans
Underground utility plans	Structural framing plans
Landscaping plans	Exterior elevations
Demolition plans	Roof plans

Cross and longitudinal
  building sections

Wall sections

Interior plumbing plans

Interior HVAC plans

Interior electrical plans

Room finish schedules

Door/frame schedules

Window schedules

Other pertinent schedules

Reflected ceiling plans

Interior elevations

Fire protection plans

Detail drawings

Security system drawings

Drawings by Content

While the role of the entire drawing set is to depict the project work in toto, each drawing sheet and/or each individual drawing has its own subrole that entails showing various-size portions of the project work. Subsequent chapters contain a general discussion of the various drawing/sheet types and their roles. Additionally, a checklist is included that lists what information/drawings usually appear on the type of sheet being discussed. Usually, though, both for convenience and for saving of space, each single sheet in the set will contain more than one type of drawing. Some drawings, such as floor plans, are so expansive as to utilize all available space on a single sheet; for very large projects, floor plans may require a series of sheets to depict just one single level.

The method for producing working drawings is setting a series of procedures for accomplishing various portions of the work. Techniques are specifically selected from the many available, whereby each element of the procedures is done. Refinement of information and work is necessary and valued, so that precision, subtlety, and polished characteristics are established. This process makes project documentation clear, credible, coordinated, accurate, and easily used.

The intent of this chapter is to provide a general outline and set of basic guidelines as working drawing standards. These are aimed at assisting the young professional and drafter in correctly arranging and depicting information pertaining to the drawing documents. As an immediate guide and reference for working drawing information, the following is one of many resources available to provide sound, fundamental information for readers of this book: Ralph W. Liebing. *Architectural Working Drawing*, 4th ed. New York: John Wiley & Sons, 1999.

Working Drawing Standards (Note: The following list is not all-inclusive; see subsequent sections for specific checklists of items to be included on drawings.)

1. The theory of working drawings: An art of communicating; the method used by a design professional (a registered architect

or engineer who is engaged in the design and construction of a bulding project) to convey graphic information to the contractor(s) regarding a construction project; in particular, information on materials, methods of assembly, quantity, location, extent, configuration, and design intent (concept) necessary to construct the building project. The drawings (along with the contract agreement and the specifications) are part of the contract documents; hence, they are legal and binding documents.

2.   A building project = building + structural system + all building services (mechanical) systems and utilities + site modifications

3.   Working drawings are a combination of words and pictures, which convey different types of information to the contractor(s). These documents are drawn to scale (a small unit of measure is used to represent one foot [12 inches]): they are usually two-dimensional, and drawn to the correct size and in correct relationships (no distortion nor foreshortening as in perspective drawing). They do not, however, contain all of the information required to build the project; a set of written "specifications" is also required. The specifications add more, but new information, and really supplement and complement the drawings. Only by using both of these documents can the contractor(s) truly review, see, and understand all the work they are to perform.

4.   On the working drawings, there are several different types of notes:

   ■ *Demolition notes*, used for removal of trees, vegetation, fences, existing structures, earth, et cetera, necessary to permit completion of the new project.

   ■ *Construction, or plan notes*, used to "call out" (indicate; designate; show; name) materials, methods of assembly, quality, or design intent (concept) information needed to define a particular item or situation found on the sheet on which the note occurs. Be very specific with the information given to the contractor in these notes.

   ■ *Landscape notes*, used only for extensive vegetation, plantings, and earth (contour) modifications. Call out both existing and new vegetation (size and quantity when applicable) and, as necessary, planting information or modifications to existing work.

   ■ *General notes*, used to transfer information that is common to either the sheet, discipline, or project on which it is found; usually refers, in general terms, to numerous items shown in other types of notes.

5. All sheets must be given a distinctive sheet number to permit easy access, reference, and coordination between information and persons utilizing the drawings. (For example, persons talking on the telephone can easily refer to a specific sheet merely by citing its number.) Numerous systems are in use, and each professional office has a standard of some sort that it uses. For example, on fairly large projects (more than ten drawing sheets) sheets could be numbered as follows:
   - *A series*. Architectural drawings, defining dimensions, aesthetics, materials, and methods of the project.
   - *S series*. Structural drawings, defining everything to do with the structural features of the project (footings, foundations, columns, beams, joists, etc.).
   - *C series*. Civil drawings, showing and defining work of a civil engineering nature, such as grading (contour modifications), drainage, roads/drives/walks. Used only on extensive, more complicated projects, or when breaking civil work out (defining it) on the site improvement plan to improve and simplify communication.
   - *L series*. Landscape drawings, defining landscape work and vegetation modifications. Used only on more extensively landscaped projects, or where such work is to be specifically called out on the site improvement plan to simplify communication.
   - *P series*. Plumbing drawings, showing and defining the materials, methods, locations, equipment, fixtures, piping, and intent of the plumbing system (including storm drainage) for the project. May be combined with HVAC information where work is limited in scope.
   - *M series*. Mechanical drawings showing and defining the materials, methods, locations, systems, equipment, and intent of the HVAC work on the project. On small projects, the plumbing work may be included, provided that work is modest in extent.
   - *E series*. Electrical drawings, showing and defining the materials, fixtures, methods, locations, equipment, and intent of the electrical system for the project.

6. A cover sheet is used on most projects and is quite helpful in many cases. This may be a separate sheet, or may be simply a portion of a sheet that has some construction work shown on it. The cover sheet contains the following:
   - Vicinity or location map clearly showing the project site; can be a state map (where necessary), and/or a portion of a local street map

More extensively detailed drawings and specifications = **More control** by the designer of aesthetics, quality, and durability of a building project

Less extensively detailed drawings and specifications = **Less control** by the designer and owner of aesthetics, quality, and durability of a building project (and more control by contractor, whose main concern is minimizing cost and maximizing profit)

This is a *very important* point: the design professional is an agent for the owner (acting in his/her behalf), and control is the key to a fully successful project that meets all requirements of the owner. Control *cannot* and *should not* be released, given over to, or abdicated to anyone else, particularly the contractor(s). This is also an important aspect in the work of any drafter working for a design professional in any capacity; it is fundamental, and needs to be understood and followed.

- Complete name of the project and any pertinent information such as project number, phase of work, etc.
- Full address (street and number, etc.) of the job site
- Names of design professionals and consultants
- Name of owner (board of directors, pastor, company president, mayor, city council, department members if they apply to the project)
- Registration seal of the design professional (this is required in several states by law, on all sheets of all projects except residences)
- Date project is issued and goes out for bidding (also occurs on each sheet)
- Index of all drawings contained within the set, showing sheet titles and sheet numbers
- On some projects (as an option), a rendering of the project

Individual Drawing Requirements

The following listing can be modified, added to, or deleted from, as deemed necessary. Order may be varied from project to project. The following is but one example of sheet numbering (use of a decimal system allows for inserting of other sheets at later date) and possible content (varied as the project requires). Working drawing numbering as noted in 5 above is not magical; with less than approximately ten sheets, numbering should be simply consecutive.

The Site Improvement (Site, Plot) Plan

1. Using a drawing containing actual survey information (by a registered land surveyor), show all property lines with a heavy line (long dash, two short dashes, long dash) and the bearing (meets and bounds) for each line (for example, N85°32′41″E, 158.94′; this denotes the direction of the property line and its length). At property corners (the point where property lines change direction), indicate the intersection of the property lines with a small dot or a hollow circle. Show bench marks (points that show grade elevations as used by the surveyor) with a solid circle or target bull's-eye, and a note. (See Figure 4-2.)

2. Show and call out all concrete paving, aprons, curbs, curb cuts, stoops, sidewalks, et cetera. Thoroughly dimension as appropriate (width, height, etc.). Indicate as appropriate by plan note all finishes, control and expansion joints, and so forth.

3. Show and call out all existing items (trees, structures of all types, fences, etc.); note specifically, or show in dotted line, those to be removed for the new construction.

4. Locate new building with dimension to two property lines (one to side of building, and one to front or rear). This should indicate the foundation wall locations. Indicate the building in one of two ways:
   - As a footprint, using a heavy, bold line around the perimeter, showing exterior columns (if any).
   - As a roof flan (bird's-eye view), indicating slopes of roof, drains, parapet (top of wall), caps, et cetera. Dash in the building footprint where it sits inside the roofline (this shows any roof overhang); dimension to footprint, not to roofline.

5. Show north arrow. If there is a wide difference, note both magnetic (true) north, and building (or plan) north, which aligns with the walls of the building plan.

6. Show grade elevation of all contour lines (lines that connect points of like elevation above a bench mark, or sea level). Show existing contours in a medium-weight, dashed line, new or modified contour routes and locations in a heavy, dark, solid line. Note the numerical value of each contour line in at least two places. Indicate the grade elevation of the first floor (or "grade level") of the building, within the building footprint; crosshatch the entire footprint of the building in a medium tone.

7. Show the locations and sizes of all existing utility lines, on the property and in the adjoining street; show new utility lines into building from existing source; be sure to note the type of line

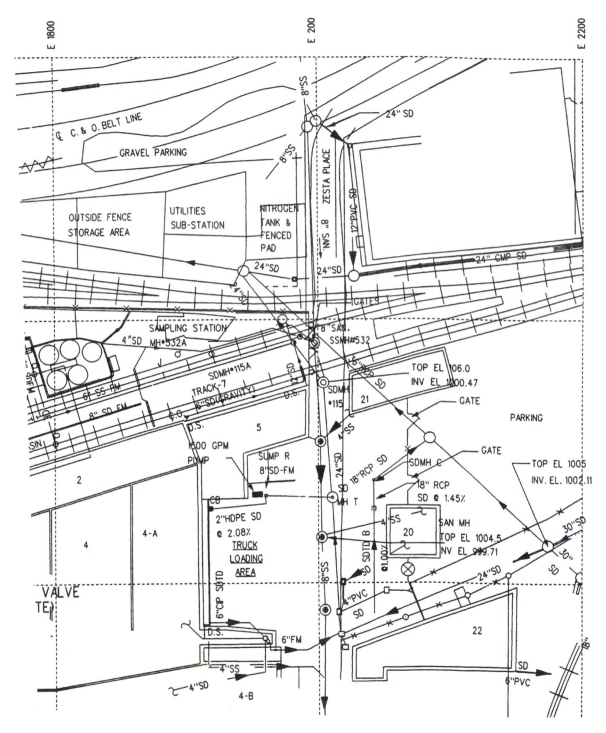

Figure 4-2 Example of site improvement plan.

(water, sanitary sewer, storm sewer, gas, etc.). Show utility meter, and shutoff valve locations if outside building. Where appropriate, show the siamese Y valve location for the fire sprinkler system. This must be accessible to all fire apparatus on a paved surface, with back-up area, turn-around, or continued access around the building.

> For some projects, it is advantageous to include a separate site plan devoted entirely to the utilities and the mechanical and electrical trade work. In some jurisdictions, the fire service requires a fire protection plan. This is a modified site plan showing fire protection equipment, sprinkler connections, annunciators, fire pumps, utility shut-offs, building exits, driveways, radii, fire hydrants, fire mains, and the location of trees, high-tension wires, and other items that may impede or affect fire-fighting access or other emergency services.

8. Indicate and call out site drainage system; piping, area wells, dry wells, culverts (including diameter and material), surface drainage swales, retention/detention basins, and underwalk drains. Roof drains and collection drains should be taken to daylight or tied into a storm drainage system (call out and so indicate). Many residences use splash blocks beneath downspouts (call out where used).

9. Show, indicate, and call out in detail all new site improvements: drives, walks, parking areas, handicapped ramps, fences, decorative features (pillars, light posts, archways, entrance features, other structures, etc.), bridges, fountains, and so on; detail these features and locate properly. In particular, dimension parking areas in relationship to the building proper. Call out and show wheel blocks, paving materials, striping, planting areas; dimension the parking bays and aisles in a string dimension and call out the total number of parking stalls in each bay. Note and locate parking area lighting standards, and all signage, both painted and erected.

10. Call out and note all new landscaping materials by legend or plan note; indicate type, quantities, and spacing (if required) for each plant type. Note all sodded, seeded, or hydromulched areas and show extent.

The Floor Plan(s)

1. If information is available, lay out the structural grid (column centerlines) for the building; then carefully, and as accurately as pos-

sible, scale out and draw in the walls and partitions for the building; establish and indicate door, window, and other wall openings. (See Figure 4-3.) Designate column grid centerlines with $1/2$"- or $3/8$"-diameter circles on the ends of the centerlines, *outside* of the building's dimensions. (These can be widely spaced away from interference with the drawing information.) Assign numbers to one set of column lines, and letters to those perpendicular to the first. Draw in all columns—proper material, cover, and so on.

2. By single string dimensions (as much as possible), locate and align all interior wall dimensions from face of studding to face of studding; call out wall finish materials, and show thickness

Figure 4-3 Example of floor plan.

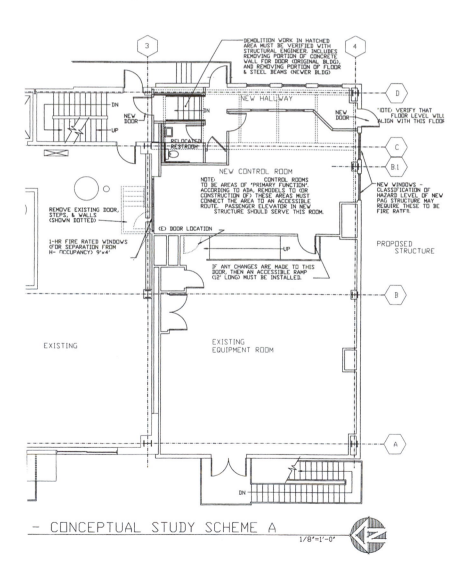

by plan note or by general note, with plan notes as the exceptions to the general.

3. Indicate fire walls, fire separation walls, and other special walls/partition types; change in hatching for change in detail or construction; call out locations (dimension), methods, and materials. All walls and partitions in 2 and 3 above should have a distinctive hatching applied via hand drafting, CAD drafting, or reproducible adhering tapes, to distinguish one type from another and make plan reading easier.

4. Envision four distinct lines of dimensions around the exterior of the building:

   ■ The outermost line is out-to-out (overall) of the extremes of the building walls.

   ■ The next line (moving in toward the building wall) would dimension between column centerline (grid) lines and to edge of wall corners (indicate to what location dimension is taken); this line may not be required on every project.

   ■ Next closest to the building is a line that dimensions the "wings," offsets, "jogs," angled walls, and major portions of the building.

   ■ Closest to the building is the dimension line that locates door, window, and other wall openings in relation to each other and to the corners of the building masses. Indicate rough opening (RO) or masonry opening (MO) (use dimensions to the centerline of openings in wood frame walls *only*). Where bands of windows or glass are used, these should be dimensioned to the center of the mullions (vertical members between glass panels); call out type of system, glass type, and thickness, et cetera. (Note should be made of panels, etc., which are typical—i.e., used repetitively around the building.)

5. Indicate *all* rooms and spaces with an area name and/or a room number. Most professional offices will have a standard regarding room/area/space indications. In the main, though, assign room numbers in clockwise order, in adjacent fashion, beginning at the main entrance, and working around the building perimeter, then toward the interior. In many instances, it is helpful to use a number that indicates the floor or level on which the room is located (example—Room 112 = floor 1, room 12). Ensure in any event that every space is numbered, without duplication; rooms added after numbering can be designated as 112A, 112B, each in relation to the numbered room near by.

6. Indicate and call out fire extinguisher cabinets, drinking fountains, counter and work tops (including in restrooms), fixtures,

built-in cabinetry, shelving, closet shelves and rods, electric panel locations, phone panels, utility entrances, telephone booths, and all other features to be built or supplied under the contract. If the above occur in an area that is to be enlarged in plan (larger scale), show the feature on the larger plan *only*.

7. Call out and indicate (heavy dashed line) portions of the floor plan that are to be enlarged for detailing and clarification purposes in another location within the working drawing set (for example, restrooms, kitchens, specially equipped rooms).

8. Provide distinctive door or window symbol/designator for *each* opening. In residential work, the window and door sizes and hardware information may be located at the opening. In larger and commercial projects, a designator should be used, and the complete associated information listed in a window and a door schedule. Many different systems are in use, but *it is not wise to use any system that counts the number of units* (this should be left to the contractor).

9. Locate, indicate, and call out with heavy, distinctive designators, building sections (cross—and longitudinal) cut through the entire building. Also, use other distinctive designators for identifying details in the construction.

10. Ensure proper title and scale indication for each floor plan. In some cases the complete plan of a building will not fit on the sheet. Here, match lines can be used to sever the building into several portions, each of which is shown on a sheet; a "key plan" at small scale showing the entire building is required, with an indication of what portion of the building is shown on the sheet. Match lines require heavy distinctive designators, also.

11. Call out, if and where appropriate, radical changes in ceiling height(s), floor levels, critical beam locations (bulkhead) if no reflected ceiling plan is planned/used; exposed features, beams, et cetera, should be located and called out. All work in this paragraph shall be shown with dashed lines, and dimensioned as necessary.

12. In the chapter on floor plans there is a checklist of specific items relating to floor plans, and which should be depicted, where used or required.

The Exterior Elevations

1. Exterior elevations are orthographic views of the outside faces of the building (two-dimensional); they are always projected at 90 degrees to the surface being viewed. The required number of

elevations varies with the layout (shape) of the building. Where walls are angled, they should not be shown in the angled or fore-shortened manner; an additional elevation view is required at a 90-degree projection to the angled wall. Curved walls should be drawn as if they were pulled out flat (i.e., show the true arched length of the wall). Elevations should be drawn at the proper scale, with vertical verticals and horizontal horizontals (i.e., nothing should be optically correct as in perspective, and nothing should be distorted or foreshortened. (See Figure 4-4.)

2. Call out critical vertical dimensions at both sides of each elevation as appropriate; ensure that dimensions extend to an actual point or establishable level (top of masonry, joist bearing, etc.). These vertical items need location:
    - Bottom and top of footing (indicate depth below grade)
    - Top of foundation wall
    - Top of sill plate; top of double top plate (wood)
    - Top of wall, masonry, parapet
    - Bearing level of roof joists
    Use a distinctive designator at each grade/elevation note (a "target" ⊕, for example).

3. Indicate roof pitch (slope triangle or slope per foot) for sloping and pitched roofs; do not indicate top of ridge as an elevation on pitched roofs.

4. Properly locate and call out wall section designators where they apply; run designator down into the wall, but not through the entire wall height. Indicate detail cuts or other locations.

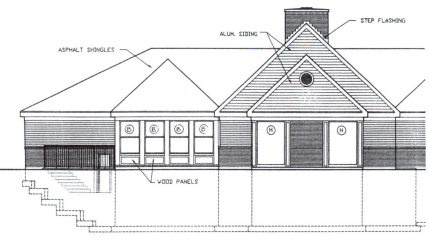

Figure 4-4 Example of exterior elevation.

REAR ELEVATION

5.   Show configuration of new, finished grade line, as it is to appear at completion of the project (uneven, sloped, graded, raised, lowered, etc.); this is the heaviest line on the sheet (and is *not* a flat drafted line). It should extend well beyond the ends of the building, in its proper location. Existing grade is often shown as a dashed line, somewhat lighter, but also in its proper configuration.

6.   Indicate all spread footings, foundation walls, column pads, pilasters, stepped footings, and other features that would appear on the outer face of the building; do not show interior features. All work below the finished grade line should be dashed.

7.   Show and call out special vertical locations as necessary for clarity: windowsill and head heights (indicate RO or MO as appropriate); centerline of circular windows or arches; vents or louvers; and major items of mechanical equipment on the surface of the building.

8.   Poché ("cross-hatch"; use standard symbols for materials in elevation, not in section) only on selected and confined portions of the elevations (not over the entire drawing, unless this is office standard); help to define design intent, and call out location of all exposed materials, joints, and so forth. Be specific, but do *not* use specification language or extensive notes (the specifications writer will usually assign proper terms to be used).

Building Sections—Cross and Longitudinal

1.   Building sections involve cutting the building across the short dimension (cross section), or lengthwise (longitudinal section) to reveal both construction and relationships of construction systems and areas. The principle of sectioning is much like slicing a sandwich, which then reveals all the details of the interior construction. (See Figure 4-5.)

2.   Show, usually at the scale of the exterior elevations, the overall mass section(s) of the building at the point of the cut. The section (cut) line may be offset to go through a variety of spaces; offsets must be taken *only* at right angles to the cutting plane.

3.   Show and indicate major structural features, using minimal detail (slabs, walls, floors, trusses, roofs, beams, girders, foundation walls, footings, etc.). Think of the section as an index to the construction.

4.   Indicate each space cut by the section by its name and room number. In these spaces, show interior elevation(s) of walls beyond (those you would see looking in the direction of the cut-

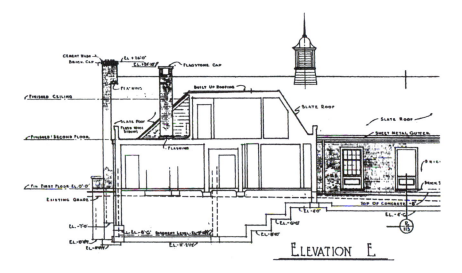

Figure 4-5 Example of building section.

ting plane) *only* if there is new or critical information resulting, which is not revealed elsewhere in the working drawing set.

5. Indicate and call out (by a heavy, dashed line or a solid line) those portions of the building section that are "blown up" (increased in scale) into details.

6. Indicate and call out with designators (targets, bull's eyes) all critical vertical dimensions similar to elevations; extensive dimensioning is not required.

Wall Sections and Details

1. The concept of wall sections is to section (cut) the building vertically, from the bottom of the footing through the roof or parapet construction. To reduce the extent of the drawing, portions of the wall construction that are redundant or repetitive can be deleted by inserting a pair of break lines (usually this occurs about midway between floor assemblies). (See Figure 4-6.)

Figure 4-6 Example of wall section.

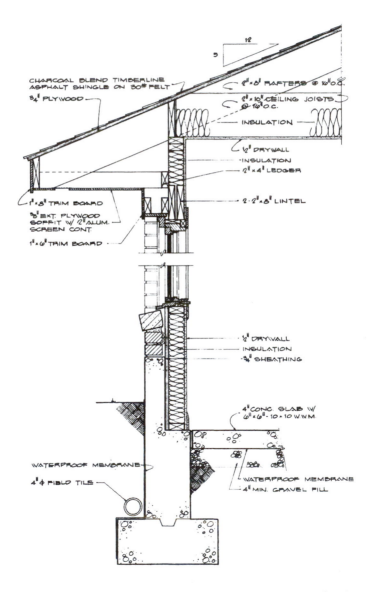

CHARCOAL BLEND TIMBERLINE
ASPHALT SHINGLE ON 30# FELT

¾" PLYWOOD

2"×8" RAFTERS @ 16" O.C.

2"×10" CEILING JOISTS @ 16" O.C.

INSULATION

½" DRYWALL

INSULATION

2"×4" LEDGER

2-2"×8" LINTEL

1"×8" TRIM BOARD

⅝" EXT. PLYWOOD SOFFIT W/ 2" ALUM. SCREEN CONT.

1"×6" TRIM BOARD

½" DRYWALL

INSULATION

¾" SHEATHING

4" CONC. SLAB W/ 6"×6"-10×10 W.W.M.

WATERPROOF MEMBRANE

4" ⌀ FIELD TILE

WATERPROOF MEMBRANE

4" MIN. GRAVEL FILL

BRICK VENEER ¾"=1'-0"

2. There is a relationship between the scale of wall sections, and the use and scale of blown-up details; the smaller the scale of the wall section, the greater the need for associated details. (Obviously, where work is shown at a small size, there is need for more, better, clearer, and larger-scaled information.) This relationship, and the scales and drawings involved, are usually described in the office standards manual. Scales of $1^1/_2$", 1", $^3/_4$", or even $^1/_2$" = 1' − 0" can be used, as deemed proper.

3. There is no fixed number of wall sections; this varies with the complexity of the construction and the number of different wall types and detailing involved. Wherever wall construction changes (even in fairly minor ways), another wall section is advisable if not required. This does not mean that every note, et cetera must be reproduced, but the new information must be shown, and proper references to other information can be made.

4. Identify materials both by call-out note, and by material symbol; use proper line weight variations to distinguish between materials, especially thin materials; do this an adequate number of times to eliminate any doubt as to if and where a material is used. A new method (if the office allows it) for callouts on wall sections is to use a numbered designator for each item, device, material, or situation, with one set of notes applied or typed on the sheet. This greatly reduces the amount of lettering required, and offers a cleaner, more easily read sheet.

5. Provide, call out, and designate pertinent vertical dimensions in a manner like those on the exterior elevations.

6. Provide and call out all pertinent horizontal dimensions, aligning identical levels in the various sections across the sheet.

7. Locations of details can be identified by heavy dashed or solid lines around the area in question, or by note. There should be no reluctance to creating another detail; remember, we are trying to communicate a lot of information without speaking directly to the other person(s). We must be clear and complete. We need to define our intent so we can maintain control of the project.

8. Some parts of details *direct* work ("Provide masonry wall ties @ 24″ o.k., each way") or *require* some work ("Flashing") through their notes and by leader lines that literally point to and touch the particular item. In general, details show and indicate (1) items required, (2) work required, (3) methods of placement, (4) attachment required, (5) a better view of the work involved, and (6) other aspects of the design professional's intent.

The Foundation Plan

1. The foundation plan is really a form of floor plan, in that it is a horizontal section that looks down on the foundation and footing system. The scale is usually the same as other floor plans; in fact, there must be a direct relationship between floor plan and foundation plan (match lines similar, etc.). Often, instead of laying out the entire plan again, one can overlay the floor plan and use it as the base for the foundation plan; this ensures coordination and correlation between these plans.

2. In many instances, the footing/foundation layout and information can be overlaid (superimposed) on the basement floor plan. Where this becomes too involved and complex, separate plans should be utilized.

3. Show foundation walls, with pilasters (where used) and other extraordinary features, in a solid line; indicate cut-outs, slots, beam pockets (wall recesses for steel beams), masonry and slab ledges, and other features that must be formed into the concrete foundation. (See Figure 4-7.)

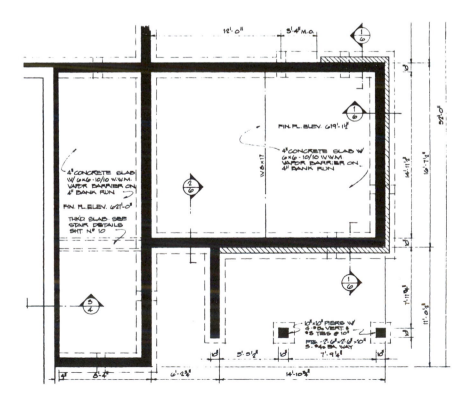

Figure 4-7 Example of foundation plan.

4. Indicate all bearing walls, column piers, columns, et cetera, that provide support for the floor above.
5. Show all spread, isolated, continuous, and other footings in their proper location, size, and configuration, in a dashed line.
6. Indicate slabs-on-grade; note slab thickness, reinforcing, materials, penetrations, moisture protection, subsurface treatment, perimeter expansion joints, other concrete joints, et cetera.
7. Completely dimension plan: interior string dimension to locate all walls, wall thickness, openings, et cetera; exterior dimensions same as the floor plan. Locate and dimension steps in footings, joints, and openings.
8. Identify, detail, and dimension crawl space areas and unexcavated areas (for slab-on-grade).
9. Add the proper material symbols in several, but isolated areas; at sides of openings, changes in materials, corners, et cetera.
10. Show detail and section cuts; draw associated drawings as necessary to define foundation systems. Show and call out location and types/number of reinforcing used. Call out and indicate beam and CMU lintel locations, and similar related items and construction.

The Framing Plan(s)—Floor(s) and Roof(s)

1. Show the footprint of the building with all bearing walls and columns (which support the framing) in medium-weight, solid lines; call out all members with proper industry designators; provide overall dimensions as indicated on the plan. (If all interior walls and partitions, bearing and nonbearing are shown, do *not* show door openings, etc.) (See Figure 4-8.)
2. Indicate with heavier lines the centerlines of beams (wood, steel, composite), with proper call-out notes. Over the beam system, draw in heavy line the centerlines of a portion of the floor/roof joist layout (every joist need not be shown); dimension as and where required, otherwise indicate repetitive spacing of members; call out manufacturer, specification number, industry designator, and so forth. (A proper note would be 2" × 10" joists @ 2'0" o.c. = 88'0".) Indicate by an arrow, with two half arrow heads, the span of the joists (need not touch each bearing) in each bay.
3. Define completely the system and all associated items and construction—bridging, decking, sheathing, accessories, anchors, trim (eave, ridge, edge closure boards)—to provide a complete structural system.

Figure 4-8 Example of framing plan.

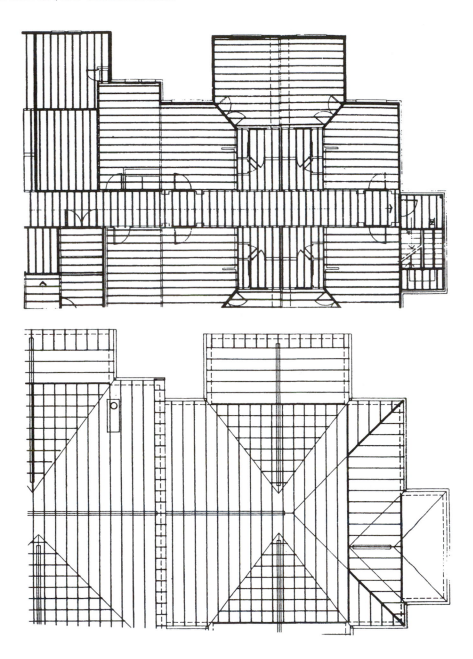

4. Indicate applicable details, building and wall sections; show additional detail to clarify installation.
5. Framing systems other than joists (glu-lam beams and arches, steel bar joists, light steel framing, composite beams, trusses for floors and roofs, etc.) are depicted in essentially the same manner.

Schedules (General)   There is a tremendous amount of information that must be incorporated and shown on a set of working drawings. This is made more complex where the project in toto, or the construction in itself, is very involved, complex, and intricate. Often drawings become overburdened with both written and graphic material, to the point that the documents become almost unreadable. This will have an adverse effect on the work, and perhaps on the project as a whole.

The use of schedules allows for the display, in a very orderly fashion, of much of that information. In fact, one should always be looking for opportunities to combine data into a chart (schedule) form, always seeking to aid in clarifying the information and making it more readily readable and usable.

Examples of schedules are room finishes, doors, windows, openings, louvers, lintels, beams, columns, reinforcing, equipment, hardware, footings, piers, caissons, test borings, light fixtures, electrical panels (several types), partitions, fixtures, symbols, and so on. Most professional offices will have standard formats that they use.

Room Finish Schedule

1. Room finishes can be displayed in either legend or schedule form. In legend form, the information is placed within the space in question and appears as a note, perhaps utilizing abbreviations to reduce the size of the note.

2. In some formats, the Room Finish Schedule is part of a sheet or sheets devoted entirely to various schedules. Where this is true, it aids use of the schedule and relating it to various spaces, if it is placed at the extreme right side of the sheet; here the set pages can be folded back to reveal the schedule and, with only slight manipulation, the space being reviewed. In some projects the Room Finish Schedule is typed and bound into the Project Manual.

3. This schedule can be either a bar or matrix type. The form used usually will reflect a concern for minimal time for preparation, and ease of use.

4. Lay out the schedule from left to right as follows (see Figure 4-9):
    - Room number (from the floor plan)
    - Room name
    - Floor covering (structure can be left exposed)
    - Base(board)
    - Wainscot (if applicable for partial wall coverage)
    - Walls (subdivide into four columns for N, S, W, and E walls)
    - Ceiling (subdivide into "material" and "height" columns)

Figure 4-9 Example of room finish schedule.

ROOM FINISH SCHEDULE

RM. NO.	ROOM NAME	FLOORS				BASE		WALLS							CEILING		CLG HGT	REMARKS
		CARPET	THIN SET CERAMIC TILE	EXPOSED CONCRETE	SHEET VINYL	4" RUBBER STRAIGHT WALL BASE	4" RUBBER COVE BASE	5/8" DRYWALL	PLASTER	THIN SET CERAMIC TILE	EXPOSED CONCRETE BLOCK	3/8" TEXTURE PLYWOOD 1-11	5/8" FIRECODE DRYWALL	CHAIR RAIL	1/2" DRYWALL	PLASTER		
65	KITCHEN							•							•		8'-0"	
66	ENTRY							•			•				•		8'-0"	
67	DINING ROOM	•						•							•		VARIES	
68	LIVING ROOM	•						•	•						•		VARIES	
69	VESTIBULE							•							•		8'-0"	
70	LAUNDRY		•					•							•		8'-0"	
71	TOILET		•							•					•		8'-0"	
72	BEDROOM	•						•	•						•		8'-0"	
73	CORRIDOR	•						•	•						•		8'-0"	
74	SHOWER		•							•					•		8'-0"	
75	TOILET		•							•					•		8'-0"	
76	TOILET		•							•					•		8'-0"	
77	VESTIBULE		•					•							•		8'-0"	
78	BATH		•							•					•		8'-0"	
79	TOILET		•							•					•		8'-0"	
80	SHOWER		•							•					•		8'-0"	
81	DOUBLE BEDROOM	•						•							•		8'-0"	
82	DOUBLE BEDROOM	•						•							•		8'-0"	
83	BEDROOM	•						•							•		8'-0"	
84	BEDROOM	•						•							•		8'-0"	
85	BEDROOM	•						•							•		8'-0"	
86	CORRIDOR	•						•						•	•		8'-0"	
B2	MECH. EQUIP. ROOM			•							•					•	8'-0"	

- Remarks (a sizable column for notes, details, specifics, modifiers, references)

5. General notes can be used that refer to the Room Finish Schedule, but they must not contain specification text or information (do not, for example, note the name and color of the carpeting). Usually these notes will be few in number and will address specific/unique conditions or will apply general principles in the form of a reminder.

Door and Window Schedules

1. Show and call out doors and windows in both written and graphic form—i.e., show elevations of each type of unit, and use a written column format for associated information (size, material, manufacturer, model number, etc.); cross-reference the two formats. (See Figure 4-10.)
2. Choose a scale for the graphic portion of each schedule that adequately depicts the units in detail.

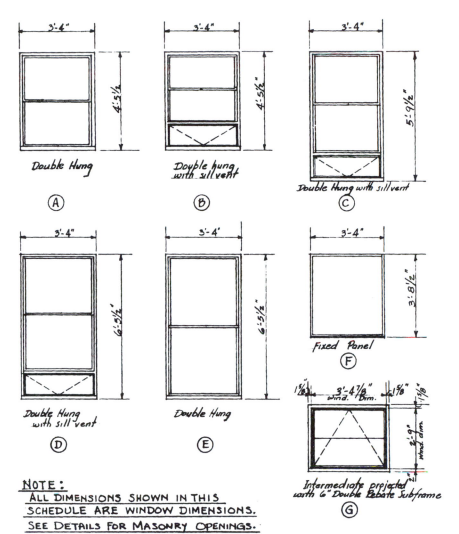

Figure 4-10 Example of window schedule.

NOTE:
ALL DIMENSIONS SHOWN IN THIS
SCHEDULE ARE WINDOW DIMENSIONS.
SEE DETAILS FOR MASONRY OPENINGS.

WINDOW SCHEDULE
Scale: 3/8"=1'-0"

3. Show head, jamb, and sill details for both types of units; show vertical and horizontal dimensions, and specific features (louvers or glass lights in doors; special hardware or glazing in the windows).

4. The door schedule is best formatted as follows (columnized left to right):
   - Door number or mark (designator used on plan)
   - Number of doors in opening (single, pair)

- Size (width, height, thickness [in this order], in feet/inches as applicable)
- Material (face material and core construction—solid, hollow, insulated, lead-lined, or other special construction)
- Glazing (explain any glass panels in door)
- Finish (painted, aluminum, plastic laminate, prefinished)
- Type or style (taken from the elevations)
- Frame (material and type; special features)
- Details (list separately the title of the head, jamb, and sill detail for each door)
- Fire rating (of opening; applies to both door and frame)
- Hardware set (list set number as described in specifications for finish hardware)
- Remarks/comments (list special conditions/exceptions/refurbishing/replacements, etc.)

5. Also include all special doors and frames (e.g., roll-up window closure over service counters); show elevation(s) and make proper entries in the door schedule itself. Call out thickness, width, height, material, and other pertinent dimensions. Note: Care should be taken to observe standard conditions; for example, in a CMU wall, the frame height is best set at 7'-4" since this corresponds with block coursing.

6. The window schedule is also set up in a grid pattern, with columns left to right, as follows:
   - Window number (and mark or designator used on plans)
   - Manufacturer (coordinate with specifications)
   - Size (rough or masonry openings; usually width by height)
   - Material (as specified)
   - Glazing (type as specified)
   - Details (usually in three columns—head, jamb, and sill). Note: where several detail conditions apply to the same window unit, use a different symbol on the plans.
   - Finish (as specified)
   - Remarks or comments (ample space to list unusual conditions, requirements)

7. Window wall and storefront glazing systems are not included in the schedules. Use notes, elevations, et cetera, on the plans themselves. Require field verification of opening sizes.

8. In simple (smaller) projects, these schedules can be modified and reduced to simple elevations, with proper detail references at the head, jamb, and sill.

All of these drawings are interrelated, cross-referenced, and fully coordinated so the information is easily accessed and is placed in its proper context and relationships. All of them are to scale, i.e., drawn so a 12-inch or one-foot distance is represented by a smaller distance on the drawing. The scales do change to best depict the work involved—generally, the more to be shown, the smaller the scale. For example, floors plans (showing the overall footprint or configuration of the project) quite often are drawn to $1/8$" = 1'-0"; details (showing a small portion of construction) may be drawn at 3" = 1' = 0".

This is all well known to the construction trades performing the actual work and is a long-accepted practice. Even now with CAD production of drawings, these principles still apply. With the coming utilization of three-dimensional modeling, it is not all that clear exactly what the working drawings will look like. The prognosis is that much more information will be set out in the database for the 3-D modeling, and will be transferable to the working drawings for use in field operations.

The size of these documents can vary from a single page to bound sets of several hundred pages; some drawing sheets are sized 42" $\times$ 48" each, with numerous individual drawings quite varied in size, but the majority are small. The illustrations show the types of drawings involved and how they augment each other by sharing information or showing added detail.

The specifications then add a wealth of information that is physically impossible to show on the drawings. (Some very small or simple projects do utilize typewritten specifications on the drawings, but this is much more the exception than the rule.)

Since every aspect, piece, system, detail, and nuance of the project must be shown or described, these documents take on a heavy responsibility. They cannot leave gaps or create any confusion on the part of the constructors. They must explain, in the clearest and simplest terms possible, even the smallest part of the project (the use of a comprehensive checklist is advised). The cost of the project is directly dependent on how well these documents are executed. As complexity in the project escalates, so does the need for commensurate documentation—and the cost will reflect both. This is in no way an easy or off-handed exercise—it is the crux of a successful project.

The following excerpt from "Selling Stone Products to Architects," by Dan Ouellette (*Stone World,* May 2003) gives some insight into the challenge involved and the massive breadth of the task of project documenting:

> Architects, as we all know, create unique structures and suitable environments for their clients, and have a tremendous amount of *control* and impact on what products are used to construct their designs. Historically speaking, architects are responsible for selecting 95% of the products installed on *an average-sized project.*

A recent (2002) study designed to uncover how architects make product decisions yielded a particularly interesting fact:

> . . . architects, **on average**, must select **1,500 products** and make over **17,000 decisions** on what is best for the project and the owner. That's **17,000 answers to 17,000 important questions** . . .

How big? How high? What color? What shape? What style? Moreover, what products will give the owner exactly what they have paid the architects to design? The list of questions about what products to incorporate in a project can be overwhelming for architects and their clients.

It is impossible for an architect to know every detail on all these products. By nature, architects are generalists, but they carry a complexity of responsibilities. Architects are design creators who desperately need trusted product information providers on whom they can rely to provide objective answers and help them determine the right product for their project. An effective stone strategy, for example, should not center on selling to architects. Instead, it should focus on influencing architects to incorporate stone products using the three E's: Education, Ease and Execution.

In addition, a staff team must be brought together with a variety of skill levels, experience, and expertise. Led by a project architect/engineer, an associate, or a principal, the team is best co-located (if at all possible) and should embrace as many disciplines as necessary. Where the firm is a single-discipline entity (an architectural firm, for example), there is a deeper need for very close ongoing coordination with other offices that will provide the services of the other required disciplines.

Considered by many as the nitty-gritty work of the project design sequence, this process entails the research, development, analysis, and incorporation of the multitudinous details required for the project construction. The work is wide-ranging, rigorous, complex, intensive, and in need of steady and dedicated persons. Here is yet another point that could be a major contribution to any eventual project failure in function, longevity, weathering, soundness, and/or aesthetics. While constantly striving to maintain faithful execution of the design concept, the construction work must provide all that is needed for that concept to become reality, and to remain intact, and pleasing to the eye, over the entire long-term life of the structure.

By way of explanation, consider two identical art prints that are to be treated in two entirely different ways. One will be treated as a finished item, mounted in a suitable mat and frame, and hung on the wall—finished, ready for viewing and appreciation, in need of only periodic dusting.

The other is to be cut up into a thousand pieces, fabricated so that they can be boxed and sold as a jigsaw puzzle. Here the picture is taken from its original configuration, and refashioned into another form that has to be reassembled to be usable and viewable by anyone.

Looking at building construction, reality tells us that there is no way in which we can receive a finished building—like the first picture—and merely set it in place and use it immediately. Of course, there is no way to transport such a structure, and really even to provide the services and work necessary to get to the place that it is built and ready for transport.

Looking at the second picture, but in a reverse sequence, we can build the picture by merely fitting the various pieces together in proper sequence and location so as to produce the picture we started with. This is closely akin to the construction process. But in construction the pieces are various full-size portions of work, fitted properly together to form the finished project.

In architecture and construction, the overall design is created to meet the goals and program of the owner. This is a concept—an idea—about how the facility can be built, and what it will look like when finished. Notice that there is a gap between the initial idea/concept and the finished product. As noted above, we cannot physically fill this gap with a finished project merely transported to the site. Every project, no matter its size or complexity, must be reduced to, viewed as, or broken down into a series of interrelated detail drawings—that is, limited-area, isolated, large-scale drawings that show the intricacies of construction and when properly placed and connected depict the whole of the construction required.

In the same way that we build the jigsaw puzzle into a complete and whole picture, we can construct and build the structure into a whole, complete, and usable facility by placing a series of small portions of construction together—fitting them properly, attaching and applying them as necessary, and creating the whole project out of the various pieces. The finished project—building, facility, structure, and so forth—will truly be the "sum total of its parts"!

The "parts," or portions of construction, are developed and built in accordance with the overall working drawings and specifications for the project. Within the set of working drawings are the myriad smaller drawings called "details"! The "parts" are fashioned in real size and fitted together to erect the completed building—safe, usable, and in keeping with the project program.

Detailing and Details It is impossible to depict any size project with overall drawings, which are drawn at small scale. Following the axiom, "the general [information] must become specific," these indispensable large-scale drawings are produced through a process called "detailing"—and individually, they are called "details." (See Figure 4-11.)

In its simplest definition, detailing is the process whereby an inordinate amount of very technical and intricate information is developed by the design professional and transmitted to the trade workers who build the project. It is the functional interface between the design concept of the professional, and the instructions and descriptions that the field personnel need to build the project as designed. It is the translation and transmission of information, without which no project could be built, and built true to the expectation and concept approved by a third party (the owner/client). This arrangement is crucial to successful construction at all levels and in all disciplines.

While fundamental, the process is certainly not simple. To facilitate successful construction is a matter of developing, refining, and converting conceptual information into usable information, and then properly conveying that information to the trade workers who will execute

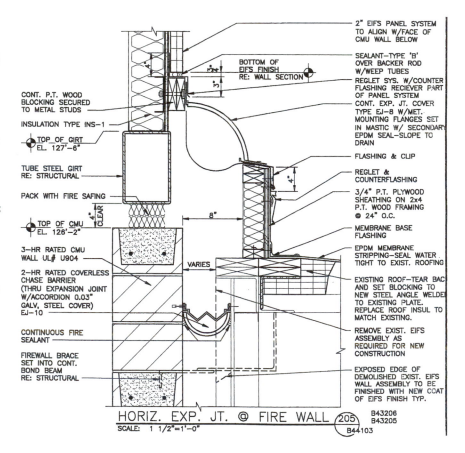

Figure 4-11 Example of a well-executed detail on a working drawing. Note the specific directions and detailed information it presents. This is a detail for the expansion joint between an existing (to the right) and a new building (to the left). Part of this work involved the expandable chase barrier, located down in the joint. Note existing EIFS to be removed and then redone; also note requirement for firestop sealant on the underside of the chase barrier. How can this EIFS repair work and the sealant be installed in this narrow joint area?

the work. No longer will general comments, innuendo, assumptions, and vague, incomplete information suffice. The time has come where decisions—thousands of them!—must be made, and the results portrayed in graphic form, in numerous small vignette drawings, and properly published with associated written specifications, as the contract documents. Later these documents will be utilized in the bidding/costing process, and still later in the field by the managers, estimators, expediters, superintendent, suppliers, forepersons, and individual trade workers.

In the whole scheme of architectural practice and its vast array of tasks, detailing could be easily dismissed or relegated to a minor or seemingly inconsequential role. Surely, it is not more important than design; not as important as client relations and securing new commissions. Surely, it could be perceived as a "throw-around" activity, which is imposed on junior staff, or the "do-its" in the office. But detailing does have a distinctive, recurring, and truly indispensable (though not supreme) role in practice. The best of design ideas and concepts created in the office will never see the light of day or be completed without at least a minimal detailing effort.

Many professionals and offices have sought all sorts of ways to extricate themselves from this demeaning task—the almost unprofessional effort of almost getting one's hands dirty in duties relating to the actual construction process. Detailing is repulsive to some, flatly repugnant to others—but the reality of architecture to still others. To those who revel in putting building together—detailing is their way of bringing the wonderful design creations to their final form and to the satisfaction of the client, both initially and long-term. The cause and effort of detailing is noble, it is needed, and it is part and parcel of the complete architect, who can envision both whole concepts and the many parts that make up the whole of each project. In fact, it is paying attention to the details that counts. Currently in our society, we talk about "detailing cars," "give me the details," and developing "detail persons." But "attention to detail" is not merely a catch phrase or motto. It is, and has been for a long time, a description of a personal attribute present in some people. Often it is developed through the work that the person does. The phrase is really an expression of caring about the work and trying to excel in its execution.

It also indicates, at least in the mind of the worker, that the work needs to be precise, accurate, and complete to be successful and to be fully acceptable to one's boss and to any client involved. Of course, this is in direct contrast to a cursory, slipshod, arms-length approach where work is done quickly but with no attempt to ensure its veracity. For example, an accountant takes great pains to see that all accounts are correct and balanced. Ignoring or dropping a penny difference here and there seems quite innocent but, over the course of time, it can add up to an intolerable imbalance.

> A detail-oriented architect optimizes the inborn value and tenacity to seek and achieve the level of precision and accuracy which is short of perfection by only the slightest of margins. Yet the quest for completeness, and the caring for accuracy and correctness is pursued in a quiet, unassuming, and most professional manner, seeking assistance as necessary (but usually rarely) as his/her command of the information, material, devices, and systems are far beyond the level of mere familiarity, but approach a fully fluent and functional level. She/he is talented, beyond imagination, in the ability to concentrate, to focus the effort, and masterful in satisfying clients with insight, professionalism, and expertise.
>
> *—Anonymous*

Is this a description of a superperson, or of a reclusive Caspar Milquetoast? Neither, really—just a rather flamboyant view of the characteristics that many people carry with them to work (and more than likely use in their home life, too). Note the many facets to this person and how they all combine to produce work of high quality, which tends to maximize client satisfaction.

Obviously, there are details in every line of work, but the phrase really reflects how a person deals with information or techniques while performing tasks. Most work can be done in an adequate manner with relatively little regard for detail. This quite often is satisfactory, but may be less than desirable in the long term. Dealing with detail and resolving loose ends and other problems tends to provide a better, longer-lasting product and a higher level of client satisfaction. Adding exactness aids the effort.

In architecture and construction, though, a less than vigorous effort at detailing will directly result in suspect work, perhaps inadequate or unsafe, and quite often not satisfactory to the client (and clients are, now, more demanding with each passing day). In many projects, the level of client satisfaction has been raised to "precision." Yet construction remains as it always has been—an imperfect science. With worker-developed skill levels diminishing, and with less worker dedication, self-esteem, pride of work, and productivity, construction is trending toward even more imperfection. On many projects, almost any quality of work is accepted, so long as the work is finished on time! There is little regard for any level of quality above adequate. Also, there seems to be some correlation with larger, more costly projects that are pursued on almost impossible time lines. Obviously, there is a strong element of attitude and perception in this, where motivation is low and the worker is simply working for a pay check, not to produce work for enhanced self-esteem and satisfaction. This is most unfortunate, since it is a common situation, with, of course, some extremes that defy the norm.

This trend has to be addressed, early-on and in a most positive manner, on projects where the client and indeed the project itself demand near-perfection because of both client and regulatory requirements. Every project needs to be perceived by all participants as a new opportunity to excel and to produce better work than before. Often the type of project sets the demand for higher quality design and work. Projects where consumer goods, and particularly food products, medications, and similar human consumables, are made or processed, impose an elevated requirement of perfection. This appears in sanitation, cleanliness, freedom from infestation, cleanability, wearability, and so forth.

However, in every project there is a need to establish a level of quality involving a search for near-perfection for proper construction and client satisfaction. No design professional should have, at any time, the attitude that "barely adequate" is the correct level of expertise and quality permitted. Even where building codes set out only minimum standards, providing better conditions and more substantial construction is in order to the point where they are still supportive and reflective of the budget and client demands. Doing more than required by code is admirable, extremely helpful, and certainly to the benefit of the client.

The trade worker, too, needs renewed motivation to produce the highest quality work he/she is capable of, within the context of the project demands as expressed in the contract documents. While motivational talks, high-tone direction from supervisors, and firm instruction on the job site may induce some effort for increased quality in the work, the work depicted and described on the contract documents also sets the tone of the project. If these documents are clear, direct, instructive, positive, informational, and in a format for easy assimilation, they set demands on the workers. There may be a need for a reminder that work is to be done in strict accord with drawings and specifications. Freeloading and lackadaisical efforts simply will not produce the work required and will, therefore, not be tolerated—no threat, just fact!

Much of the imperfection in construction lies in the fact that professionals can draw details with such great accuracy and exactness. This is especially true now, with CAD-produced drawings. Often the precision seen in the drawing simply cannot be achieved in the field. Even with power tools and skilled workers, the actual work will contain slight variations, which are of no consequence in the end product. The imperfections are not a matter of unsafe or inadequate construction, but rather a lack of the precision that can be achieved in creation of the documents—a matter of the theoretical versus the actual. It is noted here, though, to defuse any impression in young readers and professionals that what they include or see on the drawings will exist in exactly the same way in the actual construction. While quite similar, there will be normal and natural irregularities in the work. Realizing this is part of the experience that must be acquired to better understand construction as produced to meet the contract documents.

This also shows the direct impact that the professional has on the project by virtue of what is shown and how well it is shown on the contract drawings. The drawings themselves set the level of quality the professional desires in the work (and by extrapolation, what is desired by the client in the finished project). This is an aspect of the work that is not readily apparent to the casual observer, but it is a real and important part of the professional effort. In fact, it is better called a crucial part, since it is here that the professional provides the linkage (sets out the scheme or format) for matching actual work with the final finished project anticipated by the client by virtue of the approved design concept. This matching is worked from the beginning of the work and moves toward completion. It consists of doing the work as depicted on the drawings in a manner whereby the unseen ("rough") construction provides a proper backing for the finishes, and hence the complete and finished project.

The fundamental concept here is that as in a great many efforts, the underlying frame, structure, or construction simply must be fashioned and installed correctly and soundly. If done, this then provides a base, matrix, or substructure whereby the thinner finish products can be installed or applied, forming the correct shapes, features, and planes. Much like a photograph, if the negative (the fundamental structure) is faulty, the final print will be less than desirable. Misalignments, incorrect planes/shapes, lack of true/plumb/level work, improper sizing, weak construction, and other nuances in the underlying construction play havoc with the final appearance of the project. Therefore it is essential that the professional be well aware of these maladies.

Being so aware, it is incumbent on the professional to eliminate or prevent such conditions from occurring in future projects. The details of the projects may change, but the underlying principle in the details must survive and be accounted for, project by project. This is one of the considerations for determining whether a detail is a good candidate for storing and establishing as a standard repetitive detail. Obviously, where variation is wide and slight circumstantial conditions are variant, the detail will not be more than a project-specific detail, valid for a single use.

Renowned architect Frank Lloyd Wright is a good example of one giving proper attention to detail, in some portions of construction projects. He has been both saluted and widely and rounded criticized for his details. How can this be? His projects were cutting-edge in design concepts and in many cases, structural ingenuity. Many consider his designs to be revolutionary, distinctive, and far ahead of their times. It would seem to follow that Wright must have been concerned and involved in the details of each project, to produce work of such regard and stature.

Wright did paid close attention to details in his designs, but apparently ignored or failed to follow through with many of them. This matter of detail in Wright's designs goes to the level of his personal involvement. He was meticulous in unique furniture design, exact placement of furniture, accurate locations and orientations, precise matching of motifs, specifically designed concrete block to support his design concept, accessories, and the other appurtenances that served to enhance his concept. Many of these were developed for a specific project and client and not for general use. In the main, they were cosmetic in nature—details included to serve as the "correct" (and only acceptable) accoutrements for the Wright design concept.

At the same time, the details for the construction of many of his buildings, particularly houses, have proven to be quite flawed and ongoing maintenance problems—with leaking roofs, leaking windows, and structural nuances just short of collapse. This may be attributable to work that was done by Wright's "disciples" (his student drafting force), who were not as skilled and experienced as Wright. It may also indicate his lack of direct interest in the mundane details of construction—things that are not exposed to view, for example, or those things that did not directly affect, contribute to, or enhance his design concept. (This could be said to be similar to a man in white tie and tails, who has a hole in the bottom of his shoe!) It seems, though, that Wright's clients were of a mind to put up with such maladies, simply because Wright was their architect and his designs and high rhetoric were highly celebrated. A Wright-designed project was to be cherished and nurtured, in spite of its shortcomings.

In reality, many times more money has been spent on repairs through the years and by various owners (including charitable and historic groups) than the original cost of the house. Of course, inflation plays a part in this scenario, but nonetheless, the cost of remediation and repair has not been small. Yet Wright's reputation remains strong—strong in support and equally strong in criticism!

This general scenario seems to be a perk enjoyed, even today, by signature architects, who use rhetoric to overcome physical shortcomings in their designs and completed projects. Too often their buildings simply do not weather or wear well, or prove insufficient in some way, which tends to downgrade the overall impression of the project and certainly the appearance and function of the specific area(s) in question. Often such failures are pointed to as construction failures attributable to the lack of care and expertise by the trade workers who installed the work. In fact, more often than not the trade workers are hamstrung by detailing that is incomplete, inadequate, inappropriate, or otherwise flawed in its concept. The workers are obligated to erect and install work "in full accord with the plans and specifications." So if the documentation is faulty, the resulting work will also be faulty, unless someone recognizes the problem(s) early, and takes added action. Case law supports the workers in this matter, since the workers do not conceive the details and are obligated as noted.

In Wright's case, a good lesson can be learned: that there are different types and levels of details to which the architect must attend. Wright carried some of these (placement of furnishings, unique concrete block shapes, accessories, etc.) to an extreme, and so was able to satisfy the client's desire for a totally Wright-created living atmosphere. That said, the client unknowingly was also handed a bevy of problems that would appear over a period of time (leaking roofs, structural inadequacies, etc.). These would take more effort (than moving a chair), time, and money to resolve—but still the clients remained Wright advocates.

Most of Wright's peers, and architects both then and now, followed other courses. They attempted to present their clients with substantial and reliable buildings first, and then if asked, provided interior design services. Most got close enough to their clients to understand them and to ascertain the client's true wishes and convert them into project features. Where done, this is a crucial exercise, and results in accurate and proper programming. However, this is extremely difficult to do in a corporate environment, where personnel reflect corporate and not personal tastes, ideas, criteria, and demands.

Nevertheless, the lesson is that details are of several types, and proper attention to each, in its way, leads to a far better product and one that more closely matches the complete array of client requirements. Obviously, design statements can and should be made in both the building and the interior furnishings and finishes. But at the same time, the same due regard for detail is necessary in seeing that the roof and windows do not leak, and that the construction overall, in a portion-by-portion review, functions correctly and is capable of long-term endurance.

This construction detailing process is not reserved for certain clients or certain projects. Rather it occurs, or should occur, on each and every project, from the smallest residential remodeling to the most massive, elaborate, and imposing structures. The extent, scope, time, and effort for the process will vary. However, the concept and need for detailing remains intact despite all other project requirements.

The following is a typical description for a college course in architectural detailing:

> Course Objectives: Students use history and theory to gather and analyze information. Students are made aware of architectural detailing as a manifestation of cultural, environmental and technological factors, which modify architectural expression in time and place. At a more specific level, students explore principles, which affect the science of building construction to learn and understand assemblies as an integrative process in which details are related to a larger linguistic whole. Students develop an aesthetic and technological awareness about the craft of making architecture as well as the ability to articulate and communicate their observations.

While this description is of the highest academic caliber and incorporates the full range of detailing impact, it is a somewhat overblown and complex explanation of detailing. To explain in simpler terms:

1. Detailing does bring the technology to the project and the cultural and environmental aspects that are already addressed in the project concept.
2. Detailing, by necessity, reflects time and place, as it is necessary to adjust the details to the specific project and the materials and systems to be used, all of which usually are tied to current trends, styles, and methods.
3. Detailing both affects building science and applies building science—the effect being new uses or applications of building materials or methods, as a byproduct to their application to the project at hand.
4. It is true that each and every detail is an "assembly" of work, which is a part of the "linguistic whole," just as any single piece of a jigsaw puzzle is related to the completed picture.
5. Through detailing does come an understanding that one must know the technical aspects of the profession in "making architecture," and one must develop the ability to carefully, completely, and properly form and transmit both observations and conclusions, directions, and information about the work.

There is, of course, a correct perspective for the detailing process. Detailing is a necessity, though not the dominant or overwhelming process within the project sequence. True, appropriate attention must be paid to detailing; and true, it does provide a distinct and vital link between the design professional and the trade worker, and between the concept and the reality of actual construction. Perhaps it is best described as a necessary buffer or a required translation.

The buffer aspect derives from the detailing as a means to carry out the owner's wishes, and the attendant requirements of both the project program and the design concept in a proper format. It is a process that must understand all that goes before *and* still all that follows, in that it produces new and quite different information as its primary product.

In producing that new information, the detailing process is indeed a process of translation. Here requirements for ideas, concepts, and major elements of the project are converted into portioned servings of reality-oriented construction information. Often items that seem quite innocuous in the owner's program become major detailing complexes, to ensure that the proper work is delivered as required.

Moving to construction information, with its distinctive nomenclature, is in itself a challenge. The design professional is charged with taking ideas, concepts, and general references, which are rather meaningless to the trade workers on-site, and converting them into useful data. The workers are immersed in their particular perspective, their materials, and their assigned work. Few understand the project as a whole; rather, they concentrate on their specific portion of the work. But in addition to properly communicating to the workers, the design professional is required to express the deepest requirements of the project contract. This involves depicting or enumerating exactly what is required and how the project (and its numerous pieces) is to be executed, to remain in compliance with the contractual obligations of the contractors, manufacturers, suppliers, installers, fabricators, and so on.

The role of detailing is one of direct and meaningful assistance, and a buffered translation of one set of information into another set that is usable on-site and remains faithful to the owner's wishes and the design concept. Its highest value is in its ability to facilitate bringing the project to reality. It is a needed interface between aspects of the project and the project parties, which understands the requirements of them all and provides methodology to meet them.

Clients, not being fully familiar with the phases of work under the architect's purview, are for the most part unaware of this phase of work. Indeed, while they may have some insight, they do not really understand detailing or the purpose for it. However, detailing is fundamental to the success of the project in more ways than any other phase of work. This is why for many years the traditional breakdown of the architect's fee allotted almost half to the production of contract documents—including, of course, details.

It has long been established in the courts that muddled information and poorly conceived designs and details executed as received by the contractors place liability on the design professional. Hence, the importance of correct detailing and communications cannot be over-stressed. Both involve levels of technical understanding, knowledge, application, depiction, and conveyance—the right information must be given the field personnel in a fashion fully usable and executable by them. The route taken to accomplish this is of very relatively limited importance—content rules greatly above method!

What is needed is pertinent, concise, complete, and eminently clear, helpful, informational/directive/instructional detail drawings, and associated specifications. The goal is to be of value and direct assistance to the construction project's trade workers, professionals, and managers—and to produce a high level of satisfaction in the owner.

Precision is required in the detailing so each line, plane, surface, angle, recess, edge, texture, intersection, material, joint, color, and other nuance of the design concept is in its assigned place, proper, well-executed, and sound. "Attention to detail" is an understatement in describing this work effort.

5

THE DOCUMENTS AND CODE COMPLIANCE

DOCUMENTS

Responsibilities for Documentation

It is the owner's responsibility to provide all of the necessary documentation for the project to the contractors. This is only common sense, for it is the owner who knows what is required in the final, completed project. The owner sets out the grand vision or scheme for the project and hires the design professionals to create the appropriate design concept and produce the vast array of construction information required in the documentation—i.e., drawings and specifications. The basic responsibility remains the owner's. It is just that the owner does not have the personal or staff skills to design a building and document its construction. That is not a shortcoming, but merely a statement of fact.

Form of Project Documentation

The complete, final documentation of a project is classified into four groups, specifically directed to the project. In some cases, the groups of documents contain sets that are used in other groupings.

Project Manual   The Project Manual contains the following documents:

- **Bidding requirements**
  - Invitation to bid
  - Instruction to bidders
  - Information available

- Bid forms and attachments
- Bid security forms
- **Contract forms and conditions**
  - CSI Division 00
  - Contract (agreement)
  - Performance bond
  - Payment bond
  - Certificates
  - General Conditions
  - Supplementary Conditions
- **Technical specifications**
  - CSI Divisions 01-49

Bidding Documents   The bidding documents include the following:

- Project Manual (see above)
- Construction Drawings
- Addenda (information/drawings issued during the bidding period, added after the documents are complete

Contract Documents   The contract documents include the following:

- **The bidding documents** (*excluding* the bidding requirements)
- **Contract modifications** (changes made after award of the contract for construction; may add, delete, or change work)

> The contract documents are most crucial, since the contract between owner and contractor is based on the proper execution of these documents, in a provision such as "construct project in accordance with contract plans and specifications."

Construction Documents   The construction documents include all of the documents above, including the bidding requirements.

Within the design professions, there are various systems for forming the set of drawings—how they are formatted, how they are numbered, and how they are interrelated. Some clients, in addition, have their own particular requirements. For the most part, drawings concerning the site development work will be located first in the set, followed by foundation drawings, floor plans, structural layouts, building elevations (exterior views), sections (cross and longitudinal), wall sections (showing wall construction), finishes, schedules, and then the engineering drawings for plumbing, mechanical (HVAC). Usually a cover sheet is used to list all of the drawings in the set, in the order of their appearance.

PROJECT (CONTRACT) SPECIFICATIONS

For many years, the specifications were not quite so simple. Each design office had its own system for locating information (something of an understatement) that only led to confusion among contractors. Information about the same product never seemed to appear in the same location in the specifications booklets for different projects. Finding information was puzzling, frustrating, and confounding to quick and easy retrieval. Professionals who were engaged in the production of specifications, many full-time, formed the Construction Specifications Institute (CSI). Over a period of years the group developed a format of sixteen numbered divisions, each of which was assigned a material or trade designation. This format caught hold, and is now very widely (but not yet universally) used.

In 2004, a major revision of the divisional system was completed and a new MasterFormat document published (see Table 5-1). Here the number of divisions was increased to 50 (numbered 00 through 49), with some realignment of divisions and some additions. In the main, the architectural (general trades) divisions were retained with minor revisions. The mechanical divisions were changed rather drastically; new divisions were added for specific purposes and projects.

The fifty divisions remain constant for any and all projects; the sections contained within the division vary in number and content, as required by the project work. The sections have a fixed format of three distinct parts; text, provisions, materials, et cetera, vary within the parts as required to convey all pertinent information about the specific material or system.

The project manuals (bound books of specifications) can take on an onerous appearance for large and complex projects. Many firms utilize a set of such documents: one for the administrative material and "front-end documents;" another for the general trade work; and the third or more for the various mechanical building systems. There is a tremendous amount of information in these documents that complements and supplements the drawings—and in that they are indispensable and inseparable from the drawings and graphic representations.

TABLE 5-1—50-DIVISION SPECIFICATIONS FORMAT

00 Procurement and Contracting Requirements	28 Electronic Safety and Security
01 General Requirements	29–30 Reserved
02 Existing Conditions	31 Earthwork
03 Concrete	32 Exterior Improvements
04 Masonry	33 Utilities
05 Metals	34 Transportation
06 Woods, Plastics, and Composites	35 Waterway and Marine Construction
07 Thermal and Moisture Protection	36–39 Reserved
08 Openings	40 Process Integration
09 Finishes	41 Material Processing and Handling Equipment
10 Specialties	42 Process Heating, Cooling, and Drying Equipment
11 Equipment	43 Process Gas and Liquid Handling, Purification and Storage Equipment
12 Furnishings	
13 Special Construction	
14 Conveying Equipment	44 Pollution Control Equipment
15–20 Reserved	45 Industry-Specific Manufacturing Equipment
21 Fire Suppression	
22 Plumbing	46–47 Reserved
23 HVAC	48 Electrical Power Generation
24 Reserved	49 Reserved
25 Integrated Automation	
26 Electrical	
27 Communications	

Published 2004 by The Construction Specifications Institute [CSI] with MasterFormat 04]

Context

The general public is more readily familiar with the drawings—still known to some as blueprints. These are rather fascinating, graphic displays or drawings of the building overall, in different views, and with a large number of smaller, interrelated drawings. Literally, the drawings show the workers how to put the building together. But with closer and more enlightened scrutiny, one sees that, even with a large number and wide array of drawings, a tremendous amount of information is not included.

So . . . what are specifications? And why do we need or use them?

There is a vast trove of information that is required for the construction of any project, no matter the size. A good deal of this information can be depicted graphically in a range of drawings, differing substantially in scope, size, scale, and complexity. Some major projects entail hundreds of sheets, many in the range of 36" by 48" and literally covered with different drawings.

But it is impossible to depict or draw every piece of information, especially when it is a description, listing of an attribute, and other such visual or intangible information. In fact, some information defies drawing in any form. The additional information that is required is provided in one or a series of bound books called project manuals. The contents of the manuals are an array of written material and information called "specifications" ("specs," in the vernacular). This written material augments, explains, and describes aspects of the work that simply cannot be drawn graphically. Since there is a tremendous amount of information—too much to include on the drawings—and a lot of information that is best written, the specifications become most valuable documents, and in fact are coequal with the drawings. Note: No project can be built with drawings alone, nor can they be built solely from the written words in the specifications.

Concept

Any discussion of construction specifications needs to start with an open view and frank analysis of the prevailing and overall concept. There is a general lack of knowledge of these documents among the nonconstruction public. To those in the construction industry, there is a mystique about the creation, writing, use, and value of these documents, and the role they play in bringing building projects to fruition.

Despite the lack of general knowledge of these documents, specifications are not handy, nice-to-have, offhand, peripheral documents that play only a marginal or sporadic role in the construction of a project. It is essential to understand and appreciate that the specifications are a *necessary, important, pervasive, and viable part of a project's documentation.* They are a complement and supplement to the drawings, and a major and imposing instrument.

Function of Specifications

The specifications for a construction project are one-third of the contract documents required. In that context, they contribute needed information necessary for the correct construction of the project. In their status as "complementary and supplementary" to the drawings, it is essential that the specifications augment and enhance the information on the drawings. Further, they must be as complete, clear, and concise as possible, so their use by the various construction personnel is helpful and without ambiguity.

The preeminent function of the specifications, in the long view, is to round out or complete the documentation of the project through the use of specific information in construction terms.

Specifications are proactive instruments—not preventative, punitive, or afterthoughts. Their function is to provide decisive construction information specific to the project, which cannot be shown graphically (i.e., on the drawings), but which nonetheless is important and necessary. In addition, they provide detailed information that precludes the need for extensive or massive notations on the drawings, which tend to obscure or impair reading of them. By reducing the mass of the notes and providing information in a more appropriate form, specifications are a vital member to the set of contract documents.

The specifications should not be given the misdirected charge of being the prime method for preventing cost expansion, et cetera. They establish quality of product and method, which can affect costing. But it is other factors that cause cost expansion or growth. Specifications need to be complete, but not speculatively all-encompassing, anticipating every possible scenario for modification of the project work. In the same context, they should not be done in an open-ended, slipshod manner, with gaps, ambiguities, incomplete project information, or other discrepancies that allow the bidding contractor to "interpret," or flatly guess at what is required or intended.

It is necessary to understand the importance and the function of the specifications, but it is wrong to assign unattainable expectations on them, or to try to convert them into instruments that function in an altogether wrong manner. Their proper function is to provide certain attributes and give certain information to the project, but this does not expand their primary direction or function. In certain types of specifications, however, a slightly different perspective may be appropriate, depending on the end results required.

Another ancillary function, often overlooked, is the legal implications of the specifications as applied to the project work. Much of the front-end, "boiler-plate," or red-tape portion of the specifications is devoted to relationships and responsibilities as well as project-wide controls, regulations, and other parameters.

Other Documents

A most imposing document that covers a vast number of issues and procedures project-wide is AIA Document A201, *General Conditions of the Contract for Construction.* This document is designed to augment and expand the provision of the basic contract and provide detailed information about responsibilities and duties of the owner, design professional, and contractor. Basically, it sets the general ground rules for the project.

In addition, there are added and more specific, detailed, project-related requirements in the various sections of Division 01 of the specifications. Too often disregarded by the contractors (in bidding and afterward), all of these provisions are crucial to proper, cohesive, and smooth-running execution of the project, within the strict limits and direction of the contract (agreement) in effect.

The Impact of Project Cost

A secondary, yet important objective of specification writing is to facilitate the completion of the project with as little change in cost as possible. In construction, "cost growth" shows up as Change Orders (COs), and Construction Change Directives (CCDs). Both of these documents are provided for in AIA Document A201 and are good examples of the depth of information in that document. The documents and their procedures are set forth to provide a logical and continuous accounting of all changes, plus or minus, in the cost or time for completion of the project. They are specifically designed to forestall claims, disputes, and other legal actions regarding modifications to the original contract.

Most COs arise legitimately from changes in project scope, changes in design concept and features, discrepancies in the documents, and changing mission requirements. Some, however, arise from time pressure and inattention to detail in the project phases prior to contract award. Claims often happen because of inattention to administrative matters during the project work, and because of disputes over the meaning of the specifications. Note: Engineering projects build upon the work as it is completed, much as a building is built from the ground up, starting with the foundation.

When an error is made, the cost of correcting it is greatest when it was made early in the process and not discovered until subsequent work has been done. The earlier in the process that the error was made, the more work has to be done over. This is why design professionals must pay very careful attention to project planning and specification writing; they are the foundation for all the rest of the work.

The worst possible cost-growth situation occurs when a contractor pursues legal action like a contract appeal or a lawsuit. Care in specification writing is one of the most important measures a design professional can take toward preventing such situations. Note: Before you write the specifications, find out all the details you can about what your product should do and what it should not do. Also, find out what materials and methods the manufacturers may use to make the product. Then, determine for certain that what you are going to specify is doable.

Armed with good up-front engineering information, the design professional should be able to prepare a good set of specifications and facilitate a credible cost estimate. This, in turn, allows all parties to establish a common basis for the project cost, which can be adjusted as further documentation is issued during the course of the project.

The moral is to be constantly business-like, diligent, and thorough, and try not to overlook anything.

The Function of and Necessity for Contracts

A contract is an agreement between two parties involving the mutual exchange of things of value, known as "consideration." Ordinarily, it's simply money in exchange for goods or services, but sometimes it defines a complex set of duties and compensation for both parties. Such is most often the case in engineering contracts, of which the specifications are the core. When you write specifications, you must therefore be aware that you are writing a contract, which is subject to a stringent set of concepts and rules. Consequently, you should keep the following contract fundamentals in mind when drafting specifications:

Your contract will be presumed complete at the time of contract award. If you have inadvertently left something out and want to add it after contract award, you will have to negotiate a supplementary agreement and furnish something, like more money, to your contractor in exchange. Explicit requirements to agree about something at a later date violate this principle.

Changes to contracts are never unilateral. The only exceptions are rare situations in which the government uses its sovereign power to respond to an emergency. Even in those cases, both parties have to sit down later on and agree upon equitable compensation.

Also presumed upon contract award is the unlikely premise that both parties fully understand and agree upon all the words written in the contract. The truth with engineering projects is often that neither party fully understands what work has to be done until the work is actually under way. Only then do myriad details become evident, and only then do you find out that the contractor has interpreted some of your words differently from what you had intended.

> **Whose interpretation prevails?**   The rule is that
> the contractor interprets the specifications,
> as long as the interpretation is reasonable.

The owner is responsible for furnishing sufficiently clear and complete language to evoke the intended understanding. The owner is also responsible for any expenses that may be incurred if the contractor does not interpret the specifications as intended.

Legal authorities like courts and appeals boards are usually very liberal in deciding whether or not a contractor's interpretation is reasonable. If there is any way at all to read your words differently from what you intended, there is a chance that a contractor will choose it and later on require redirection in the form of an engineering change. Occasionally, one will encounter contractors who take full advantage of their power to interpret, when it provides them with more profit than merely doing it right the first time. In such cases, there are three elements of cost: first, doing the work incorrectly; then undoing what was done; and finally, redoing the job correctly.

Legal Status Specifications are at least co-participants—a fully authorized and endorsed equal to the drawings in the execution of the project. Therefore, they require as much attention and care in their production as the drawings, and the very same display of material and information in such form as to be well-displayed, clear, easily used and assimilated, and readable. This involves as much care as the use of the CAD attributes that are brought to bear on the project drawings.

The specifications are not an academic exercise—a paper written to set out research or fundamental information in report form. Rather, they are a form of the highest communication of valuable and vitally needed information crucial for the actual construction and administration of every construction project. Their informational content ranges from the general, project-wide provisions to the highly legal, intricate, and meticulous; to the minute, detailed, and nit-picky information that provides the essence of the nuances of the project. They cover massive pieces of equipment, complex systems, and the smallest of individual devices and implements.

Contract drawings are so commonly known and familiar that they tend to overshadow the specifications. In turn, the specs are rendered even more remote by the lack of instruction about them—from understanding them and their fit into projects, to their actual writing and legal standing. Although these maladies are most prevalent among young professionals and students, they are not totally resolved even among professionals of longer experience.

The intention here, however, is not to even attempt to relate "everything-you-ever-wanted-to-know-about-construction-specifications." Rather, it is to present the fundamentals without venturing too deeply into the innumerable nuances, variations, quirks, concepts, formats, approaches, directions, techniques, opinions, and perspectives regarding these documents. This is an overview and introduction to a process that has no fixed system and to which there are many differing approaches. Each professional office and each project sets different parameters for the specifications and their production.

RELATIONSHIPS AMONG CONTRACT DOCUMENTS

It is of paramount importance that design professionals—both architects and engineers—learn as early as possible in their careers (even midway in their academic preparation) about the fundamentals of the contract documents. Beyond the basic three elements (drawings, specifications, and contract/agreement), young professionals need to understand the interplay and distinctive impact of the drawings and the associated specifications. The drawing functions, of course, come to the student early on (perhaps even as secondary school classes) and can be easily translated, extrapolated, and refined into the working drawings required for construction. The ready availability and zealous selling and teaching of CAD operations to already computer-astute students has escalated this aspect of the work—but it is not without its own set of quite imposing and increasing problems (for discussion elsewhere).

At the other end of the spectrum lies the mysterious contract/agreement, which is vitally important to all parties, but cloaked in legalese and case law concepts that are well beyond young professionals. Since they do not usually prepare that document, the immediate need for understanding is of a far different ilk. This is reinforced by the lack of meaningful business and practice instruction and academic preparation on these topics. The specifications also remain as a murky unknown, too often with little else known than the name of the document. But the integral interrelationship of the specifications to the drawings is crucial. For all intents and purposes, drawings and specifications are inseparable—a vital point often lost on the young professional.

While the student or young professional may never engage in actual specifications writing, the understanding of the function, the content, and the resource value of those documents needs to be part of every professional's knowledge bank—if for no other reason than to know where to go to find the information required. To understand how information is processed and included in drawings and specifications is an invaluable time-saver and a matter of professional expertise. Knowing about one document and not the other shortchanges the young professional, narrows perspective, and forces reliance on only one source of information.

Drawings and specifications, though, are the functionally interdependent methods whereby design concepts, designs, and calculations are converted to construction terms and information that are directly usable in the field—on the job site. No matter the medium of this transformation or the form of communication, it is the communicative value that is of paramount importance. Young professionals must know that these two sets of documentation have very distinct and separate aspects, yet they are inseparably related, intertwined, complementary, and supplementary.

Certainly one could, given enough time, describe in writing how a project is to be constructed. But the massive array of information, the possibility for misinterpretation, the single direction of the verbiage, and the turn of the phrase could imperil easy use of such novel-like "construction narratives." Hence, the wide use of the concept that "a picture is worth a thousand words"!

Count the individual drawings on the numerous sheets of a set of construction drawings, and you can see the overwhelming collection of words that would be required to replace them. This does not even take into account the interconnecting words to make the "construction words" meaningful, understandable in their context, and fully usable. From here it is quite easy to see why certain words have arisen to modify the "word documents" of construction—namely, clear, complete, correct, and cross-related.

It is quickly seen that a construction narrative is far too complex to do, and the resulting uses of it are not even marginal but are inadequate to the task. As far back as biblical times and before, there have been drawings/diagrams scratched in the sand, and drawings on trestle boards used as the means to show construction, with appropriate verbal instructions to augment, complement, and supplement them for full and accurate understanding. But the verbal instructions could be easily forgotten, misinterpreted, or unwittingly modified, producing unwanted results. There was a need for continual instructions—words that "would not go away."

So we come to specifications. But what, exactly, are specifications? Simply put, they are written descriptions of various construction devices, materials, systems, and pieces of equipment. They provide specific and detailed information about things as small as a brad or clip, and as large as massive and complex pieces of equipment; they provide precise physical descriptions or performance data. They differentiate between similar items and choose from the array of possible choices. There is, as has been noted, a vast array of such items, and a goodly number are used on any one project. See Figure 5-1, for an example.

Specifications are communications that remain—they do not "go away"; they are not easily forgotten or difficult to reproduce. They can be referred to repeatedly; they can be used to measure work to ensure its propriety and completeness. They can provide information that cannot be depicted or that is too voluminous to be placed on the drawings.

They are the instructions about how to put the project together. They include both administrative and legal matters, as well as the technical work items. Usually they are bound in booklet form and called the

Figure 5-1 Sample page from a specification that includes the CSI prescribed three-part format (General; Products; Execution) for individual Sections within the appropriate Divisions. This Section would be located in Division 09, Finishes, since it specifies material used as finishing elements in a project.

SECTION 096513 RESILIENT BASE AND ACCESSORIES

PART 1—**GENERAL**

1.1 **SUMMARY**

    A. Provide resilient wall base and accessories, as indicated on drawings.

1.2 **SUBMITTALS**

    A. Product Data: Submit manufacturer's product data and installation instructions for each material and product used.

    B. Samples: Submit two representative samples of each material specified indicating visual characteristics and finish. Include range samples if variation of finish is anticipated.

    C. Submit extra stock of each material equal to 2% of total used.

1.3 **QUALITY ASSURANCE**

    A. Comply with governing codes and regulations. Provide products of acceptable manufacturers, which have been in satisfactory use in similar service for three years. Use experienced installers. Deliver, handle, and store materials in accordance with manufacturer's instructions.

    B. Performance: Fire performance meeting requirements of building code and local authorities.

PART 2—**PRODUCTS**

2.1 **MATERIALS**

    A. Manufacturers: AFCO Rubber Corp., Johnsonite, Roppe, or VPI Floor Products

    B. Resilient Wall Base: ASTM F 1861
        1. Type: TV (vinyl)
        2. Group: I (solid, homogeneous)
        3. Style: Cove
        4. Thickness: 0.125 inch
        5. Height: 4 inches

    C. Resilient Stair Accessories:
        1. Rubber Stair Treads: FS RR-T-650, Composition A
        2. Type 2 Design: Raised-disc pattern
        3. Nosing: 2 inch high, square profile; 0.125 inch thick

    D. Installation Accessories:
        1. Adhesives: Water-resistant type.

PART 3—**EXECUTION**

3.1 **INSTALLATION**

    A. Comply with manufacturer's instructions and recommendations. Install in proper relation to adjacent work.

    B. Install base and accessories to minimize joints. Install base with joints as far from corners as practical.

    C. Clean, polish, and protect.

END OF SECTION
RESILIENT BASE AND ACCESSORIES
09651-1

Project Manual. Today, there may be several volumes in a Project Manual, because of the complexity of the project and work, and the tremendous quantity of information required. This has created an atmosphere in which extensive organization of the information is a necessity for easy retrieval and use.

The writing of specifications for construction projects has long been a task left to the experienced, more senior members of design firms, those with the experience and knowledge to produce quality technical documents in the necessary legal context. In many cases, a person becomes a specs writer by virtue of their experience and interest in materials, systems, research, and the written word. This has become not so much a tradition as a question of placing the best expertise in the area where high responsibility and liability lie. For the most part, this has not changed.

Unfortunately, instruction about specifications, their function, and their contribution to construction projects has long been either ignored completely or given only token exposure in all but a few architecture and engineering schools. With a dearth of practice-related instruction in the schools, specifications remain low on the priority list. This is also seen in the criteria of the National Architectural Accrediting Board (NAAB), which monitors and sets basic criteria for accreditation of architecture schools. In recognition of these facts, emphasis has been placed on specifications in the Intern Development Program (IDP) of the National Council of Architectural Registration Boards (NCARB) and the state registration boards. That is quite telling! Nonetheless, it seems basic that student professionals should be familiar with, at the absolute minimum, the existence of specifications, how they are created, how they impact projects, and in general, the context in which they function.

Of course, being a collection of words with legal impact, specifications have become matters of interest in the law schools. In fact, there has been an emerging specialty in construction law among the nation's attorneys. That in itself gives a strong indication of the status of specifications, and the nuances and problems that they may resolve—or create! Certainly, it is a distinct warning sign to the design professions that their "word products" need to be properly conceived and well executed. Most lawsuits revolve around words, phrases, and other written material that is more familiar to the attorneys and which often provide latitude for varied interpretations, ambiguities, and of course, honest differences of opinions—all fodder for legal proceedings.

The precious little, if any, practice instruction given in the schools, and the almost total lack of addressing of legal topics, leave the professional specification effort at a tremendous disadvantage. The fact that specifications writers are usually elder statesmen in the profession is a true indication that, for decades, design professionals have been learning the legal parameters of their professions via on-the-job-training. Rarely is there any instruction that addresses the legal context in which the professions operate, or the legal implications of their services and documents. Specifications are second only to the fundamental construction agreement (contract) in legal importance, and may, indeed, be the more important due to their breadth, depth, and obligation setting.

The specification effort is daunting, but one must simply know what they are about and how best to produce them, in terms fair and proper to all parties.

Evolution of Specifications

At one time, specifications were produced by using a "back-carboning" process and translucent onionskin paper. Here the carbon paper was reversed so the imprint was made on the back of the onionskin sheet on which the text was typed (yes, "typed," as in typewriter). The sheets were then reproduced by the traditional blueprint method (white images on blue background). Gradually, a change was made to sensitized paper "ditto masters," which used a reproduction process that provided purple-colored copies, then to early photocopying, where some material was actually moved from the master matrix and placed on the copy. This was a heat-related process, which tended to fade and disappear over a period of time. The pages were made into booklets, bound with large binding staples, or punched and held with strap-like fasteners.

Two developments greatly aided the production of specifications—rapid mimeographing (using gelatin stencils through which the ink was pressed) and plastic spiral binders. The entire process was speeded up and the results were far more usable and durable. Some offset printing was done, as project manuals came into vogue, and they used heavy, often colored covers that were imprinted with pertinent project identifications.

Not only were these processes crude by today's measure, but the content was equally disparate. Construction firms were confounded by having to work with documents that placed similar information in widely different locations. The process was time-consuming, confusing, and mostly quite irritating.

Still, the primary issue was the content of the booklets. What should be said and exactly how?

THE CONSTRUCTION SPECIFICATIONS INSTITUTE

The Construction Specifications Institute (CSI) was started in 1948 by professionals active in writing project specifications, but with little mutuality or guiding concepts, principles, or standards to work by. Specifications were being produced at will, with no continuity, prevailing rationale, or commonality in the location of information. It was a wide-open, helter-skelter process, with each office doing as it pleased—much to the chagrin and dismay of contractors who were forced to spend inordinate time trying to read and assimilate the information (a situation that led to and still casts specifications in the state of being generally dismissed and disregarded).

The primary purpose of CSI, then and now, is to bring greater uniformity and understanding to the process of writing specifications, and to provide a common-ground clearinghouse for, and exchange of information between writers of specifications. It is a mutual-aid organization, so to speak, where the collective minds could assist the single practitioner with the task of writing better specifications. Part of this was the relating of "war stories" and sharing of experiences both good and bad, which served to form general principles, standard practices, prudent phrasing, and sounder, more enforceable specifications. The goal was to get one's thoughts and requirements across in better terms, more commonly understood in the field, and providing the client with the anticipated configuration and quality of project.

Even today, despite the strong CSI initiative, there is widespread acceptance but no mandated consensus as to a specific format, style, or content for specifications. This has produced a very wide range of opinions formulated mainly by those who work as consultants or full-time specifications writers. Their processes are designed to meet the needs of their clientele, in-house or out. There are well-accepted principles in many aspects, and time, along with lawsuits, has modified language, legal implications, and the direction that specification has taken. It is not now a matter of avoiding legal problems, but rather one of doing things in such a manner as to forestall problems, based on previous incidents and case law. You "just don't do dumb things"!

Nuances, tricks of the trade, variations, versions, manipulations, indications, short form, and streamlined language all are used as tools for specification production. To provide instruction other than in general terms is likely to provide more exceptions than rules—more strongly held opinions than precise, unassailable, or mandatory facts. Instruction is "spec writing" is largely organized "opinionization." What one does, or how one does it is generally based on what the individual or office perceives as the preferred method. There are truisms and guidelines, but nowhere is there a document that issues strict rules.

In a sense, there is no right way. Rather there are better ways, and ways that produce more cogent and reliable results—more professional and astute specifications—and reduce liability exposure by being clear, complete, relevant, fair, and fully enforceable. But the primary direction was to produce a proper document in keeping with the needs or desires of the clientele, by applying professional expertise to the task and by generating acceptable products that incorporated that expertise.

The methods, direction, formats, and styles still are varied, and also innumerable. Good, well-founded information is still adapted to correct image and packaging to meet the anticipated uses by the client. Underlying all this is the need for understanding the content and intent, and the manner in which correct information can best be transmitted to the users—the trade workers on the construction site. At that point the words and the specifications and the drawings must be assimilated into the tasks and actions of construction work, from which the structure rises. That sounds grandiose, but nonetheless it is accurate.

Specifications are not gamesmanship or "wordsmithing," but rather they are communication instruments that simply must get all of the information to the proper location and to the proper personnel. They can be complex but must be refined to truly communicate, and must never be used or intended to create adverse situations, to be punitive, or to cause undue trepidations among the contractors. Note: It is only the total complex of drawings *and* specifications that truly and wholly conveys the complete range of the project work.

CODE COMPLIANCE REVIEW AND PERMITTING

The construction industry as a whole and its work are highly regulated. This involves, where the work is concerned, the enacting of laws (building and other codes) and other regulations with regard to fire resistance, life safety, structural capacity, adverse conditions (seismic, climatic, weather events, etc.). In the United States, there are some 19,000 jurisdictions (states, counties, cities, villages, etc.) that enforce building codes; most are adaptations of one of the three current model codes available. The agencies who wrote these codes (Building Officials and Code Administrators [BOCA], Southern Building Code Congress International [SBCCI], and the International Conference of Building Officials [ICBO]) combined their efforts and produced the International Building Code (IBC) and associated other codes, for publication and enactment starting in 2000. Each of these model code groups had their codes adopted for use in several other countries, but it is still unclear what pattern of use and adoption worldwide will be forthcoming in response to this new array of codes. Ideally, there will be wide adoption worldwide, which will provide uniform control of construction from area to area.

As an aside, it should be noted that the construction industry, because of its inherent safety exposure, is regulated by the U.S. Occupational Safety and Health Administration (OSHA), as well as by state workers' compensation provisions, industrial relationship rules, and other occupational and workplace constraints. All of these, however, are aimed at the workers and their welfare, and not at the project work itself.

Quite often, the completed contract documents are submitted to the regulatory agencies for their review (of the methods used to comply with the regulations) and issuance of required permits. The filing of the application may be done prior to the bidding period, since changes that are required can then be incorporated into the project via the issuance of addenda. Good practice would note that there should be an ongoing rapport with the regulatory agencies, to ensure that the project progresses in accord with the various requirements. It is not prudent to make a code search early in programming, and then never approach the agencies again until time for permits. There are almost always items of design and work that require some interpretation of the laws, and best effort would call for resolution of these situations so they can be correctly incorporated into the final documents. Additionally, regulations are changed periodically, and there may be new provisions that apply to the project; these may aid or inhibit the project as designed.

This application sequence is critical so the time required for review of the documents does not slow or inhibit project progress. This is even truer when there is a need for an appeal or variance from the regulations, to meet the specific circumstances of the project. These procedures should be initiated as soon as it appears they are needed, since they can be time-consuming and could delay the anticipated start of work. Hence, the design professional often will file the permit application(s) and will field any questions coming back from the agencies. Usually the contractor is required to receive the permit and pay for it as part of the overall project cost—in fact, in some cases the permit fees are known and noted in the bidding documents.

RESPONSIBILTY FOR CODE COMPLIANCE

The matter of codes and code compliance is not isolated or assigned to one group alone. Of course, the government code agency is required to enforce the law (i.e., the codes) as deemed appropriate by the enacting jurisdiction. In that enforcement there is little discretion, and the work is a matter of assessing whether or not the construction proposed in the documents (drawings and specifications) is compliant with the regulations.

The fundamental, bottom-line responsibility for code compliance lies with the owner, even though the owner may not be aware of this fact, or know how to achieve compliance. The project work, the design professionals, and the contractors appear for but a short period, but the property remains with the owner for a much longer period. Hence, initial compliance and the maintenance of it is the owner's bailiwick.

The establishment of initial project compliance is the responsibility of the design professionals. Code considerations need to be part of the basic project programming early on, as they can affect other decisions about the project. It is this group that knows the conditions being utilized or proposed for the project, who in turn must assess those conditions within the requirements of the codes. Design professionals must have a commitment to comply and then must create a "pattern of compliance"—i.e., details, product selection, and construction that provide code compliance in various aspects of the work. Design professionals then are required to ensure that the work of compliance is incorporated into the actual project work.

The contractor also has a responsibility in code compliance. In addition to following the drawings and specifications (which show compliance), the contractor is required to reveal any situations that arise that are not code-compliant. Contractors, through the depth of experiences on a wide variety of projects, gain great insight into code requirements and compliance. Their keen eye needs always to be assessing the actual work that may be inadequate to code compliance. This is not a mandate to carry out extensive and searching investigations, but merely a responsibility to be carried in the normal run of things on the project.

CHAPTER

6

BIDDING, AWARD, AND CONTRACT

CONTRACTOR SELECTION

This outline of project sequence is predicated on the traditional design/bid/build configuration. Most of the processes listed here are also required in other contractual arrangements, but in differing order.

There are now numerous different types of construction contracts and project delivery systems from which the owner may choose. These vary as to how and when the contractor is brought into the project sequence.

Contractors are the persons or organizations that actually perform the construction work on the project. The term is most commonly used to mean the traditional "general contractor" (GC), who oversees the entire project work, may perform only portions of it (called general construction work), and hires and supervises the work of specialty subcontractors (see detailed definition below). The term can also be used to indicate huge corporations who both design and build. The term can also refer to any person who is under contract to perform a portion of the work; in some cases, the term can include design professionals.

There is a more current term, **constructor**, which means much the same as contractor. It is thought to be a more accurate and descriptive designation in that it emphasizes "constructing" (building), and not so much "contracting" (being a party in a contract), which is the old generic term to describe the overall purview of the contractor. No doubt the newer term is quite valid, but it carries no meaningful change in responsibility, expertise, or legal status. The constructor has a different perspective of the project than that of the design professional (the professional architect or engineer). Both, of course, are seeking to make a profit through the work and services they provide to the owner through the project work. It is the route by which they each proceed where the difference occurs.

By contract language and definition, the constructor is responsible for the "methods and means of construction." The design professional is responsible for the overall concept, design, and documentation of the project. The constructor's effort must be in filling in the methodology that is used to execute the requirements of the contract documents, that is, the drawings and specifications. This is done by taking portions of the work, and determining who will do that work, exactly how, with what equipment, who will supply the materials, when the work will be done, and so on. Oddly enough, the planning of the work site is just the beginning of this work, and can be either a tremendous aid or a hindrance to the work. The placement of the tower crane, the location of contractors' storage areas, loading and unloading areas, location of office trailers, access roads (temporary or permanent)—all play a part in this first function.

A GC must determine what portion(s) of the work will be done by her/his own workforce, and what other portion(s) will be accomplished by subcontractors. During the initial bidding process (in a traditional scenario), the GC will receive numerous bids from subcontractors ("subs") who seek to do portions of the work. The GC must formulate the construction team of these contractors based on price, but also taking into account previous work done jointly and knowledge of the subs (finances, work ethic, expertise, etc.). To ensure a maximum profit for himself or herself, the GC will seek to establish a team with compatible and skilled subs who will work well together, will coordinate, and will meet all schedules and cost situations.

Often, a single area of work will entail a number of subcontractors. The GC must ascertain the correct sequence of the work, while ensuring that there is no conflict created between the work of the various trade subcontractors. For example, it is foolish to allow finish work to proceed before the building is covered, enclosed, and suitably heated. Many finishes are sensitive to damp and cold; they will not perform as desired if conditions are not optimal, or as required by the product manufacturers.

Obviously, the larger the project, the more critical the coordination of the work portions among the various contractors. This requires added personnel on the GC staff to coordinate, expedite, order, and process various billings, schedules, product/material orders, and so on. Also, this entails having the right array of subs on the project at the right time, working in the proper areas.

Within those areas of work, the GC (and the appropriate subs) must determine what materials are required, what amount of each is necessary, whether all of the material is required at one time, where excess can be stored until needed, and finally, just exactly how the work will be done. This is the key issue for all of the constructors. Despite complete and rather meticulous drawings and specifications, the design professional is not responsible for and does not show every minute item of the work. The documents show the overall concept for the work area, the configuration, the materials required, etc. They do not necessarily show all the detail of how connections are made, the sequence of what is installed first, etc., nor exactly how the work should be accomplished; this is all part of the "methods and means of construction" under the purview of the constructors.

The contractor, for the most part, is awarded the work after a successful competitive bid, and is then held responsible for executing the project in accord with the construction contract. In essence this means to build the project as designed and depicted, for the amount of money agreed upon (with the owner) and in the time frame established (to mutual satisfaction). How to do this is also the sole responsibility of the contractor.

The contractor's or subcontractor's **project manager** is an office staffer who coordinates all aspects of the work assigned or under contract, and acts for the contractor when necessary. This person may handle more than one project at a time, depending on project size, complexity, and timing (a new project may have to be started well before one in progress is complete). The project manager schedules crews, adds/assigns staff, orders materials, and negotiates with suppliers and sub-subcontractors, et cetera. In addition, the manager usually supervises the superintendent (or foreperson in the case of a subcontractor) and provides assistance by facilitating work process and flow. This also involves handling the paperwork (general administration) aspect of the project work, and in general supervising and running the project from the contractor's point of view. The project manager attends progress meetings, and convenes meetings with subcontractors when necessary for problem resolution or other coordination matters.

The contractor's primary on-site person, the **superintendent**, has the overall responsibility for the construction of the project. There may be a small staff (one to three persons) to assist with scheduling, cost control, and so on (where the project warrants it). Ideally (and usually), the superintendent does not perform any actual construction (trade) work but oversees all work by all trades and coordinates subcontractors.

Basically, the charge is "to run the job," and all that goes with that. Almost without exception, the superintendent is a trade worker—generally a highly experienced carpenter—who is trained to envision not only the project as a whole, but also the process to produce the project. She/he acts as the contractor's eyes on-site when the project has no construction manager, and represents the contractor in meetings and communications; although somewhat limited in authority, the superintendent can act and speak for the contractor to a large degree. This person works very closely with the contractor's project manager, to provide the full range of service required for administration of the project.

The **foreperson** is the individual who is in direct charge of a work crew or a subcontractor's entire work force on the site, usually a worker experienced in a single trade who can resolve problems and assist the workers in the correct execution of the work required by contract documents. This person has the expertise to adjust work as necessary to meet changed or unusual conditions encountered on the site, and to still meet the contract requirements. Also, this person is responsible for coordination with other trades, where their work interfaces, relies on, or supports the work of the subcontractor. Through experience this person fully understands all ramifications of the work assigned, the materials being installed and how best to install them, and in general, how the work/installation fits into the overall project.

On the staff of the contractor or construction manager (more commonly, although this person could be a separate consultant) may be a **value engineer**. This person seeks to identify unnecessary costs in both design and construction, and seeks or proposes alternative schemes or technology, without sacrificing project requirements or quality. Obviously, this must be an experienced person with a broad knowledge of construction methods, materials, techniques, systems, equipment, capabilities, and other technology. The value engineer could be considered a major advocate for the contractor/manager, who is committed to providing the services outlined above. This person and work is best utilized prior to the start of the construction phase. As one of the preferred aspects of construction management, utilization of a value engineer early in the project's design sequence is becoming more common, and is producing better project value and cost control.

The **estimator** is one of the contractor's most trusted employees, whose task is to gather and maintain actual costs of work items, materials, and subcontractor bids and prices. This person may also track costs as they appear on each project. It is important for the contractor to have a reliable and wide-ranging set of actual prices and costs for various items of work. The estimator must know individual prices for small pieces of work. These are called "unit prices," for example, the cost to excavate one cubic yard of rock material from a depth of 15 feet below grade. Other examples include not only the cost of a door, its frame, and its hardware, but the labor cost for the time it takes a carpenter to apply the hardware and hang a single door. Changing wage rates, added benefits, or the normal upward rise of construction costs adjusts these prices overall. All this is necessary to properly establish the actual cost (both reliable and anticipated) of the door installation. The contractor relies on such information, as the individual prices are then assembled with the many sub-bids and formulated into the primary bid the contractor submits on a project. This pricing is most important to the contractor, so he or she can be confident that the work can be done as required, but also in a profitable manner. Consequently, the estimator must have a large number and a wide range of resources and sources of materials, information, cost data, etc. All this must be tempered by an intelligent understanding of the construction work and process as it impacts cost, and vice versa.

In some cases contractors have separate staffers, **expediters**, on the payroll who are specifically assigned to "make things happen." Such a person may absorb some duties performed by the project manager (depending on the company and project size and type). The expediter schedules crews, acts as traffic manager, schedules material deliveries, and coordinates operations with deliveries and crew availability. The fundamental goal is a formal and ongoing program of bringing people and things together so work can be accomplished properly and quickly.

Construction managers (CMs) are part of a newer group of people in the construction industry. These are individuals or firms placed under separate contract with the owner to evaluate design approaches and contractibility, and to provide value engineering and management on a project. This added oversight serves to bring better value to a project by identifying potential problem areas and offering alternative solutions. Although there are several forms that construction management can take (for fee, Guaranteed Maximum Price (GMP), at risk, etc.), the firm usually will not perform any construction work, but will oversee all contractors (usually without contractual relationships, although other forms involve contracts). The CM may act as the owner's agent during construction and also has an expeditor/coordinator role to facilitate every aspect of the project regarding cost, schedule, and prompt, successful completion.

Owners always like to have a single person who is responsible for the entire project. The use of a construction manager has a wide and varied range of possibilities, and often is formulated in a manner specific to the needs or requirements of the owner. There is no single configuration for CM work; the owner can decide what set of contractual arrangements best suit his/her needs. However, it does set out the CM as the single point of responsibility.

The CM is active during the design and documentation processes and from the outset of the construction phase. The degree of involvement varies as desired by the owner. For example, in the design sequence the CM can offer cost-comparison information, which helps to ease the decision making for systems and materials. Alternative construction methods can also be suggested. The construction manager (be it a firm or a person) can be inserted into the design/construction portion of the project progression at any point. The CM can act as an advisor in the design work; can advise and input aspects of the construction depicted in the documentation; can participate in the bidding process; and can either monitor and administer construction or, with the proper contract, can act at risk and actually hire the subcontractors (a role similar to that of the traditional general contractor).

While the CM is not the primary design professional, the hope is that under a CM the design will be more easily established and will be truer to budgetary constraints, while still providing a satisfactory appearance and function to the owner. In late 1998, at least one state (Idaho) enacted a registration system for construction managers. Primarily aimed at publicly funded projects, this appears to be a growing trend. The criteria for such registration includes training, education, experience, etc. Further, the law sets out certain required contract configurations and relationships, so public agencies have less discretion in how the CM will work on their projects.

Much the same interface occurs during documentation. Some cost impact data is helpful, and alternative construction methods, sequences, and details can further better implementation of the basic approved design. Here again, the CM is not the primary functionary, but rather is in an advisory role, if that is what the client desires. Normally, construction management is not set out as a policing function or one that creates dissension among the professionals. Each professional has a role and an obligation to the owner. Their best effort is one that is fully coordinated and respectful of each other. There will be differences, but the final authority on the project is the owner.

Perhaps the most dramatic changes, in the scheme of construction management, occur during construction. There are several methods and many variations in which the CM can be established on the project. The primary issue with the CM in construction is whether the CM performs some of the construction work and has a contractual relationship with some or all of the contractors, or whether the CM is in strictly an advisory, oversight, coordinating role with no contractual relationship to the various contractors. Again, the explicit form used depends on what the client desires, and on what the resulting contract obligations of the CM are.

The work of the design professional and the construction manager complement each other, interface for better coverage, and provide the owner with a different scenario for responsibility in the various phases of the project. There must be a full and continuous exchange of information between these parties, to ensure that the project's direction is maintained and that progress is proper and consistent. In the main, owners will contract with both parties for complete overall project administration and improved project attributes.

The **subcontractors** are individuals, persons, and organizations with expertise in a very specific and narrow range of work required on the project (supplying and installing ceramic tile, for example). By concentrating their efforts in a narrow range of work and materials, these organizations become more expert and can perform with good speed and good quality work. In a sense, they are experts in their field. Usually a project team is an array of different subcontractors combined in their effort by being placed under contract by the general contractor (or construction manager), and not the owner. They are beholden to the general contractor for their work, their payment, and a correct technical and administrative interface with others on the project. Their contract comes, in the norm, through a competitive bidding process, wherein the subcontractor bids against others for the portion of the work. Their contract is with the general contractor (GC). The sub is under the administrative control of the GC as to schedule, direction, quality of work, interface with others, etc. The primary (general) contractor makes periodic (usually monthly) payments for the subcontract work done.

Worker is the general, all-inclusive term to describe a person who has particular skills, ability, education, training, and knowledge about specific types or portions of construction work. This includes the employees of both contractors and subcontractors. Although training and direction vary, trade unions prefer to confine their training to single-task orientation. Other groups prefer cross training in several tasks, resulting in workers who can function in many specific ways. For example, one worker might be trained to install framing for partitions, but not the drywall (which is installed by other workers), or the same worker might be trained to perform both functions with equal skill.

Tradesperson is the term applied to workers trained and skilled in a narrow-scope trade, usually involving a single or a fairly limited range of materials or systems (glaziers for glass installation, carpenters for several tasks, but not an extremely large range of work). These persons are well-versed in the best methods for installation of the material(s) or system(s) using the latest techniques and technology, and they draw on their personal skill/knowledge/experience in applying previous successful solutions to new circumstances. They usually have an in-depth understanding and working knowledge of all of the work they are to perform. In many instances, the jurisdiction of a trade has been established, primarily through a collective bargaining contract, that is, unionization (e.g., bricklayer, electrician, carpenter, painter, tile setter, concrete finisher, etc.). Some in the industry advocate cross training and multitasking, but in the large majority the concentration is still on a single portion of area of work.

The term **journeyman** is used most commonly within the unionized construction trades, and indicates a worker (male or female) who has served a term of prescribed apprenticeship and has acquired the requisite training, knowledge, skill, and a level of experience in the trade. This is usually tied into the wage rate agreement and benefits package offered through the union contract with the construction industry. For the individual, it is an indication of a level of expertise that when coupled with years of experience denotes a well-skilled worker who has progressed well beyond the novice level of the apprentice.

Apprentice is the term, name, and program that has been carried over from the historical system of a young person learning a trade in a shop, or working with a guild (an early form of the union) craftsman, who was highly skilled and experienced in the work. Primarily a function of the construction trade unions (of about 30,000 American apprentices in 1995, 75 percent were union), the program is the prime feeder into the trades. Of journeyman-level workers in the unionized trades, between 75 percent and 99 percent are apprenticeship graduates; in nonunion trades, this figure is only 7 percent to 25 percent. Apprenticeship involves a progression of mentoring in physical work and a teaching/learning process of maintaining and carrying forth the quality work, skill, and reputation of the trade. This system remains today in a similar form in even nonunion, home-building, and professional situations (co-op students, for example). The major change is that the teaching/learning is a more formal and structured program, in many cases carried on in vocational, community college, or even full university programs. The apprentice now works during the day and attends classes in the evening or on weekends. Apprenticeship programs are usually regulated and controlled by the states. The period of time varies but is usually in the range of four years. During that time, the apprentice works at a reduced rate, gaining insight and experience in the chosen trade.

The construction work force is a blend of a sizable number of different groups of trade workers. Each of the groups is formed by the mutual interest and well-being of the members, based on the type of work they perform. In many instances, these groups have resulted in the unionization of the workers. This is basically the formation of formal organizations that represent the collective interest of its members, all of whom perform similar work but for different employers. Primarily, the collective function is to improve the lives, employment, working conditions, and financial stability of the workers.

In many parts of the world and particularly in the United States, construction-oriented unions form a strong influence on the work, vigorously defending members' overall welfare and establishing jurisdiction over such emerging new materials and work as can be reasonably performed by and assigned to their members. In addition, they protect the wage rates and associated benefits of the members through collective bargaining (i.e., negotiating standard wages and benefits applicable to each member of the union, no matter what employer they work for). This is necessary because the majority of the members do not work exclusively for one employer; rather, they move from project to project as the work demands. Further, most unions have apprenticeship programs wherein they train new members in the work to be performed, so there is a more uniform approach to and level of expertise in that work.

Unions now, however, do not have the same level of influence that they attained two to three decades ago. At that time, most commercial (nonresidential) work in the United States was performed by unionized labor. For various reasons, other groups, primarily contractors (the employers of the trade workers) sought to reduce their cost, increase their competitive edge, and open the labor market to far more people. The result was the formation of a nonunion work force. There is now a formidable portion of the work force that does not use unionized workers. Here workers may or may not be trained (although training is becoming more prevalent to upgrade expertise and employability). In a sense, there is a competitive atmosphere around construction workers, and a good portion of projects in the United States now have work forces that are a combination of union and nonunion crews (again, reflecting the work of the particular trade). This promotes employment for workers and allows owners to receive true value for their money.

Table 6-1 is a list of construction-related trades. There are many others that use slightly different names for their workers, which are narrower and more specific to the nature of the work performed. Also, there are within the list variations within titles, such as "Electrician, power line," as opposed to the electrician who does the wiring for a building. "Operating engineer" covers all of the drivers and operators of various types of construction equipment from road graders and scrapers to cranes, lifts, and temporary elevators. Table 6-1 includes a brief description of the typical work performed.

TABLE 6-1—CONSTRUCTION WORKERS BY TRADE

TRADE WORKER	DESCRIPTION
Boilermaker	One who makes, assembles, re-fits, and repairs boilers of various sizes and fuels
Bricklayer; Mason (see Stone Mason)	One skilled in the building of masonry walls, including brick (of various sizes and bonding patterns) and concrete masonry units (CMUs, concrete block)
Cabinetmaker	Shop worker using woodworking techniques and equipment to make cabinets of various sizes and configurations, and can be utilized to install same in the construction project
Carpenter: Rough and Finish	Worker trained in the use of wood and wood-related materials; does a wide range of work from rough wood framing and concrete form work installation of specialty and finish items; has a good general overall knowledge of construction and is often utilized as a job superintendent who oversees and coordinates all other trades; work is broken down into "rough" (work generally concealed) and "finish" (work generally exposed to view) carpentry
Carpet Layer	One skilled in the installation of wall-to-wall carpeting, including cutting, seaming, binding, trimming, stretching, and attachment to subfloor with nail strips or adhesive
Cement Mason	Worker trained and skilled in the finishing of exposed concrete; flat work (slabs) and other surfaces; various finishes and coating/grinding/finishing of formed concrete
Drywall Installer (Hanger) and Finisher	Worker applies panels of drywall (gypsum wallboard) and associated trim to the framing; and who fills the board joints and fastener depressions with compound and tape, and sandings, making it ready for finish work
Electrician	In buildings, one trained and skilled in the installation of electrical wiring, devices, power panels, lighting, etc., in accord with the national electrical code; one involved in high-voltage work in building areas and other high-power installations, including transmission lines, etc.
Electronics and Telecommunications Technician	Technical worker who installs, starts up and services the numerous electronic and communications systems now so common in buildings and their operating systems
Elevator Constructor	Worker trained and skilled in the installation of various types of elevators, escalators, other lifts, and their operating equipment; all work is involved within the shaft construction performed by others
Floor Covering Installer	Worker skilled in the installation of different types of floor coverings; often grouped by the specific type of coverings they install (i.e., carpet, resilient tile, etc.)

TRADE WORKER	DESCRIPTION
Foreman and Forewoman (also, Supervisor, Crew Chief, Team Leader)	A person with substantial experience in the particular trade, who is capable of overseeing other workers, correct installation of the work as applied to the specific project and its conditions
Glazier	Worker trained in the fabrication and installation of various glass products—fenestration, interior vision panels and sidelights, roof monitors, etc.
Hazardous Material Removal Worker	Worker responsible for removal of existing material that has become hazardous, prevalent in renovation work (most commonly, asbestos workers); also, a worker who cleans up hazardous materials on project sites to bring them into usable and environmentally safe condition
Hod Carrier	Laborer employed solely to bring materials to the brick mason (brick, block, mortar, accessories); also usually responsible for mixing of mortar
HVAC Installer/ Technician	Technician trained for the installation of various air-handling and air-conditioning equipment (exclusive of sheet metal ductwork); may also install small package boilers, VAV boxes, and other equipment for heating, ventilating, and air-conditioning purposes
Insulation Worker	Worker skilled in the application and installation of various building insulation products (exclusive of roof insulation), from blankets/batts in walls and floors to custom insulation fitted to different piping and ductwork systems
Iron Worker	One who installs structural steel framing of differing types, from lightweight steel lumber to the major framing for high-rise buildings and bridges; with skill in welding, bolted connections, and some riveting
Laborer	An invaluable, general-purpose worker, who performs any number of unskilled tasks, from direct assistance to skilled workers to clean-up; usually hired for work in conjunction with a specific trade, and with knowledge in what that trade requires
Lather	Worker who installs underlying support for wet plaster applications; can utilize expanded metal lath or gypsum board lath
Millwright	One skilled in the set-up of various equipment and machinery in a project shop or in a new project where required as part of the basic contract
Operating Engineer	General term for a worker who drives or operates heavy construction equipment (cranes, scrapers, bulldozers, excavators, loaders, drag lines, graders, power shovels, backhoes, etc.)
Painter	Worker skilled in the preparation, mixing, tinting, and application of various paint and coating products; skilled in use of brush, roller, or spray application equipment; can produce all types of finishes, opaque or natural

TRADE WORKER	DESCRIPTION
Paper (Wall Covering) Hanger	Quite often, a painter who has acquired skill in the application of wall coverings of all types—vinyl, paper, grass cloth, metallic, etc.
Pipe Fitter	Worker trained in the installation of piping for water, steam, gas, oil, chemicals, and other processing operations
Plasterer	Worker adept at applying wet plaster systems to walls and ceilings—both traditional 2- and 3-coat systems, and thin veneer systems
Plumber	Person trained and skilled in the installation of sanitary and storm drainage fixtures, elements, and systems, and in water and natural gas supply systems for buildings; also involved in major outdoor sewer, wastewater, drainage, and similar piping systems and facilities
Reinforced-Concrete Iron Worker	Often called a "rod buster," a worker who installs reinforcing bars and accessories in preparation for the placing of concrete in various elements and features
Roofer	Worker trained and skilled in the application of various roof-covering systems; some known as "composition roofers" work in sheet roofing for commercial installations, as opposed to shingled systems for residences and light commercial projects
Sheet Metal Worker	Worker who installs the sheet metal ductwork associated with HVAC systems; may also be involved in ductwork in association with other operations or machinery (called a "thin knocker" at times)
Sprinkler Fitter	A pipe fitter who specializes in the installation of fire sprinkler systems
Stone Mason	Masonry worker who specializes in setting cut stone or stone veneers, in lieu of the unit masonry laid by brick masons
Stucco Mason	Although stucco is a plastic material applied much like interior plaster, a stucco mason can be either a form of plasterer or a brick mason, who is skilled in the application of parge coatings (which is similar to stucco)
Terrazzo Worker	Often a worker who is also a tile and marble setter, but specializes in the installation of terrazzo systems
Tile Layer	Worker skilled in the installation of precut floor tile systems, or in the application of flooring (vinyl) sheet goods, which is installed using wide rolls of material cut to fit the profile of the area
Tile Setter	Skilled worker who sets wall and floor tile of various types (ceramic, various pavers, stone, epoxy terrazzo tiles, and other unitized material)
Tower Crane Operator	A special operator out of the operating engineers' realm, whose work is confined to the single-mast, top slewing tower cranes now used so widely on larger projects

TRADE WORKER	DESCRIPTION
Teamster	A collective term for all types of vehicle drivers, and associated workers; different from an operating engineer in that the vehicles are of wheeled, roadway type
Welder	Person trained, skilled, and often certified for the work of welding materials together; most prevalent in steel construction, where certification is important to correct installation and adequacy of the steel members

*For further explanation of trade work and opportunities, consult the Web site of the U.S. Dept. of Labor, at http//stats.bls.gov/oco/ocos1009.htm

The major challenge of the general contractor or the construction manager is to find companies who employ the various trade workers. A combination of these companies (and their employees) then forms the construction team. Here the various players must be brought into a coordinate and directed effort to complete the desired project on time and within the owner's budget—and certainly in a profitable manner for their employers.

In reality, the formation of the team is based primarily on cost, the amount of money the various firms have issued as bids to perform the work. This is where the competitive aspect of construction comes into play.

Construction firms retain meticulous cost information to ensure that they can perform given tasks for "x" dollars, which will yield them a profit and will also cost less than other firms, but all in the performance of project work as required by the contract documents. This is a strictly disciplined activity, in that cutting cost (on the part of the contractors) adds to the risk of losing money, which cannot be avoided by failing to perform in accord with the contractual obligations.

Technicians appear in several different forms in the construction context. The designation involves two differing groups of people. First, this is another name for a worker in a specific area of work; also, a mechanic or a person doing repair or other work of adjusting, testing, calibrating, etc., to place an item of equipment into proper operation (as opposed to the person who actually installs the piece). Secondly, in the design professions, a technician is a person trained, perhaps to the associate degree level, who operates in a technical support role to a design professional. For example, this could be a CAD designer who has a good level of technical knowledge as well as CAD skills, but has not been educated or trained, and does not have the experience of a registered professional. Oddly, the first group is usually trained to a higher and more technical level, to contend with all of the various systems that may be encountered in different equipment. The second group has been fashioned and trained formally in an area that previously was confined to persons of high school education, who trained through on-the-job training, rising in status as their skill level increased (for example, a young person hired as an entry level drafter, who gradually gained expertise through on-the-job training).

An **installer** is a trained worker whose principal function is to receive, or take delivery of, materials, equipment, or apparatus, and locate, assemble as necessary, anchor, and adjust the same for full and proper functioning. The installer ensures through prescribed procedures and/or a troubleshooting process that all items or pieces of equipment are complete (and as specified) and ready for use by owner/occupant/user(s).

Depending on business philosophy, staffing level, and type of project, a contractor often will have a **job clerk** on-site, whose purpose and efforts are to track documents, monitor costs, and generally engage the documentation involved with the progress of the work (but not the design/contract documents). This staffer may act in any of several ways, from an assistant to the superintendent, to running necessary errands, filing for permits, and to some degree, to act as expeditor; but in total, the clerk is more a technical clerical than anything else.

On projects of some extent or complexity, a contractor and/or the construction manager may provide a **site secretary** for on-site administration. This person would be heavily engaged in the more highly clerical pursuits (handling correspondence, in/out, keeping current files, recording meeting minutes, coordinating and publishing meeting notices, proper distribution of documents and information, including various computer functions) but might be assigned some of the functions of the job clerk. Also, on a particularly active site, the site secretary may act as receptionist and executive secretary to the manager, superintendent, or even the clerk-of-the-works. In general, the site secretary assists with, and relieves the superintendent and others from, day-to-day administrative duties.

In many repects, the **clerk-of-the-works** is the predecessor to the construction manager. Mainly hired as a full-time, on-site representative of the owner, the clerk ensures compliance with contract documents through daily exposure to and inspection of the construction work and process. Quite often, the clerk is hired by, and placed on the staff (and payroll) of, the design professional, with all salary and costs involved reimbursed by the owner (or could be hired directly by the owner). The clerk-of-the-works works closely with the design professional (and the project representative) but is not the professional's on-site presence or representative. With the clerk on-site daily, the professional may be able to utilize just a part-time project representative, relying otherwise on information and observations from the clerk. Usually, this is a highly experienced construction person, who can aid in identifying and solving problems, with limited bounds somewhat similar to the project representative. While titled differently, a person in this assignment or position is a major player in the process of contract administration, acting as the CM's full-time site presence.

PREPARATION FOR BIDDING

It is essential that all parties have a mind-set that the bidding process must be executed in a strictly controlled manner and on a level playing field. That is in regard to the atmosphere and demeanor of the parties on the owner and professional side, since at this point, the contractor(s) are not yet involved. There can be *no* mysteries, side deals, or second agendas that inhibit the contractors from bidding in a fully equal, straight-up, and competitive environment.

Fairness is the preeminent key word in the bidding process. The concept of the bid documents requires that every bid be based on exactly the same documents. This, of course, is the reason for the reproduction of drawings and specifications using methods that produce identical copies of the documents. While there may be variation in the actual construction methods and procedures between bidders, projects must be bid in a manner that will provide the project work in full accord with those same documents.

The concept is that the bid price will be reflected in the construction contract and used in that document as the basis for it. Such contracts have language such as, "for the price/cost noted herein, the project work will be executed in full accord with the contract drawings and specifications." That language is so blatantly clear that it virtually eliminates any attempt to subvert the concept by charging more for the work or providing less appropriate, substantial, or quality work than that shown or described. Also, it is an open expression of the fairness and equity of the contract and the expectations of both contractual parties (owner and contractor).

Part of the fairness issue in bidding is that the estimating and costing of a project for use in a bid is an extremely time-consuming and expensive process for a contractor. For contractors, bidding is a high-risk exercise—extensive, expensive, meticulous, highly competitive, and frequently disappointing. There is no fee paid for the bidding, it being done at the contractor's cost to search out new projects for their workforce (and profit). Bidders, therefore, are deadly serious in seeking the contract for a project (and recouping part of the expense of bidding) or they will not take the time or spend the money to bid. In the end, one bidder will be successful, while the others will be left with no recourse but to understand that bidding is merely part of the cost of doing business. This scenario for bidders is the keenest, strongest, and most imposing part of this work—an "all or nothing at all" prospectus. Therefore it had better be part of an absolutely fair, open, and equitable process with no room for any shady aspects.

ASSISTANCE IN BIDDING

In soliciting bids, the owner must make project documents (drawings and specifications) readily available for the bidders to use in their take-offs. Common sense shows that if the owner is asking for contractors to bid the project, the bidders must have access to all pertinent project information—otherwise the bids will be fatally flawed from the outset. And in addition, every bidder must have access to exactly the same information, in both amount and in content. The competition lies in how each bidder perceives the work and how they feel they can execute it.

Normally, a deposit is required to ensure that documents in the hands of unsuccessful bidders will be returned. These can then be reused by the contractors who are selected to work on the project. Most of the bidding contractors will have limited amounts of work, and will not seek full sets of documents for bidding. To allow them access, however, sets of contract documents are placed in public "plan rooms." These facilities are offered by local construction industries offices (Associated General Contractors, Allied Construction Industries, American Building Contractors) and by F. W. Dodge, Inc., which is a construction-reporting agency and provides the service as a courtesy to local contractors.

This is a distinct aid to subcontractors or material suppliers who do not need full sets of drawings (which usually involve a refundable fee for use). At the plan rooms, they can make a quantity take-off of the items with which they are concerned, without a fee (this is really a service to attract additional bidders for better competition). They then can formulate their bid and call it in to the general contractors they choose to bid to. In this way the owner is not made to pay for an overabundance of documents that may never be needed. The documents are made available to the entire array of contractors on an equal basis, which leads to better and closer pricing—stiffer competition—which in the end benefits the owner through the lower cost of the project.

In many instances, there is a requirement for a list of subcontractors to be provided with the bid. This is aimed at locking in both the contractors and their submitted costs. If a list is not required, a general contractor may submit one subcontractor and the associated price, but then "shop" that price to reduce it on his/her behalf, without changing the amount in the bid. Here the owner is required to pay (if the bid is accepted as submitted) in excess of what the actual cost to the general contractor is. This is, of course, highly suspect and underhanded (to say nothing of poor business practice) but is not necessarily of high legal impact (without a list, the owner never is made aware of the change of subcontractor and the reduced price).

Prebid Meeting

This is an essential part of the level playing field atmosphere and getting everyone on the same page for bidding the project.

This meeting is called after the documents are distributed in an attempt to clarify information, to make certain points clear, and to receive and answer inquiries about the project and the work. In many cases, it also involves a walk-through of the existing facility (where the new work is an addition or alternation) or the site to familiarize all with the conditions of the project. In the case of a new building and site, the bidders are held responsible for visiting the site and becoming familiar with it and all its attendant features (ignorance of site conditions is not a valid basis for extra compensation).

Although the meeting is quite detailed, it is aimed at the overall project scenario and not at highly detailed provisions of the documents, in exact and precise terms. It deals more with procedure than with document content, since it is usually held early in the bidding period, before the bidders have had a chance to really uncover all the nuances of the project and documents. Generally it is a familiarization and a setting of the record so everyone knows what is expected.

Addenda

When bidders begin their in-depth review and precise examination of the documents, questions, ambiguities, and gaps will be discovered. All of these should be routed to the design professionals for explanation, clarification, and answers, to a point. That point is that all queries of all types must be answered identically to all bidders—again, to maintain a level playing field where everyone uses the same information. A formal written document is developed and supplied to all bidders of record (those who have acquired documents for bidding), noting any changes in the documents, along with suitable answers, interpretations, new information, and clarifications to the inquiries. A query made by one bidder must be answered to all.

The formal document is the addendum, usually on a form developed by each professional office. There may be more than one addendum (called addendas), if the volume of inquiries merits such action. However, no addendum should ever be issued closer than ten days to the bid receipt date, giving ample time for delivery, analyses, pricing, and adjustment of the bids to the new or revised information.

RECEIPT OF BIDS

Many construction-related organizations have their own set of guidelines and requirements for bidding their construction projects (see Figure 6-1). It is important to know about these early on and to conform to and comply with them in every aspect. This is particularly true for publicly funded organizations and projects. Here bidding is extremely sensitive and must be executed exactly as prescribed. Private sector bidding is a little more informal, but still in need of precise execution.

Because of the time and money involved, bidders are highly competitive and give no quarter to any bid that is done outside the requirements or in any way cuts corners or uses procedures not clearly available to all. Equal is equal among bidders. The competitive spirit makes for a high level of scrutiny and the slightest irregularity is cause for comment, questioning, or complaint. Unfortunately, all too frequently strong litigation is taken over the smallest nuances in the bidding process.

Although not firmly entrenched, there is a general strategy for setting the date and time for receiving project bids. This, too, is part of the level playing field concept, as well as making the process as adaptable and easily executed (for the bidders) as possible.

In general, it is a good idea to incorporate the following into the bidding process:

- Do not receive bids on Mondays, Fridays, or days immediately before or after holidays (this allows time for the bidders to get back to their work in an atmosphere without distractions).
- Do not receive bids before noon (again, giving time during the morning for the bidders to receive the host of sub-bids they normally receive, and for their analysis and adjustment; often the same sub-bidder will revise the price several times within several minutes).

Most construction projects in the United States are competitively bid. However, bidding procedures from one geographic region to another frequently vary widely. This variety has become an increasing industry problem as owners, design professionals, contractors and subcontractors more frequently move from construction market to construction market.

As a result, there is a need to establish more uniform guidelines for bidding competitively-priced projects in order to reduce confusion, increase fair competition and lower construction costs. Some key concepts for bidding are summarized below:

Advertisement for Bids

Owners should advertise the availability and distribution of bidding documents as far in advance as possible, but no later than 30 days prior to bid document issue. An advertisement should contain a short description of the project, including bid date, time, approximate contract amount, approximate size, project location, licensing requirements, plus bid and performance and payment bond requirements. It also should state the date of document availability, location of documents, and deposit and refund information. The advertisement should be circulated to both individual prime and major subcontractor and material supplier prospect bidders, placed in construction publications and posted in plan rooms.

Bid Documents

Bid documents should be complete before they are issued. For small or simple projects, at least two weeks should be allowed for bid preparation. If a project is large and/or complex, four to six weeks or even more may be necessary.

Bid documents should be made available to a sufficient number of bidders to foster competition. Thus, the owner should furnish each local plan room with at least four complete sets of bidding documents. In addition, the owner should provide each prime bidder with at least four sets of bidding documents for its use and the use of its subcontractors and suppliers. Major subcontractors also should be provided, by the prime bidders, with a copy of the bid documents. Any prospective bidder should be afforded the opportunity to obtain complete sets of documents through a plan deposit system and/or to purchase partial or complete sets directly from a printer or the architect.

Recent developments in the use of "electronic plan rooms" have increased the availability of project information to multiple users. Owners and General Contractors are encouraged to investigate and implement web-based plan access to maximize plan availability while minimizing cost.

Plan Deposits

In order for an owner to receive the best possible price on a construction project, it is important that all bidders on the project (prime contractors *and* subcontractors) have access to the most accurate and complete plans and specifications. It is in the interest of owners to provide sufficient sets of drawings and specifications to permit all interested contractors, subcontractors and material suppliers to prepare accurate bids. A fee for the use of such plans, when added to the contractors' other estimating costs, can be a factor limiting both quantity and quality of the bids on the project since only successful bidders can recover these costs.

Deposits, not exceeding reproduction costs for the plans, are reasonable. There should be a provision, however, for prompt refunds in full to anyone who pays the deposits and who submits a bid or sub-bid on the project and returns the plans within 30 days after bid opening (if its bid was unsuccessful) or who returns plans promptly after examining them and making a decision not to prepare a bid.

Further, it is reasonable to charge reproduction costs for plans to those material suppliers or bidders on smaller subcontracts who wish a set of plans for their own exclusive personal use, yet for whom plan room or borrowed sets of plans would normally be adequate for careful bid preparation.

With these facts in mind, and in order to promote the best, most careful and complete bidding on all projects, an adequate number of plans to permit careful preparation of bids should be provided to interested parties at no cost to bidders who return such plans within 30 days after bidding.

Scope Letters

Each sub bidder should submit a written scope letter to the prime bidder at least 24 hours before the bid time.

Figure 6-1 A document published by the Association of General Contractors (AGC) that details the procedures to be followed for ensuring good, competitive bidding, to the owner's benefit.

The scope letter should contain any information the prime bidder needs to evaluate the sub bidder's bid, including its proposed scope, alternates, unit prices, addenda, and/or bulletins to be included. The scope letter should reference specific divisions or sections and specifically identify any omissions or additions. Each sub bidder should submit its final bid dollar amount and any necessary clarifications to the prime bidder at least four hours before the prime bidder's bid hour. The prime bidder should establish a cutoff time for receiving sub bids, make it known, and adhere to it.

Ethics in Bidding

The bid amount of one competitor should not be divulged to another prior to bid time, nor should it be used by the prime bidder to secure a lower bid proposal from another bidder on that project. A subcontract bidder or supplier also should not request information from the prime bidder regarding any sub bid prior to the award of the subcontract (*see B.4 Bid Shopping and Bid Peddling for more details*).

Owners should publicly open and read aloud the bids. Construction contracts should be awarded to those responsible and responsive bidders, at all levels of the project, which submit the low bids for their portions of the work prior to bid time. Bids should not be held longer than 60 days without an award being made.

Bid Errors and Adjustments

If, after bids are opened, a low bidder claims it has made a material error in the preparation of its bid and can support such a claim with satisfactory evidence, it should be permitted to withdraw its bid, without forfeiting its bid security. Under no circumstances should a bidder be allowed to adjust its bid price as a result of an error in its bid. If the owner opts to re-solicit bids for the project, the erring contractor should not be allowed to bid for the contract, unless precluded by local, state, or federal law.

Some construction owners allow a low bidder who can demonstrate an error in its bid to upwardly adjust its bid price to the extent of the error. The low bidder will be awarded the contract at the adjusted price so long as that price, as adjusted, is still below that of the second low bidder.

Allowing a low bidder to adjust its price under any conditions, other than change orders issued after the contract is under way, undermines the entire system of competitive bidding and is an open invitation to abuse.

Use of the following procedures is recommended when a bid error is discovered:

When an apparent low bidder discovers an error in its bid price, it shall have the following options:

1. The low bidder may, at its option, confirm its original bid price; or
2. The low bidder may withdraw the bid, without penalty or forfeiture of bid security if it establishes that a valid computational or transcribing error resulted in an unintentionally low bid, but shall not be allowed to re-bid the job under any circumstances.

The owner shall then have the option of awarding the contract to the second low bidder or of re-soliciting bids for the project. In the event the project is re-bid, the former low bidder shall not be allowed to bid for the contract. Unless required by statute, no adjustment in bid price should be allowed a bidder as a result of an error in its bid.

If a subcontractor bid is so low in comparison with other bids as to suggest clearly an error, the general contractor should notify the subcontractor immediately that its bid appears to be out of line. The subcontractor should either withdraw or confirm its bid, but not modify it. The American Society of Professional Estimators has prepared even more detailed *Bidding Procedures for Competitively Bid Construction Projects.* Copies of the document can be obtained from ASPE, 11141 Georgia Avenue, Suite 412, Wheaton, MD 20902, telephone: 1-301-929-8848 or online at *http://www.aspenational.coml*

Other references include:
Recommended Guide for Competitive Bidding Procedures and Contract Awards for Building Construction published by AGC and the American Institute of Architects:
http://www. agc. org/contractdocuments/
http://www. aia. org/documents/

Recommended Competitive Bidding Procedures Construction Projects published by the Engineers Joint Contract Documents Committee:
http://wwwpubs.asce.org/contract.htm

Guidelines for a Successful Construction Project. Copyright © 2003, The Associated General Contractors of America/American Subcontractors Association, Inc./Associated Specialty Contractors.

Figure 6-1 (Continued)

- Do not receive bids in downtown or congested traffic areas, particularly at lunchtime when parking can be a problem (bidders need to have enough time to get to the place of bid receipt *before* the due time).
- Ensure that all doors leading to the room where bids are to be received are unlocked if not open; install signs and directions to the room (leave no doubt where the bidder is to deliver the bid).
- Have a time stamp, correctly calibrated to verifiable or corrected local or other acceptable time standard; stamp each unopened bid envelope as it is received.
- Close and *lock* the room door at the precise time when bids are due; do not open it for anyone, and do not check the halls for any latecomers (late is late! lawsuits have been filed over the giving of any latitude in this regard).
- Open bids in order of time received.
- Have one person open the envelope; another extract the documents; another check for all required documents; and yet another read the bid numbers, including alternates, slowly and clearly.
- Have sheets available for the recording of the numbers by the receivers and by all bidders (these may contain columns, but no pre-inserted information).
- Make no comparisons, draw no conclusions, and make no comment about any bid, or the bids in total, at this time. Merely receive the bids without comment; take them under advisement.

An emerging scenario for receiving bids is through electronic means, i.e., facsimile or e-mail transmissions. Of course, either of these allows for the submittal of bids without some of "people issues" like parking, etc. However, there is need to properly and firmly control these formats. Following is one set of requirements for these transmissions.

SUBMITTAL OF BIDS

1. Bids may be submitted using postal or other delivery service, or as noted below.
2. All pages of the bid form shall be fully executed with all attachments, signed, and received at the destination prior to the date and time stated (controlling time is that at the destination).
3. Where bid is faxed or e-mailed, an original copy of the bid form, including original signatures and all required attachments, shall be subsequently received no later than noon of the following business day.

4. Bidder is responsible for allowing ample time for the transmission of the forms, and for ascertaining that all pages of the bid and bid-related forms are properly and completely received. Partial bids or those with difficulty in transmission or opening will be considered flawed in the preparation and/or sending procedures, and may be deemed nonresponsive and void.

Select one or both methods below for submitting bids:

<u>Faxed Bid Forms</u>, sent Attention: _____ at (000) 000-0000.

<u>E-mail bid forms</u>: Bid may be submitted via e-mail, provided it is completed using Adobe Acrobat software, password-protected against editing, in PDF form only, and it is part of an e-mail message with a recorded time, at the destination, prior to the bid receipt time.
Send e-mail bids to: _____@_____.____

Bid Forms

Most project manuals (books with project specifications and other important documents) contain the actual bid form that is required (see Figure 6-2). This form is usually a "fill-in-the-blanks" type. Pertinent information required includes the project bid (cost) and the time for completing the project work. This form is created to present the information the owner requires to evaluate the bidding, as well as other information that could be utilized under other project circumstances.

For example, there may be a request for unit prices (i.e., cost per unit measure) for extra excavation. This may be included when the underground conditions are suspect and could require added work. In lieu of taking the time to gather new cost information, the bidder merely in-

Figure 6-2 Bid package documents, from Halpin, *Construction Management*, 3rd Edition (John Wiley & Sons).

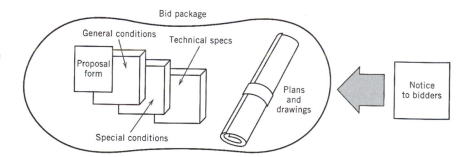

cludes a price—perhaps a price per cubic yard for rock excavation—that will automatically be used if needed.

BIDDING

This process for determining the overall cost of the project's construction is adapted and carried out in a manner as desired by the owner. However, the majority of the actual estimating process is a standardized, routine operating procedure specific to each contractor. Each bidder/contractor has in place a procedure, software, forms, and techniques for the collecting of cost information and ancillary subcontract bids. Each uses those processes that best serve their interests and have held them in good stead with previous bidding experiences. In addition, each contractor has a vast array of reference information regarding cost, including the unit costs that are developed and kept from project to project. Each of these indicates an exact, minutely detailed account of money, labor, and material required for a portion of work. For example, the installation of a door is broken down into hours of work required and the wage rate in effect, and that cost can then be added to the cost of a door to ascertain the cost of the door, installed.

While the processing and preparation of bids is rather uniform in concept, there is a rather dramatic difference between public bidding and private bidding. The fundamental difference, first, is that anyone may submit a bid on publicly funded projects. The laws prohibit closing out any bidder who has the wherewithal and the inclination to submit a bid. The same laws usually require awarding of the contract to the "lowest and best" bidder, which is cause for much consternation and a high level of extracurricular activity. Obviously, the lowest bid is the one asking the least amount of money for construction of the project. But the best bid is much more difficult to determine. This hits at the ability, skill and capacity of the bidder to accomplish the project.

For example, a large or complex project can be bid by a small, minimally staffed, ill-prepared contractor who appears to have no capacity for accomplishing the work. There is, of course, a scenario in which this bidder "jobs out" or utilizes myriad subcontractors who are capable of doing their assigned work; the bidder would only coordinate those contractors and generally oversee the work. Still, the contract award stands, and the project work becomes highly problematic. Any action to remove or replace the bidding contractor becomes entangled in legalities and directly affects the project. Proving a contractor with little history in the appropriate level of construction is extremely difficult, until there is open evidence of inadequacy (which may well not appear until well into the project work). All this impacts the owner and the other parties, who have no choice except to expend added effort, time and money to make the project work.

This example, is of course, only one scenario, since the vast majority of public projects are well executed in all aspects, and are tightly controlled by various regulations and procedures to ensure that public funds are not wasted or poorly used. This protection is quite valid, but does not account for the many cutting-edge design projects using public funding—university buildings, for example. Here justification of the design often is left to the bidding process—i.e., if you can build the proposed design within the stated budget, there will be no particular concern; going over budget or misusing the funds will cause grave concerns.

Private bidding is carried out in a much more relaxed and less restrained atmosphere, but is no less competitive. The owner involved sets the tone of the bidding process by the project delivery system chosen and the other procedures that are set out for both bidding and constructing the project. Usually none of this is nearly as involved as publicly funded construction. On private projects, bidders can be restricted to those on an invited or otherwise prequalified list, developed jointly by the owner and the design professionals (none others need apply). Such lists usually contain names of firms that are known to have the necessary capacity to produce the projects in a timely and correct manner.

Usually this list contains contractors for the four major trade contracts (typically general construction, plumbing, HVAC, and electrical for a design/bid/build project delivery system) who are familiar to the professionals and who have performed well on other projects. This process allows the owner and design professionals to fashion a project construction team that is a known quantity and promises to be more productive and less contentious than with wide-open bidding. Of course, the more compatible the project team members, the more coordinated and smooth-running the project work will be. This, in turn, fosters project delivery on time and on or under budget.

There are other forms of more open bidding whereby any interested general contractor can submit a bid for the work, but the owner retains the right to write the contract as seen best for the project and is not constrained in making the award as in the public sector.

Also, depending on the choice of project delivery systems available to the owner, other bidding scenarios are available. Some owners choose to avoid the nuisance of bidding and merely negotiate a construction contract, but the vast majority like the idea of competitive pricing and the ability to secure the project at the lowest possible cost. It obviously is a measured process, pitting low cost against contractor aplomb and skill, and how the various work contracts (subcontracts) are executed.

CONSTRUCTION EQUATIONS

1. Good Design + Poor Construction = Good appearance and function; short-term durability
2. Poor Design + Good Construction = Poor architecture (well-built, but ugly, malfunctioning building)
3. Poor Design + Poor Construction = Probable litigation
4. Good Design + Good construction = Good architecture (good appearance, function, and durability)

There is a distinct and highly developed methodology, technique, and bank of knowledge in bidding; prices for units of work (installing a door and hardware, for example) must be known and must be reliable. These must then be applied to the correct number of items as taken from the drawings and specifications (called a "take-off"). Items missed or miscounted are at the contractor's expense, be the error a shortage or an overage. This is high stress/pressure and intensive work to ensure that every item, no matter how small, is accounted for. Additionally, the contractors seek to assess, visualize, completely understand, and envision how they would approach and execute the project. This entails understanding not only the construction but also the various nuances and encumbrances that will (or could) impact the project work. Estimators can make or break contracting firms; they are held in high repute, and are a valuable asset to an active firm. They must know construction methods, materials, sources, equipment, techniques, politics, and all of the nuances in order to convert contract documents into an appropriate, accurate bid, and hopefully into a new contract. In reality a good estimate is a plan for the project, ready to execute.

Additionally, much of the work will be given over to subcontractors—specialty contractors who perform work of limited scope, usually in a specialized field or material installation. The sub-bids must be received by the general contractor (usually from several firms of the same trade) and analyzed so the best and lowest (most reliable and favorable) sub-bid can be factored into the overall bid. Many times the general contractor will use a sub-bid that is a little higher just because the sub is known and has worked well previously. All subcontractors do not usually bid to every one of the general contractors who may be developing bids—here competition is again extremely high as the subs vie for more work.

BID REVIEW AND ANALYSIS

The owner, in consultation with the design professionals, attorneys, construction manager (if utilized), needs to very carefully review, analyze, compare, and understand all of the bids and how they could influence the project (see Table 6-2). If bound by law ("lowest and best" bid usually must be used for publicly funded projects), the owner needs to know the type of organizations that are represented by the low bid and their expertise.

Actual selection of the contractor is at the will of the private owner, and is usually unencumbered, legally. In publicly funded projects, the list must be opened to all, which makes ascertaining the "best qualified" contractor a difficult task. Public work frequently also requires the acceptance of the "lowest and best bid" regardless of qualifications (lowest is the numerical lowest; best is much more difficult to ascertain, and often leads to many disputes, including litigation). This process can lead to difficult (slow, disrupted, inadequate, improper, etc.) projects, as the contractor endeavors to recover costs on at least a "break-even" basis.

TABLE 6-2—BIDDER SUMMARY

BIDDER	BASE BID	ALT NO. 1	ALT NO. 2	ALT NO. 3	ALT NO. 4
McCorkell and Company	$3,254,890	$42,510	$7,000	$30,000	$91,208
Henderson Construction, Inc.	$3,330,000	$41,000	$7,900	$29,990	$90,800
Concept Building Company	$2,999,000	Deduct $10,000	$21,000	$37,754	$98,990
Burke-Meadows, Inc.	$3,310,890	$38,300	$8,050	$31,405	$89,450
Springer/Weye, Inc.	$3,050,000	$39,000	$7,850	$28,100	$78,250
High-Point Constructors	$3,284,100	$42,890	$7,900	$35,000	$89,999
Langer Brothers	$3,175,642	$40,500	$7,750	$30,669	$79,250
Parker Construction Co.	$3,500,000	$42,000	$7,300	$29,110	$85,000

Low bids most often are created by pure error on the part of the contractor in putting together the bid: leaving work out, transposing numbers, misplaced decimal points, forgetting tax/wage rate changes, etc., and/or cutting margins and subcontract funding too close.

If an error is claimed (usually by the contractor very soon after the bidding) there needs to be a resolution as to the impact and severity of that error and whether or not the contractor can overcome the problem and execute the project. If not, proper action must be taken to void the bid and move to the next lowest bid for the same consideration. Sometimes a bid is extremely low, and the contractor claims no error. Here, obviously something is wrong, and an attempt must be made to find out what. Construction is not the place to seek, or take advantage of an apparent bargain by default—simple equity and correct pricing is the better route.

Should an apparently errant bidder be awarded the contract, there could well be a very adverse situation sometime later in the project. Problems can arise when the contractor attempts to recover from the error, such as substandard work to cut costs, a slower progression of work, shut-downs by unpaid subcontractors, or other financial problems detrimental to the project. In addition, the progress of other contractors can be affected (who may well seek to recover for their unanticipated extra costs).

Other Bidding Formats

There is an interesting bidding method used quite extensively in Europe on a voluntary basis. Here bidders are informed that the contract will be awarded to the bidder who is closest to the "actual cost of the project." That cost is established by eliminating the highest and lowest bids (as being erroneous or unresponsive) and averaging the remainder. The bid closest to that number (either slightly under or over it) is awarded the bid. This process is intended to achieve smart and straightforward bidding without the discounting and adjusting in an effort to manipulate the price in the bid. While still competitive, it tends to eliminate the jockeying and gaming involved in much of the bidding in the United States.

AWARD OF CONTRACT(S); NOTICE TO PROCEED

Awarding the contract should be a very thorough and careful process, so no assumptions are made, and so the contract can be formulated with all of the proper provisions. Here is where the client's attorney comes into the picture, to protect the client, and to produce an equitable contract, fair to all but to the ultimate good of the client. Quite often, the attorney will use standard contract forms from such organizations as the American Institute of Architects (AIA), or the Engineers Joint Contract Documents Committee (EJCDC) of the National Society of Professional Engineers (NSPE). It is not all that infrequent that the client will require a specific contract form, written to the needs of the client (such as governmental agencies), or the peculiarities of the project, or the contractual configuration. Such forms must be made available for review during the bidding period, so the contractor can assess what the project entails. If, however, the contract proves to be too extraordinary, the contractor may balk at signing it—particularly if it appears to place hardship or added risk on the contractor alone.

Many times the client will issue a notice to proceed (or notice of award), telling the contractor(s) of the client/owner's intention to enter into a contract based on the bid price (and any negotiations that may have taken place subsequent to bidding). With this legally binding notice, the contractor can start mobilization of his forces, and begin to formulate the project team. Often this process starts with the subcontractors listed on the bid form (List of Materials and Subcontracts) being given similar notices, or their contracts. Fairly soon after the notice, the formal signing of the contracts with the four major contractors (again the D/B/B delivery system) will take place, and the contractual relationships thus established; also, the project clock starts running, ticking off the days until completion of the project (as required in the contract).

PRECONSTRUCTION CONFERENCE MEETING (KICK-OFF)

All concerned parties to the project can best be aligned and familiarized with each other and with project conditions and procedures, through the use of a pre-construction conference or meeting. As part of the mobilization process, the contractor in conjunction with the design professionals calls for this conference. Usually at least a notice of intent (to issue a contract) is required to get the parties to attend the meeting. Formal contract signing is not necessary, but is preferable. However, the meeting should occur before actual construction (and even on-site mobilization) is started.

If not already done, an accurate and current directory of all parties should be compiled and distributed, including company name, contact persons, addresses, phone numbers, fax numbers, and other such data. There should be a formal agenda for the meeting, which includes personal introductions of all parties, and short presentations by the owner (or the designated representative) and design professionals (including construction manager and consultants). Topics specific to the project should be included and resolved—communications, distribution lists, site security, assigned storage areas, site operations, site office/trailer location, temporary services, and peculiar parameters regarding excessive noise, dust, traffic control, parking, safety issues, et cetera. Additionally, there can be a distribution of documents, review of contractual obligations, the Conditions (both General and Supplemental), and Division 01 General Requirements of the specifications; and there should be an open discussion of how the general contractor intends to run the site and the project.

While this is not strictly a social meeting, neither should it be a dictatorial, fist-pounding expounding of demands; rather, the tone of the entire project can be set by having an amicable, friendly interchange, whereby all parties can meet each other, and recognize each other by sight (and first name!). With this and a sincere, firm, and fair explanation of the need for cooperation, the project can be set on a good course. Also, it is helpful to create an open atmosphere where any question is welcome and will be resolved promptly, fairly, and in keeping with the obligations of all contracts.

PROJECT MODIFICATIONS

As actual construction begins, all parties to the project must understand that there will be modifications (changes) during that process. While the terms of the contract are firm and mutually accepted, changes occur in every project—in varying degrees. This is a common or normal occurrence and not a dramatic event.

Changes result from various circumstances, such as unforeseen conditions, requested changes in project scope (added or deleted work), revision in the work, discrepancies in drawings and specifications, substitutions, unavailability of materials or systems, other requests from contractors, and so forth.

The wisest and preferred course, for correct administration of the project, is to process all changes as they occur. Changes need to be documented, solutions need to be resolved, pricing needs to be requested, and proper approvals need to be given. This process is best handled through a standard form like AIA Document G701, Change Order. Change Orders need to be written for any variation in the cost of the project or for added time for completion—either or both.

The Change Orders become part of the Contract Documents and document the variations that need to be made in the project cost (and payment) system and the time it takes to finish the project. The owner, design professional, and contractor all need to be part of the changes to allow correct and proper processing and resolution without contention. Too often, mishandled changes result in claims, disputes, and other legal events up to and including litigation—all needless if changes are resolved correctly in a timely manner.

CONSTRUCTING, ERECTING, AND INSTALLING

CONSTRUCTION PHASE

In this phase of a project, on-site/field operations begin to run both in successive order and concurrently with each other and with office and administrative functions and activities. As the project progresses, the staffing level increases in the field to its maximum, and then gradually lowers as work is completed and contractors fulfill their obligations and leave the site.

All of the project functions are listed in order here for ease of explanation, but they are not truly linear; project work of one nature or another is performed concurrently on many fronts, at the same instant, but in different locations and certainly for different reasons. Perhaps the ideal place to see a good example of this is on the project (construction) schedule, where all tasks are set out in their correct order (see Figure 7-1).

Also, it should be stated that this text does not attempt to explain all of the intricacies of the construction materials, systems, devices, implements, items or operations—it is the general progression that is addressed here. Within each listed procedure or task there is a tremendous amount of information and work required. It is through the wider study of construction methods, equipment, materials, and systems in architectural and engineering curricula, and through experience that one acquires full, wider, and deeper insight and knowledge. This leads to flexibility of mind in designing and documenting construction projects.

As immediate guides and references for construction information, the following are but two of many resources available, which provide sound, fundamental information for readers of this book:

H. Leslie Simmons. *Olin's Construction: Principles, Materials and Methods,* 8th ed. Hoboken, NJ: John Wiley & Sons, 2007.

Figure 7-1 Example of a project schedule, showing the various tasks set in the time frame and sequence in which they must be completed.

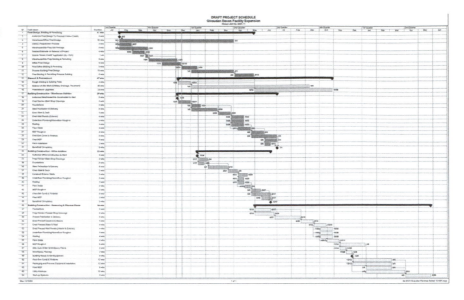

Edward Allen. *Fundamentals of Building Construction: Materials and Methods,* 4th ed. Hoboken, NJ: John Wiley & Sons, 2004.

In addition, the following is a very good Internet resource for general discussion of construction systems, procedures and methods as developed through history: www.britannica.com/eb/article-9106103/building-construction.

Reference is also made to the list of trade associations (see appendix), which can provide a wealth of information of a very specific nature; of course, individual manufacturers can and will address the full range of detailed information about their products and their correct use.

The Raw (Undeveloped) Site

Every site, and more particularly those that are undeveloped (still overgrown with trees, underbrush, existing natural and man-made features, etc.), must go through a process that opens the project site (if not the entire parcel of land) for the impending construction activities. This starts with a process called "clearing and grubbing," that is, removing unnecessary brush, trees, undergrowth, existing features/structures, and the like from the job site. Basically, this is an operation to clear an open area at least for the project itself, of all existing things that could impact the work of the new project. Not only does this involve the actual site for the project, but enough area around it to allow for access, storage and staging of materials, field offices/shops, parking, and so on.

Often large project sites will have a huge pile of discarded trees, which may be taken off-site and dumped, or perhaps sold off as firewood to the local residents. Of course, stump removal is required, and can be a troublesome activity if there are large units, deeply grown. It is not uncommon for the site to be cleared to such an extent that some earthwork and landscaping must be done upon completion, just to restore the site to a condition nearly as it started. Once the site is cleared, the various limits, parameters, and locations can be set out, and the operations turn to earthwork.

Initial On-Site Operations

The very first operation for the actual new project work is to physically lay out and establish the limits of the project work on the job site.

Prior to the design process, a detailed land survey should have been made to ascertain the various features of the property. This entails a survey and engineering crew who traverse the property and set stakes and monuments on all property lines and corners. Just prior to the start of construction, it is best to verify the survey data. There is then a need to physically establish all bench marks, easements, or other legal (but mostly invisible) encumbrances impacting the work site. Also this surveying/engineering work should establish clearing lines (the edge of an overgrown or wooded area which is to remain) and mark the plants, trees, et cetera, that are to be removed for the project. Additionally, all utility lines should be located (this is best done by each utility company, who maintain accurate records). It is important that this matrix is set out so no part of, or party to, the project will violate any of the parameters (which could have legal consequences).

Prior to moving on-site, the contractor will have determined how the temporary construction facilities (storage trailers and area, parking areas, office trailers, work sheds, toilets, water supply, electric service, etc.) are to be located. This must be done in a manner that allows adequate work area for the contractors in the construction area, but also allows for maneuvering of equipment and for receipt and storage of various materials (see Figure 7-2). If done improperly, the site layout can be a direct impairment to good work progress and completion.

Building layout is an engineering task usually done by a surveyor or an engineer who has a background in surveying. This involves the establishment of measurements and the turning of angles to establish the corners of the structure(s). This must be done in reference to specific landmarks and other such points set forth for the project (bench marks for height and elevations, property lines and corners for the lines).

Figure 7-2 View of a construction site, illustrating the extent of the work areas and the complexity of using the site in a productive manner so that the various operations do not infringe on each other. Sites require study to ensure that placement of temporary facilities do not conflict with the work. *Courtesy of Jupiterimages Corporation.*

From the layout marked by corner stakes, the contractor sets a pattern of batter boards to each of the corners. These are stakes or pipes, but mainly horizontal boards on stakes, each way at each corner. The lines of the building (usually the outer faces of the foundation walls) are then transferred to the boards, which are set well outside the building and excavation area and remain undisturbed throughout the project. These become the reference points for all contractors so they all work to the same points and lines and their work then is coincident and correct. On both very open and tight (inner-city) sites, and where appropriate for the type of building, column centerlines will also be established and indicators set. In essence, this is a full-scale "site plan" come to life; it is placing the project structures physically on the land area.

Mobilization

This is the process the contractor uses to energize the project, with both physical and administrative activities—both on- and off-site. Administratively, the process involves securing insurance and bond coverage, acquiring permits, preparing progress schedules, and so on. Additionally, the list includes a number of activities and work items that are performed or provided on the actual site.

On-Site Mobilization and Staging

Some earthwork operations may be required on-site, to allow for setting of office trailers, opening storage areas, and so forth. This may entail clearing, grubbing, scrapping of topsoil, et cetera, if these facilities occupy a portion of the project site, and there may be need for restoration of these areas at the completion of the project.

Site mobilization is the task of the contractor and at times can become a major increment of the project. Remember that every project is not of modest size and located on an open tract of land with road access. Some projects are executed in tight quarters, in a busy downtown city environment with tight spaces, streets, traffic and pedestrian concerns, no storage space, extreme heights, and myriad other important concerns, occurring daily. Indeed, the mobilization situation is a direct reflection of the size, complexity, location, and restrictions of the new project.

Starting with a home or isolated commercial building, the chances are good that the site will have road frontage (direct access for trucks and personnel) and will be large enough to accommodate site storage of equipment and materials. Even here the contractor must plan the utilization of the site so as not to impede or encumber the work. It is foolish to store materials only to have to move them to allow the work to proceed in the very same area.

Large projects like schools and shopping centers also are of such size that the site, if planned well, can be an asset to the work. Care must be taken, though, so storage does not conflict with paved areas like parking lots, roadways, recreation areas, et cetera. Although that work would be performed late in the project sequence, material storage must be planned. Chances are most of the material will be expended by the time of paving, but waste, excess materials, and equipment can interfere with those operations if not dealt with carefully.

Most projects can make good use of temporary trailer offices and tool sheds, temporary worker parking, track access, and material/equipment storage. In some cases, though, this is a major problem and can have a very drastic adverse impact on the project if not well considered and planned. For example, a remote site for a major structure may require that new access roads be installed to allow construction traffic. Not wanting to place the base materials for future permanent roads, the access roads are purely temporary and are eventually removed. That, of course, can be a hefty cost to the contractor. This situation can also be a requirement for smaller projects, again depending on the size of the property and the configuration of the project (and perhaps existing structures).

Two types of projects where mobilization is a tremendous problem are inner-city projects—a high-rise office building in a downtown area, for example—and a bridge, dam, or navigational lock project on a major stream.

In the first case, it may be necessary to block off lanes of the roadway to allow both access and some storage. Perhaps there will be a need to off-load all materials directly from the delivery truck to the place of installation, avoiding any need for on-site storage. That requires a tower crane in a very careful and calculated location (mobile truck-cranes would have to be placed too close to the work, and would not have clear open access all around the project).

In the case of a project in a stream, part of mobilization is to establish the work areas out in the streambed itself. This involves the construction of cofferdams. These are usually a round cylinder with steel piling for walls, which are driven down into the streambed and rise above the level of the water. This cylinder is then pumped out to create a relatively dry area literally under the water, in which foundation and pier work can be conducted. When that work is complete (or at the completion of the entire structure), these facilities are removed and the new pier is located out in the stream, but founded below on good bearing soil.

The following mobilization activities (and perhaps others) are required, and in some cases are required in the project specifications:

- Move plant and equipment onto site
- Furnish/erect plants and temporary buildings
- Install temporary construction power, wiring, lighting
- Establish fire protection
- Install construction water supply
- Provide furnishings and utility services to offices
- Provide on-site communications
- Provide on-site sanitary facilities
- Establish contractor storage areas, furnish/install/ maintain storage buildings/sheds
- Post all OSHA and other required labor/employment placards; establish a site bulletin board
- Establish all safety programs, safeguards, signs/instructions, and placards
- Have project superintendent on-site full-time
- Plan and submit design, provide and erect project sign
- Install fencing, gates, parking areas, truck delivery locations, tower or other crane(s), hoists, debris and waste collection facilities, garbage facilities, eating/break/smoking areas, traffic controls, et cetera

Mobilizing for Renovations

Mobilization takes on an even more imposing look when the project is one of renovating an existing facility—particularly when the owner intends to maintain full production and operation.

Here the task of accommodating construction within the production operations is often quite complex and daunting. Extensive temporary work is needed: dust and/or soundproof partitions, barricading, rerouting or maintenance of exits, and so on. In many cases, fairly intricate and elaborate measures must be taken to allow for the owner's continued operations and production, as well as for the construction. In the extreme, the construction may have to be scheduled during off-hours of the plant (second or third shift; even weekend work). Often convoluted configurations are required—and of course, safety for all personnel (construction and operating) takes the highest priority.

This all is greatly exaggerated if the facility is a quiet use (hospitals, nursing homes, schools, libraries, etc.) or produces food products, pharmaceuticals, or sensitive or sterile implements or materials for medical and other highly sanitary work. The by-products of construction—noise, dust, and disruption of building services—must be mitigated to the point where they are totally anticipated, planned, and controlled, imposing in no way on the production areas. Sometimes, whole departments of personnel are temporarily relocated and isolated to allow for easier and more rapid construction; often, though, this is not practical.

Of course, this all has a direct and often major impact on project cost, scheduling, and operations. But it must be done so the owner does not lose income because of shut-downs or the inability to produce products, in addition to paying for the new work. Understanding, cooperation, and coordination are of the utmost importance. But this ancillary mobilization work is unavoidable if the construction work is to be done and a better facility is to result. While not directly producing results, it is an absolute necessity, and benefits both owner and contractor.

Project Organization: Project Progress Meetings

Very soon after the first personnel from the contractors come on-site and work begins, it is necessary that there be a meeting to establish the organization of the project and the site. This should be the first of a series of periodically scheduled project progress meetings, and should be a detailed expansion of the information discussed at the pre-construction conference. The contractor should convene these meetings with a firm and appropriate agenda (this is not to be a free-for-all, rap session, or social event), distributed prior to the meeting, so all participants arrive fully prepared to discuss the project, answer and ask questions, and simply to coordinate. The participants should include all contractors currently working on-site, those to arrive shortly, and those leaving shortly; also, the design professionals' representative(s) and the owner's representative. Others may be invited as required to discuss special situations or to give specific information to all present.

Often these meetings are set for a time just prior to the deadline for submitting monthly payment requests, so there can be review and discussion of the requests, the work completed to date, accuracy of information, completeness of information, extenuating problems and circumstances, and so on. This speeds processing of the requests by the professionals and provides for prompt payment by the owner.

Project Schedule

The general (primary) contractor is responsible for the execution of the project work, and also for the methods, techniques, and process of construction. With this comes the necessity and responsibility to organize the work, and to schedule the work and the interface of the various subcontractors. Obviously the contractor is concerned that some work is not done, and that later work disrupts, removes, or mars earlier work; repair/replacement in this case is at no cost to the owner, but can be a detriment to the project.

There are numerous different techniques for scheduling, and the system that best serves the project should be chosen. Some schedules are simple bar charts, noting start and completion of each subcontracted work, or work item. These can be done by hand, but more than likely will be computer generated. There are several software programs, from simple to highly complex, that can produce the proper schedule for the project (given good data to work with). Mostly, scheduling is predicated on good weather, but factors of flexibility are built in, which can adjust the progress when interrupted or delayed by weather conditions (some projects in colder climates shut down completely during winter or other adverse seasonal weather).

Usually the Notice to Proceed (and eventually the contract) will call for work to start within seven to fourteen days after the Start of the Construction Process (the date of receipt of the notice). The schedule must reflect that date and the end (completion) date as set out in the contract; most contracts now use a number of calendar days for the work period. This schedule is used as the basis for all discussions of project progress, and is usually the topic of some discussion at every project meeting. While flexible, every contractor takes note of its provisions, and works within the time frames outlined (all this being discussed and resolved prior to issuance of the final schedule).

Initiate Purchases of Material and Systems

As soon as they have signed contracts, all of the contractors will start to order the materials, supplies, and equipment they will need to perform the work. Some of this procurement is driven by the schedule; that is, there is no need to order material that will not be used until later in the project sequence (paint would be a good example). However, it is necessary that all contractors monitor the project's progress and the schedule, so prompt ordering can be done to prevent any delays due to inadequate supplies of materials or excessive delivery time. Often material is ordered "for later release and delivery"; this is a form of reserving the materials, but receiving them when needed so as not to create a storage problem on the site.

Some materials will have delivery times in the range of ten to twelve weeks from the date of order, so care, knowledge, and monitoring is an absolute necessity to the contractors. Also, care must be taken, primarily by contractors who work with numerous items specified throughout the project manual, so all of the devices, equipment, and materials required by their work are ordered in a timely fashion. Occasionally, one item will be overlooked (or assumed to be part of another contractor's work) and not ordered in time to allow prompt and in-sequence installation. Almost all of this work is office work done by the project manager, and is accomplished while other on-site activities are taking place.

Yet another process is started as material orders are placed. This is the activity known as shop drawing production. The vast majority of the items to be used in the project are made through various manufacturing processes. Quite often standard materials or devices are specified, but even these must be made proper for their fit into the project—minor adjustments in spacing may be involved. Other items will be fabricated specifically for the circumstances of the project and must be made in special ways. For example, a countertop must be made to fit exactly between two end walls—obviously, its dimensions must be determined in the field, and then the shop must be told how to fabricate this work. Shop drawings indicate to the manufacturer's shop what is to be made, how many are required, and what special, different, or added features need to be made part of the material or apparatus. In many instances, the shop drawings will depict a specific arrangement of standard (stock) parts, pieces, or items, which matches the configuration or conditions in the project. While the individual items are common and mass produced, their combinations and relationships vary from project to project, or even in different locations on the same project.

Before giving these drawings over to the shop, the manufacturer will submit them to the design professional and contractor for review, and to ascertain whether or not the proposed fabrication meets the intention and requirements of the contract documents. No manufacturer wishes to produce an item only to have it rejected, or have it not fit the dimensions or purpose. The shop drawings, along with product data sheets (cuts, descriptions, and listing of product features), are part of the submittal required in various sections of the specifications. In some cases, samples of the material or device are also required, for assessment of quality or, in some cases, for selection of color(s). These submittals are not required and are not submitted at the beginning of the project. They are submitted throughout the progress of the work, but in a timely manner to allow for production and shipping time, so the actual material or devices are on the site ready for installation at the right time.

Earthwork; Grading and Excavation

Along with, or part of, the excavation operations is the rough grading operation, whereby the "cut and fill" and rough regrading sequence is put in place—that is, the cutting down of high spots and filling in of low spots on the site. This is not necessarily to achieve an absolutely level site, but to create flat areas (plateaus) where the building can be placed. There may still be variations in the site profile, but usually they will be more moderate than the original. Also, this is the base for the site drainage plan, which will carry storm water away from the buildings and into the various drainage facilities, both natural and man-made.

Where required, the existing layer of topsoil will be stripped off and stockpiled on the site for future use; this is an economical measure where good and deep topsoil layers are in place. Once this is done, the actual moving of dirt can occur—scrapping, pushing, moving, filling, compacting, rolling, removing soil (where excessive or of bad quality), and bringing in soil (new or additional good soil, from a "borrow" pit elsewhere on-site, or from another source).

All this is also an indication of what the start of earthwork operations must entail. No site remains intact without some earthwork involved, if only minor clearing and re-grading for positive drainage. Only very light buildings—sheds and single-car garages, for example—rest *on* the ground; all other structures and buildings (including small, one-story structures) actually engage, rest in, and bear on the soil under and around them.

Part of this site preparation work is the actual excavation—the creation of a hole in which the building foundation will be set. Two operations then follow, sometimes concurrently, sometimes in tandem, depending on conditions, extent, and areas of mutual activity and use. These are the excavation for the building substructure (foundation system) and the various trenching/excavating work for the utility lines (which entails both linear trench lines and fairly large holes, where manholes, junction boxes, vaults, etc. will be built for the utility equipment: transformers, sewer lines, retention/detention facilities, etc.).

In most areas the bottom of the foundation system (footings) is required to be set below the frost line (the depth to which the exposed soil will freeze). This is part of the regulations set forth in the applicable building code. This depth varies from a few inches to several feet and eliminates the possibility of uplift (heaving) of the structure by the expanding soil. The excavation need be only as deep as necessary to meet this requirement. In some construction (basement-less, for example), the depth of the excavation is minimal. In other cases, the excavation can vary from a modest eight- to twelve-foot deep opening for a house basement and foundation to a depth of several stories, where a high-rise building is to have several basement and sub-basement levels (for parking, storage, mechanical equipment, etc.).

In many cases of very deep and/or extensive excavation, there is a need to stabilize the perimeter of the site. In other words, temporary walls of driven piles, sheeting, and bracing may be installed to hold back the surrounding soil so it does not filter or slide into the excavated area. This is a rather costly operation but one that can save an enormous amount of time and trouble. Taking time to continually deal with earth slides, cave-ins, slippage, filtering/sifting, or collapses is both dangerous and time consuming. To box out the surrounding soil is the preferred method of creating a clean, easily worked excavated area for a project.

In the case of large and high buildings, the excavation can be so big that large excavating equipment and trucks are actually moved into the excavation. Drives and ramps may be needed to allow the dump trucks to take the excavated soil up and away from the excavation. Various types of digging, loading, and earth-moving equipment may be needed, from self-propelled articulated loaders to backhoes, clam shells, and large shovels and drag lines. It is the task of the contractor to develop the plan for excavation and to secure proper and adequate equipment to do the work on schedule.

In the case of high-rise buildings, once the lowest floor level is exposed, there may be need to dig fairly large isolated areas for massive column footings. These are often quite large and deep and are fitted with a grillage of steel members to form a resting or bearing surface for the building columns.

These operations may sound relatively simple, but they can be very extensive, expensive, and imposing. The proper foundation system must be carefully selected, to match the imposed loads of the building to the capacity of the soil at some level. It is not uncommon that a building is so big or heavy or the soil so poor and weak that a common excavation will not expose a level of soil capable of carrying the building weight. Hence, very unique, heavy, and/or deep foundation systems must be considered.

Installation of Substructure (Foundation) System

The substructure of a building is the portion that is never seen or seen only in part from the outside; it is the lowest portion of the building and usually underground. The system can be a combination of the foundation system that supports the upper portions of the building and some occupiable spaces. There can be an open area called a basement or cellar, or a honeycomb of rooms and spaces on several levels (especially for high-rise buildings) that house storage, maintenance, mechanical equipment, and parking functions. In some instances, some of these spaces are actively used as shops, restaurants, night clubs, and similar uses.

There are numerous foundation systems that can be considered to best serve the building. It must be kept in mind that the foundation system will probably never be fully exposed again, unless expensive changes or repairs are needed. It is better to select and prudently design an adequate system and have it installed correctly, as a second chance is not likely.

Two basic categories of foundation are available: shallow and deep. These are explored and explained in detail in other resources; suffice it here to list several of the variations:

SHALLOW	DEEP
spread footings	driven piling
wall/strip footings	drilled caissons
isolated footings (columns)	deep wall
combined (trapezoidal—2 columns)	mats
cantilever	mats with piles
continuous (3+ columns)	cofferdams
grade beams	vibra-flotation
mat or raft	piers
rigid	soldier beam/breast boards
thickened slab	turned-down (dropped) slab

For the most part, the shallow systems reflect light building loads, adequate soil bearing pressures, and modest excavation (perhaps one or two stories deep). Foundation walls and grade beams require a continual footing system, whereas columns stand alone or are closely located, and are carried by other types of footing combinations. Thicker or turned-down slabs indicate very light loads, like partitions or light wood frame outbuildings. Mat or raft foundations are a single homogeneous concrete mass, extremely thick (10 to 12 feet is not uncommon).

Where the soil bearing is weak, there is a need to either excavate more deeply or select an alternative foundation system. Some systems create legs for the building, with piling, piers, or caissons built or driven into the soil below the excavated level. These are made of such length (sometimes hundreds of feet) as to reach a level of soil (mainly bedrock—the strongest "soil") that is capable of holding up the building. The weight of the building itself, its furnishings, equipment, and people are taken up in the upper structural system. That loading is transmitted to columns or walls, which transfer it downward. Eventually, the load must engage the earth surface. Here there has to be an equal upward strength to match the downward loading. The load can be spread over a large area (like a column footing much larger than the column itself) or carried to stronger soil. It is for the structural designer to find just the right combination of systems to achieve a balance, so the building is adequately supported and stable (see Figures 7-3a through 7-3g).

Installation of Underground Utilities

Intertwined between the features of the foundation system are the utility lines that will serve the building systems. Commonly called "the underground," this work can be done concurrently with the foundations (usual in smaller, lighter buildings) or may lag slightly behind foundation work, so as to avoid direct conflict or intrusion. It entails the sewer (sanitary and storm) systems, water, fire protection, natural gas, perhaps steam (where supplied from another building), and of course, electrical, telephone, and other communications systems, along with alarm and security lines. These all are the larger and primary sources being brought into the building, from which they are distributed ("run to") throughout the various levels, rooms, and areas of the building.

Hidden away like the foundation system (hopefully never to be seen again), most of the lines and piping are laid in trenches on the excavation bottom and covered with fill material prior to the lower slab installation, or perhaps encased in concrete for durability. They vary in size depending on the size and number of features, or fixtures they serve or drain throughout the entire building or complex; often they are quite formidable in size, to say nothing of their extent.

They are then carried under or through the foundation outside the building area and connected to the mains or primary supply sources in the street, owned by the utility companies. This is an extensive system and must be well designed to be all-inclusive and properly sized to provide an adequate supply of all services required by the people, operations, equipment, or work to be imposed on or connected to it.

Figure 7-3a Courtesy of J. Robert Welling.

Figure 7-3b Courtesy of Jupiterimages Corporation.

Figure 7-3d Courtesy of Jupiterimages Corporation.

Figure 7-3c Courtesy of Jupiterimages Corporation.

Figure 7-3e Courtesy of Jupiterimages Corporation.

Figure 7-3a–g Series of photos showing various examples of footing and foundation work. The last pictures show the top of the foundation wall and a portion of a finished floor at a steel column.

Figure 7-3f Courtesy of J. Robert Welling.

Figure 7-3g Courtesy of J. Robert Welling.

Erection of the Superstructure (Structural System)

Once the foundation system is brought up to approximately finished (final, outdoor) grade level, the upper structural support system is started. This creates what is called the building envelope, or the enclosure of the planned interior floor space by the exterior walls and the roof. This envelope can take any of a number of shapes and forms, but in any event it is the construction that separates the outside elements from the new interior space(s). It also is the major image of the final project, as the forms and shapes become the final appearance of the building, and give it its aesthetic character and appeal.

There is a wide choice of building envelope (wall) systems:

    Masonry (see Figures 7-4a through 7-4f)
        Solid construction
        Cavity construction
        All brick
        Brick and CMUs
        All CMUs

    Lightweight framing with (see Figures 7-5a through 7-5j)
        Brick veneer
        Exterior insulated finish system (EIFS)
        Stucco
        Siding
            Metal
            Wood
            Composite
            Vinyl

Figure 7-4a Courtesy of Jupiterimages Corporation.

Figure 7-4b Courtesy of Jupiterimages Corporation.

Figure 7-4c Courtesy of Design by K4 Architecture, LLC, copyright 2006. *Photo by J. Robert Welling, Project Architect.*

Figure 7-4d Courtesy of Design by K4 Architecture, LLC, copyright 2006. *Photo by J. Robert Welling, Project Architect.*

Figure 7-4e Courtesy of J. Robert Welling.

Figure 7-4f Courtesy of J. Robert Welling.

Structural framing with subsystem (girts, struts, etc.) (see Figures 7-6a through 7-6f)
  Masonry
  Insulated metal panels
  Metal siding
  EIFS

Cast-in-place or precast concrete (see Figures 7-7a through 7-7d)
  Formed, cast-in-place
  Precast off-site, set in place
  Tilt-up, cast at site and lifted in place

Obviously, this is one of the primary considerations and creations of the architectural designer. The design elements are formed, framed, and adequately supported by the structural design of the structural engineer. That resultant framing is then encased in the selected finished covering materials.

Here again, there is a wide choice of building structural systems that can be selected for use. Framing systems fall into three categories: concrete, wood, or steel. Within these categories, numerous products and systems are available for selection, depending not only on loading but also on aesthetics, finishes, and adaptability to the function plan layout to be installed within the framing grid.

Some are very easy and natural choices because of the moderate nature of the building. The choices often are the result of the type of structural system involved. In smaller, light-duty buildings (residences, small isolated commercial buildings, etc.), the structure is partially made up of the exterior walls.

These are called bearing wall systems because the roof and interior floors (if any) bear on and are supported in part by the walls (see Figures 7-8a through 7-8d). Here, obviously, the walls must be built before the other construction can be placed. At the time the walls are built, the major portions of the surrounding walls are also installed. In houses and small buildings, this generally is done in light wood framing, either prefabricated or in some cases "stick-built" (erected member by member) and then covered by the exterior "skin." That skin or covering can be

---

Figure 7-4a–f Pictures showing masonry being installed, rubble stone masonry, a building with sharp-angled configuration, a trim detail of specially shaped brick used to decorate a build. Last is what appears to be a brick wall but, in fact, is thin brick veneer (perhaps $^1/_4$" thick) adhered to a stud wall framing system in panels. This allows masonry to be installed in a climate-friendly plant, with tight tolerance, and installed in large panels at the job site.

Figure 7-5a Courtesy of Jupiterimages Corporation.

Figure 7-5b Courtesy of Jupiterimages Corporation.

Figure 7-5c Courtesy of Jupiterimages Corporation.

Figure 7-5d Courtesy of J. Robert Welling.

Figure 7-5e Courtesy of J. Robert Welling.

Figure 7-5f Courtesy of J. Robert Welling.

Figure 7-5a–j Examples of wood framing for walls and roofs. In addition, there is a series of details in steel framing. All are typical of what can be expected on any project.

Figure 7-5g Courtesy of J. Robert Welling.

Figure 7-5h Courtesy of J. Robert Welling.

Figure 7-5i Courtesy of J. Robert Welling.

Figure 7-5j Courtesy of Design by K4 Architecture, LLC, copyright 2006. *Photo by J. Robert Welling, Project Architect.*

Figure 7-6a–f Structural steel is very common in modern construction. It is capable of being very light (small shaped, low weights) up to and including massive built-up sections (for large and high-rise construction. While using stiff shapes, steel can be adapted to odd and even rounded layouts, depending on the requirements of the project design.

Figure 7-6a Courtesy of Jupiterimages Corporation.

Figure 7-6c Courtesy of J. Robert Welling.

Figure 7-6b Courtesy of Jupiterimages Corporation.

Figure 7-6d Courtesy of J. Robert Welling.

Figure 7-6 (*Continued*)

Figure 7-6e Courtesy of Jupiterimages Corporation.

Figure 7-6f Courtesy of Oklahoma Council on Law Enforcement Education and Training, and Oklahoma Department of Central Services, Construction and Properties Division.

Figure 7-7a Courtesy of Jupiterimages Corporation.

Figure 7-7c Courtesy of Jupiterimages Corporation.

Figure 7-7b Courtesy of Jupiterimages Corporation.

Figure 7-7d Courtesy of Jupiterimages Corporation.

Figure 7-7a–d Concrete is a common material that is familiar to most people. It is adaptable for many uses and to virtually any shape that can be formed. Buildings use concrete for walls, footing foundation, framing members, and slabs. But concrete can also be used for bridge piers and other unusual shapes and uses. Concrete is made even stronger when reinforced with steel reinforcing bars, which can be very closely spaced and quite numerous as the design requires. It can be pumped using piping and cranes, or delivered by a "bucket."

Figure 7-8a Courtesy of J. Robert Welling.

Figure 7-8b Courtesy of J. Robert Welling.

Figure 7-8c Courtesy of J. Robert Welling.

Figure 7-8d Courtesy of J. Robert Welling.

Figure 7-8a–d Examples illustrating how various structural framing members rest or bear on others in the system. In some cases, the members rest on load-bearing walls for their support.

face brick, siding of any sort, or applied finishes, at the choice of the owner, designer, or builder. In other cases and types of buildings, these walls are constructed of masonry—all concrete masonry units (CMUs), all brick, or a combination of the two.

Once the bearing walls are in place (in some cases there are also interior bearing walls), the roof structure can be installed (see Figures 7-9a through 7-9h). This can vary from light wood trusses to long-span steel joists or other structural steel framing. Over this structure, there will be a roof deck—fluted metal, concrete (either precast or cast-in-place)—or some sort of sheet material. In many instances, smaller intermediate framing (purlins, tees, etc.) needs to be placed across the main framing to allow for shorter spans in the decking.

Figure 7-9a Courtesy of Jupiterimages Corporation.

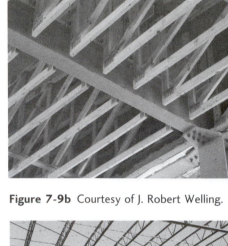

Figure 7-9b Courtesy of J. Robert Welling.

Figure 7-9c Courtesy of constructionphotographs.com.

Figure 7-9a–h Various examples of roof framing, from light wood members to a combination of wood and steel to all structural steel. There is no strict requirement that says one single system must be used, so often combinations prove to be helpful, expedient, and cost saving.

Figure 7-9d Courtesy of J. Robert Welling.

Figure 7-9e Courtesy of J. Robert Welling.

Figure 7-9f Courtesy of J. Robert Welling.

Figure 7-9g Courtesy of J. Robert Welling.

Figure 7-9h Courtesy of J. Robert Welling.

In larger and heavier buildings there is a need for very careful consideration of framing systems and selection. In addition, local custom, local expertise, and locally available materials also impact the choice of systems. It is obvious that if materials or systems remote to the site or outside the capabilities of local workers are chosen, it will have a severe cost and time impact—and quality may well suffer to a large extent.

There may be merely an extension of the foundation system (for example, installation of additional column lengths on the foundation columns). In larger structures this system is usually a skeletal grid of structural framing bays with a column at each intersection of the grid. In general, though, the framing system in plan is a regular grid pattern with column spacing as the designers determine. Normally, these bays are the 20- to 35-foot range (20 to 25 feet most common) center to center of columns on a side, with the columns and horizontal members sized to carry the imposed load accumulated over the spacing (span) between

Figure 7-10a Courtesy of Jupiterimages Corporation.

Figure 7-10b Courtesy of Oklahoma Council on Law Enforcement Education and Training, and Oklahoma Department of Central Services, Construction and Properties Division.

supports. What is a grid in plan becomes a tower of cubes—six-sided areas with a column at each corner connected to adjacent columns by girders or beams.

Normally, the framing system will be structural steel, concrete, or in some rare cases heavy timber. The system is formed by a series of columns spaced at regular intervals both ways in the building area. These columns will rest on and emanate from their own footings, designed specifically for the entire load being transferred down through the column. Variations are used where needed to account for smaller spacing, erratic shapes in the building form, and so on. Here combined or strap footings are used, formed to support two closely spaced columns.

In steel, the columns are rolled H-sections, properly sized and selected for the loading to be imposed. There is an array of sizes available, and the designers make selections from the available sections. In rare cases (bridges, for example), columns and other members are built up using smaller sections connected together to collect the massive loadings. All of the steel work must be fabricated (cut and shaped with necessary holes for bolt or rivet connections) before they reach the field. Iron workers erect the sections one at a time, and make proper alignments and connections.

Cast-in-place concrete framing is a bit more complex. Here each member of the framing system (columns, girders, beams, etc.) must be separately formed, temporarily supported with proper reinforcing installed, and the concrete placed (see Figures 7-10a and 7-10b). Suitable curing must occur prior to removal of the forms and subsequent installation of another set of

Figure 7-10a,b Concrete, being a plastic. fluid, or moldable material, needs a container or "form" to hold it in place and in the shape required. The examples here show formwork that can be quite complex if the concrete members required are extensive or complicated in configuration.

forms above to form another set of framing members. Obviously, the best of concreting procedures must be followed so the members will not have to be removed for inadequate strength or other maladies. Concrete framing is a laborious, complex process that requires highly skilled workers and added time for installation. It is, however, the system of choice under certain circumstances, as determined by the structural designers.

Precast concrete members can be fabricated in the factory and transported to the job site. This simplifies the on-site operations, as it is common to merely unload a member from the truck and immediately set it in place in the building. Connections are usually formed by welding steel plates that are set into the members as they are cast. The various members can be sized, reinforced, and configured as required to meet the project requirements. Wall panels can be cast on-site and raised into position (this is "tilt-up" construction).

Projects also have been designed in which the structure has taken the form of a cast-in-place concrete shape—barrel vault, dome, folded plates, hyperbolic parabaloid, and so forth. Here the concrete shape is the roof "framing" (really a plane) in addition to some limited portion of the walls. The key element to the production of the desired shape lies in the construction of the formwork for the placement of concrete. This, necessarily, is often a very complex, labor-intensive, and costly item.

One such venture was the terminal building at Lambert Field, the St. Louis, Missouri, airport. Built in the mid-1950s, this four-dome structure was—and remains—unique in its construction. The scaffolding and form work for the first dome was built on railroad tracks and jacked up into position. The concrete for the dome was placed, and when it was of proper and sufficient strength, the form work was lowered and then moved to the position of the new adjacent dome, via the railroad tracks. This process was repeated for placing the forms and concrete. The whole procedure was repeated for subsequent domes. And it represented tremendous savings over erecting, wrecking, and reinstalling the forms repeatedly.

Regardless of the material used or the innovation in the fabrication, the structural framing is so essential to progression of the project that it is necessarily expedited as much as possible through preordering, long-lead-time ordering, and factory fabrication (which can be done even in inclement weather). This framing is the backbone of the project, and the elements which all the remainder of the building relies on and is supported by.

Installation of Roof and Floor Framing System(s)

The completion of the roof framing and the placing of the last beam is a time of celebration. It is a long-held tradition to place an evergreen tree atop the completed structural frame to indicate its completion.

Figure 7-11a–d Interior framing is required to hold the finish covering and the decorative finishes. Such framing can be of wood or steel, as deemed proper. In addition to forming the required partitions, framing is required to enclose structural framing that is undesirable (i.e., needs to be concealed from view for the sake of appearance).

This celebration is appropriate, since once the roof's primary framing is in place, the work can shift quickly to installing the smaller framing members in preparation for the roof deck and roofing system. This short sequence adds to the enclosure ("drying in") of the building, and significantly accelerates work on the interior (see Figures 7-11a through 7-11d). Although the walls may not be totally covered, the roof does keep out a major portion of the dampness that can invade the structure. Reduction of water and dampness is a necessary element in the project's progress.

Within the primary framing bays, there is a series of smaller (more closely spaced) grids made up of girders, beams, joists, and purlins—each grid perpendicular to the one below. This pattern of construction is used as framing for both the roof and the various floors of the building. These members become progressively smaller as their spans and

Figure 7-11a Courtesy of Jupiterimages Corporation.

Figure 7-11b Courtesy of Jupiterimages Corporation.

Figure 7-11c Courtesy of Design by K4 Architecture, LLC, copyright 2006. *Photo by J. Robert Welling, Project Architect.*

Figure 7-11d Courtesy of J. Robert Welling.

imposed loads become less. In many cases, "steel lumber" (that is, light steel bar joists fabricated with small angles, and solid bars to form truss-like members) are used. These can be designed to carry various loads by changing the size of the members.

While there are a variety of ways to form these grids, the intent is to place supports about 16 to 48 inches apart, which can be easily spanned by some form of decking—metal, concrete, composite, precast concrete, plywood, and so on. The decking becomes the overall membrane that can act as the subfloor (structural floor), or perhaps the subfloor on which other finishes can be applied.

Extension of Utility Lines and Systems

As the structural frame is extended upward, the utility lines follow. They are usually run in close proximity to the columns, since both must rise with the building. Keeping the lines close to the columns minimizes the space required for these more utilitarian features of the building. Necessary as they are, the owner will want their space requirements held down to maximize the usable space, and so there is no intrusion or interruption of the work and service to be operational in the building spaces. It is standard procedure that all vertical lines and elements be bundled together; also, they can share the same floor openings, further reducing intrusion into operations.

The lines (branches or risers) at this point are reduced in size from the underground, but they will be increased in number so they can be run horizontally to provide service throughout the individual floors. As they rise in the building, there will be an incremental reduction in size, since the amount of material carried is lower due to less demand, fewer outlets, fewer people served, et cetera. At their lower ends, they will be tied together and eventually connected back to the main underground system.

Installation of the Building "Skin"

Once the superstructure framing has progressed far enough to allow other trades to work below or behind the framing crew, the outer skin (building enclosure or cladding construction) can be started. This consists of a relatively thin layer (hence the "skin" designation) that acts as the infill or covering applied over the exterior face of the structural framing system (see Figures 7-12a through 7-12h). (There are some designs where the framing is exposed on the exterior, but this is an unusual solution).

Even at this early juncture in the project, the design, aesthetics, and "architecture" of the project will begin to emerge as the wall and roof

Figure 7-12a Courtesy of J. Robert Welling.

Figure 7-12d Courtesy of www.bigfoto.com.

Figure 7-12b Courtesy of Design by K4 Architecture, LLC, copyright 2006. *Photo by J. Robert Welling, Project Architect.*

Figure 7-12c Courtesy of www.bigfoto.com.

Figure 7-12e Courtesy of Design by K4 Architecture, LLC, copyright 2006. *Photo by J. Robert Welling, Project Architect.*

Figure 7-12a–h The exterior envelope, or "skin," of the building is necessary to protect the building from the elements and to provide the image, exterior shape, or configuration or "looks" of the project. The number of material that can be used, or used in combination, is innumerable. Examples here show a variety of possible exterior skins (note the number of different design schemes in the buildings around the World Trade Center). Also, the success of the system is in the detailing and in how the various materials, systems, and elements are placed together and connected.

Figure 7-12f Courtesy of Design by K4 Architecture, LLC, copyright 2006. *Photo by J. Robert Welling, Project Architect.*

Figure 7-12g Courtesy of Design by K4 Architecture, LLC, copyright 2006. *Photo by J. Robert Welling, Project Architect.*

Figure 7-12h Courtesy of J. Robert Welling.

materials are being installed. The massing of the building will solidify, as the exterior coverings fill the voids of the structural framing and create the enclosure and the form of the designed shapes.

From a vast and quite varied array of materials, the design professionals select or create this enclosure. Simple wood siding can be used, not only for houses but also in such buildings as churches and stores that may be larger than houses, but whose construction is quite similar. As noted, such buildings can have bearing walls framed with wood or steel studs. Outer sheathing and finish material can be added to ensure a weather-tight and watertight installation. Except for finish painting (if required), this system would become the finished walls of the building.

Masonry can be used, from unit masonry (CMU or brick) to quarried stone blocks or panels. As load-bearing walls, this work would be installed initially for support, but then could be finished out as the final wall configuration. In addition, face brick could be applied to wood/metal studs to form a veneer wall, if that is the designer's choice. The use of studding in exterior walls is now common in larger buildings, where the finish materials are masonry, veneer, or other materials. This is a lighter weight solution than solid masonry walls in buildings of several stories (thus saving money by requiring lighter/smaller foundations to support the building as a whole).

Masonry panels are also an option for infill in exterior wall constructions. Curtain-, panel- and window-walls are commonly used, with a grid of mullions and crossbars attached to the framing system. Translucent, transparent, or opaque panels are fitted into the cladding system's grid. These can be colored or tinted to prevent the passage of unwanted heat and light into the building proper. The creation of this enclosure is a direct application of technology and aesthetics, in that this application will create and become the image of the project. The framing, of course, gives the project its shape and form, but the envelope gives it texture, color, weather-resistance, wearing surface, watertightness, energy efficiency, and yes, eye-appeal; it projects the wish of the owner(s) as to what he/she wants the building and consequently the owner's image to be. Obviously, a building can be a direct reflection of the owner, including the business philosophy, prestige, and image that the company wishes to portray to the public and to its customers.

Within the construction of the envelope are features that provide for insulation, fire resistance, safety, ease of maintenance, and translation of mechanical systems both vertically and horizontally to places of use. The covering can be closed, blank, and tight-fitting or open, light, sparkling. It can encourage viewing the surroundings, or create a cloistered, closed environment for protection of employees or products. Surprisingly, much of the basic impact and philosophy behind the project is manifest in this enclosure; it serves to create the environment desired for the operation of the facility, in the end.

The installation of the envelope system is a major undertaking and should not be seen otherwise. While many components of the various systems that can be used are relatively small, a major effort is needed to provide staging, scaffolding, or other temporary works to provide a workplace for the erectors.

Masonry and EIFS are particularly difficult systems, in that some type of work platform is required for each rather limited vertical area of work. Where the project is a multistory building, this is no small consideration in time and cost. There is a direct correlation between the amount of handwork and the requirements for people-oriented facilities. That is, where small units of work (like brick, CMU, or even EIFS) are used, the work area is relatively small and necessitates that safe and adequate work platforms be available for workers. Either these must be moved frequently or they need to be so extensive that the work can be carried on in a continuous manner without stopping to move the platforms. Where the work unit is panelized (i.e., precast panels or panelized brick), the installation is usually carried on more easily with a crane lifting the work and workers making the attachments by standing and working from the building floors. Obviously, all this plays into the cost and time progression of the project.

Curtain-, panel-, and window-walls all have slightly larger units, and in fact some can be prefabricated and lifted into place. But eventually smaller panes of glass or panels must be installed, and proper provision must be made for that work.

In some systems, like precast concrete, the increments or units of construction are much larger and require another technique. Here mainly the panels are off-loaded from trucks and set into place utilizing a rig or crane of adequate capacity to lift and maneuver the panels. These panels can be up to 50 feet in length, and there have been records of panels cast on-site and rotated or tilted in place that measured over 96 feet in length.

The envelope system must be designed and fabricated in such a manner as to be adapted or adjusted to variations in the substructure to which it is attached. These variations—which should be held to the tightest tolerance possible—can be the cause of adverse installation conditions and eventual failure of the system. In addition, the system must be built with suitable and proper attention to and attachments for seismic conditions and such climatic elements as wind loading. Basically, the envelope system must be rigid enough to remain in place, but flexible enough to be manipulated by natural events.

The crux of the entire project sequencing is the need for the work of one trade to be done in a manner that facilitates the work of the following trades. It is obvious that a competitive atmosphere is therefore inappropriate, and coordination and cooperation are absolutely essential. All trades, suppliers, and manufacturers need to buy into the process and contribute in a positive and fully correct manner as to their specific work.

All of these systems are not merely set side by side, or interlocked and forgotten. An extensive closing or sealing operation is needed to prohibit the invasion of wind, rain, and other elements into the system itself and, of course, into the building. So the process of installing gaskets and sealing joints is no small matter, nor one that can be relegated to minimally trained workers. The success of the envelope system lies in the process by which the components—large or small—are placed and sealed.

Installation of Roof System

Closing off the top of the structure is the roofing system. This is as varied in materials as it is in shapes, textures, and colors. The simplest roof is a single-slope flat plane, titled to drain in one direction. From here the design professional can create a multitude of planes, shapes, and forms to enhance the overall impact of the project and perpetuate the design concept. Much of this is seated in the current style or motif of the day; it varies in almost a faddish manner, based on what is the current state-of-the-art and what is both readily accepted and desired by the client. Usually, the roof formations will have some relationship to and kinship with the envelope system, and both together to the design concept— what exactly the client wishes.

Since the roof is largely forgotten, there is a need to install a system as long-wearing as possible. New materials are usually directed at extended life, but the elements play havoc with roof systems, perhaps more than those in the envelope. The roof lies fully exposed to the sun (a most debilitating presence) and receives an untold amount of water from rain and snow. Shifting of the building or parts thereof tends to open joints and cracks. All of this creates leakage and problems that the owner is not willing to accept. Perfection, of course, does not exist, but this system in particular comes in for a lot of scrutiny and criticism if not done as well as it can be within budgetary constraints.

Precision and excellence are required in the installation not only of the roofing system but of the entire building envelope. While the systems and individual materials are designed, manufactured, and diligently tested in many ways, there needs to be assiduous adherence to installation instructions and tolerances—this is not the place for renegade, free-wheeling work. The protection and function of the interior spaces rely totally on the successful and continuing performance of the exterior systems. All this must drive a motivation in the contractors, their personnel, and all parties contributing to this work.

Installation of Mechanical Systems

Following (perhaps very closely behind) installation of the outer envelope, the various mechanical systems trades will start their work. Taking advantage of the open areas on each floor (prior to installation of interior walls) these trades can run ductwork, conduit, cabling, water and soil lines, and all of the branches and amenities required for properly functioning systems (see Figures 7-13a through 7-13f).

It must be mentioned that the use of the term "mechanical systems" is highly misleading. Numerous systems may be required—electrical, plumbing, fire suppression, air handling, process piping, vacuum systems, communications (several types), security systems, alarms, et cetera. Each of these has a wide assortment of materials and equipment that can be chosen for a specific installation, varying widely in size and type. Many choices will be made by the design professionals in the design of these systems, but the installation is a critically important activity to ensure that all systems are correctly installed as required, and fully functional within their individual capacities.

There is an obvious need here for close coordination (and cooperation!) so no competition, conflicts, or disputes are created between trades (i.e., the mentality that "whoever gets there first, gets the space"). This tends to cause much discussion, anger, and disarray in the project. This coordination/cooperation activity is a primary event in the job meetings, held at least weekly and attended by all trades currently on-site (and perhaps those coming to the site shortly). It is important to have full and open discussions in this setting, in lieu of "pushing and shoving" in the work areas.

The drawings must themselves be fully coordinated, so as to present exact locations, routing, and so on for execution by the trade workers. Where the structure becomes more industrialized and more utilitarian (almost totally dedicated to mechanical systems and functions), there is an increased need for this coordination and for conflict/interference analysis. Simply put, things must be done neatly, precisely, and completely.

Where numerous interior partitions and finishes are to be installed (see discussion below), added attention and precautions must take place, to ensure that all of the mechanical functions and devices are contained and confined, so they are easily concealed by the finish work. Again, there is the need for coordination with the documents displaying the finish work.

When space is made available, the mechanical equipment itself may be installed. Usually, areas will be set aside for this work, and there will be a need for a very concentrated work effort to install the machinery and the piping and instrumentation required for its operation. It should be remembered that in all but the most utilitarian buildings, these systems must be ready for use when the building is complete. Where the function of the building is more industrial or mechanical, some equipment may be long-delivery items and could take added time (beyond building completion) for installation and start-up.

Figure 7-13a Courtesy of Design by K4 Architecture, LLC, copyright 2006. *Photo by J. Robert Welling, Project Architect.*

Figure 7-13c Courtesy of J. Robert Welling.

Figure 7-13a–f Examples of portions of the mechanical systems "roughed-in" prior to being enclosed by the interior finish systems. These items are connected to the underground systems that supply or service the system (water, drainage, electric, telephone, etc.)

Figure 7-13b Courtesy of J. Robert Welling.

Interior Walls and Partitions

The layout and installation of interior walls and partitions is usually a direct reflection of the complexity of the project (at least for the area involved). Obviously, a warehouse will have few such dividers, and they will be of more utilitarian materials—masonry, metal, et cetera. In a hospital, on the other hand, there is a myriad of areas, rooms, alcoves, niches, recesses, nooks, and so on. Each is enclosed in whole or in part,

Figure 7-13d Courtesy of Design by K4 Architecture, LLC, copyright 2006. *Photo by J. Robert Welling, Project Architect.*

Figure 7-13f Courtesy of J. Robert Welling.

Figure 7-13e Courtesy of J. Robert Welling.

and requires careful attention to meet the requirements placed on the area or the services to the area. Some require numerous and complex mechanical systems for plumbing, electrical, and ventilation, along with other utilities such as oxygen, natural gas, suction, monitoring, et cetera—despite the relatively confined or small area involved.

All this impacts the installation of the enclosure (see Figures 7-14a through 7-14c). Stud framing can become involved, with much cutting and fitting of small pieces, creation of numerous openings, or extra support framing (for grab rails or fixtures, for example). The same holds true for masonry where units must be adjusted and fitted to confined areas, unusual conditions, and the final finish and appearance.

Major or long elements, like corridors, are laid out using a laser beam, so alignment is near-perfect. This ensures that misalignment will not lead to encroachment or unanticipated reduction of space and area

Figure 7-14a–c Various examples of interior framing for walls and ceilings. Note the complexity, configuration, and interrelationships of the various design elements.

Figure 7-14a Courtesy of Design by K4 Architecture, LLC, copyright 2006. *Photo by J. Robert Welling, Project Architect.*

Figure 7-14b Courtesy of Design by K4 Architecture, LLC, copyright 2006. *Photo by J. Robert Welling, Project Architect.*

Figure 7-14c Courtesy of Design by K4 Architecture, LLC, copyright 2006. *Photo by J. Robert Welling, Project Architect.*

sizes (which could impact use, equipment size, etc.). Still, worker care is required to make necessary adjustments; to fit, attach, and fasten in a proper manner; to meet the dimensions and configurations noted on the project drawings; and to fulfill the requirements of the specifications for the work involved.

As part of the installation of the walls and partitions, there is the work of setting door frames, frames for other openings, building of bulkheads, and installation of blocking and anchorage for various devices and items of equipment. This work must be done in the sense of a negative, in that the installation will not be seen in the final project but is vital to its ultimate success. At the appropriate time, doors will be hung and their proper hardware installed; still later they will be field-finished (if they are not ordered factory-finished).

A good deal of time will be allotted to surface preparation (prior to application of finish coverings or coatings), as well as to closing gaps and cracks and creating an overall appearance of a smooth, complete series of surfaces and planes. Finish here refers to a good-looking, neat, carefully executed, complete, proper, and unmarred appearance of all surfaces, items, and devices. Everything should be plumb, level, and true to line; properly coated or covered; and neatly and carefully fitted.

This work, while no different in overall concept for all project work, does require skill and care, since so much of the project is yet to be applied or installed. Certainly, the mechanical systems need to be installed and connected (see discussion below), but their function is to supply air or water or electricity, not necessarily to present a proper and acceptable finished appearance. This is not to favor one trade work over another—it is simply that some trades involve support or contribute to final appearance, while others do not.

Connection of Branch Systems to Mechanical Equipment

In reality, much of the mechanical systems' work is accomplished by working from both ends. Ductwork may be run at the extremes of the building spaces, but needs to be connected to the basic units later in the project. The same holds for electrical wiring (later connected to lighting and power panels and equipment) and plumbing (which connects later to the sewers, taps, meters, and service supply lines). See Figures 7-15a through 7-15e for examples.

The majority of the final connection work takes place within the areas dedicated to the equipment, machinery, and service entrances. Quite often, through poor planning and short-sightedness, these areas are very confined in size (no one wanting to allow too much space to be devoted to such functions), and hence are extremely crowded, con-

Figure 7-15a Courtesy of Design by K4 Architecture, LLC, copyright 2006. *Photo by J. Robert Welling, Project Architect.*

Figure 7-15b Courtesy of Design by K4 Architecture, LLC, copyright 2006. *Photo by J. Robert Welling, Project Architect.*

Figure 7-15c Courtesy of Design by K4 Architecture, LLC, copyright 2006. *Photo by J. Robert Welling, Project Architect.*

Figure 7-15d Courtesy of Design by K4 Architecture, LLC, copyright 2006. *Photo by J. Robert Welling, Project Architect.*

Figure 7-15e Courtesy of J. Robert Welling.

gested, and greatly in need of cooperation and coordination. Piping, tubing, switches, gauges, valves, fittings, and equipment are everywhere; pads are required for many items to keep them up and free from the floor. Good systems are at their very best when their work is neatly planned, accurately and carefully executed (tight bends, well anchored, plumb, and level, except where slopes are necessary), fully identified, with fitting and connection of the best skilled work. While utilitarian in nature, these areas usually come to finale in a very professional manner, fully functional, and well executed—this being a tremendous aid to maintenance, repair, replacement, addition, and adjustment. In reality, these rooms reflect awareness and field experience on the part of the systems design engineer(s), and they are a real credit to the care, skill, and expertise of the trade workers.

Installation/Application of Finishes

For this stage of work, the array of available products is mind-boggling. The finishes involve the final, exposed decorative face or surface of walls, ceilings, floors, equipment/built-ins (see discussion below), doors, glazed areas, and other surfaces exposed to view. From the simplest of unpainted CMU to painting of exposed structural work, one can proceed at almost any level up to the massive carved, solid wood paneling of the corporate president's office suite, or the gold-leaf-covered trim in a cathedral. Variety takes on new meaning—materials, colors, textures, patterns, shapes, combinations, joinery, utility, surface finish, coatings, attachments, serviceability, and maintenance included. The design professionals have a mighty task in ascertaining how the needs and wishes of the client/owner can be met. They must resolve how utility and function can be supported by attractiveness; supported by ease of maintenance, length of usefulness, ability to repair, replace, or refresh; and purchased at an acceptable budgetary level.

The finishes, of course, require skilled workmanship so the final result is both appealing and functional. Much of the other aspects of the project are in place to support and allow the application of the final finishes. These are the interior skin, much as the facing and siding of the exterior building envelope is also a skin. Ceramic tile, for example, appeals to the eye (as the finished surface), but is applied to an underboard

---

Figure 7-15a–e Photos showing branch service portions of the overall mechanical systems (supplying service to specific areas or the building overall) just prior to enclosure by interior finishes. Notice the precise and logical layout of these systems and their fit into the overall construction and finish systems.

of gypsum wallboard (see Figure 7-16), which in turn is applied to stud work framing, which in turn is supported by the floor slab, and tied to the roof or floor structure above.

The process of applying the finishes must be carefully programmed and scheduled, with the understanding that the finer, more sophisticated, final materials cannot be placed where there is still peril of damage or even slight marring. Obviously, certain installations, even some finishes themselves, can threaten or harm adjacent surfaces and their finishes. For example, rolling out wall-to-wall carpeting can mar finished walls, if particular care is not taken. Quite often, large rolls of carpet are unrolled, even though they may be wider than the space available—hence mars and roll marks appear on the walls. If these walls are already painted with the final coat, touchup work is required (and can lead to claims as to who pays for it, since the painting contractor has finished and met his/her contract obligations).

In some cases, care must be taken to ensure that the finishing process does not add other hazards to the structure and/or the remainder of the work. Moisture from plaster, drywall, or interior (decorative) masonry work can be a deterrent to other finishes which must follow drywall, such as floor covering, adjacent surfaces, and finishes already in place. Sanding or grinding operations in one area may well intrude on new painted surfaces in other areas. Finishes in walkways used by workers and suppliers are open to great abuse, and are best reserved for application after traffic is minimized or eliminated. Cases can be cited where unlike materials impact the finishes and cause blemishes or deterioration (e.g., incompatible backing behind a finished sealant joint).

Another caution, primarily for designers, is the selection of materials and finishes that simply cannot be made to match. Staining of wood items is a good example, where different wood species appear different even when finished in the same manner. This often leads to dissatisfaction on the part of the owner and can be the cause of remedial work very late in the project.

The goal is to leave the job ready for owner occupancy, in a fresh, new, clean, unmarred, unblemished, bright, neat, sparkling, as-near-perfect-as-possible condition. This should be the culmination of, and mark of a fully successful project, from a technical viewpoint.

Installation of Specialties, Built-Ins, Furnishings, and Accessories

Intertwined throughout the final phases of the project, the contractors must provide for the timely, proper, and unobtrusive installation of quite a variety of items. Some are manufactured products (restroom acces-

Figure 7-16a,b Photos showing installation of drywall (gypsum wallboard) on metal studs—a most common interior construction. An area very close to being finished, with paint and wall covering installed, as well as the light fixtures, roof skylight, and other elements of finish work.

Figure 7-16a Courtesy of constructionphotographs.com.

Figure 7-16b Courtesy of Oklahoma Council on Law Enforcement Education and Training, and Oklahoma Department of Central Services, Construction and Properties Division.

sories, basketball backstops, etc.) that are provided in a standard form, and are accommodated by installing required openings, framing, and support for attachment of the units. Some items are made in finished form and require only unpacking and installation; others require more extensive installation and may also require finishing of some parts of the assembly. Others are custom-made to fit the project specifically and exclusively (countertops, work tops, cabinets, casework, etc.). In the main, these are fabricated by contractors or suppliers close to the job site, and are fitted to the circumstances, dimensions, and other aspects of the project work. Much of this work is prefinished or fabricated with finish materials; some items do require finishing on-site (mainly to match other features).

Still other items are installed or movable pieces, such as furniture, desks, file cabinets, chairs, tables, etc. Supplied by manufacturers remote to the site, these usually arrive on the job complete, prefinished, and needing only to be unpacked and set in place; some very minor adjustments may be required, or installation of small hardware items.

It is necessary to understand the three different types of items that will appear on the site. Where they require some accommodation, it is necessary that this be installed along the way (in its proper place, when it is convenient), so there is no need to provide the work in the finished surfaces. This involves making or framing openings, not cutting them later; installing backing, blocking, and other anchorage, and not trying to provide this in or behind a finished surface. Although many items and materials in the project require the submittal, review, and use of shop drawings, no other instances are more important (as to the value of such shop drawings) than the items noted above.

TOWARD FINALE

The construction and finish work progresses in an ordered sequence, whereby one layer, process, or application logically follows its preparation or predecessor. The fundamental axiom is that "the more finished the item or material, the later in the process it is installed." Obviously, work of a very finished nature (including work that comes to the job site in a finished condition) is installed close to the very last of the project. Here the idea is to install these items at a time when they will be virtually untouched or disrupted by other work, and where their fine finishes will not be marred or blemished.

CHAPTER
8

REFINEMENT AND ENHANCEMENT

WRAP UP, CLOSE OUT

This phase includes energizing or commissioning all contractor-supplied/installed systems, trouble-shooting, and modifying as required for proper performance. As completion of the project approaches, there is a normal process of bringing all of the various systems on-line and into operation. After all the lines, branches, accessories, and so on are installed and connected, there comes the moment of truth when the system is energized and made to run. At this juncture the contractors can check out their accumulated work to ascertain if (1) the work is complete; (2) the work is proper (everything operates as required—no leakage, proper balance, proper levels of performance or output, does what it was designed and expected to do; and (3) what, if any, remedial work must be done to achieve the expected result(s).

The current nomenclature for these operations is "commissioning." This has become more formalized, and is now quite often a specific block of requirements in the specifications.

- Commissioning is the process of verifying that specific elements and equipment that are part of the project perform as required, when fully installed and set into operation.
- The Basis of Design is a document that records concepts, calculations, decisions, and product selections used to meet the owner's project requirements and to satisfy applicable regulatory requirements, standards, and guidelines. The document includes both narrative descriptions and lists of individual items that support the design process.

- The owner's project requirements are set out in a document that details the functional requirements of a project and the expectations of how it will be used and operated. These include project goals, measurable performance criteria, cost considerations, bench marks, success criteria, and supporting information.
- The Commissioning Plan is a document created to outline the organization, schedule, allocation of resources, and documentation requirements of the commissioning process.
- The execution of commissioning process activities is usually verified using random sampling. The sampling rate may vary from 1 to 100 percent. Verification includes, but is not limited to, equipment submittals, construction checklists, training, operating and maintenance data, tests, and test reports to verify compliance with the owner's requirements. When a random sample does not meet the requirement, it should be reported in the Issues Log.

There may still be some other work in progress; usually this is work that is benign and has no real operation or operating parts (for example, paving, curbing, landscaping, etc.). Each trade has a distinct and specific end point at which the workers know that the work is finished or ready for running. Some trades may have to run active tests to ascertain if their work is complete and proper (e.g., checking temperature and volume outputs, filling a pool and seeing if it holds water, etc.).

This also is the point where managers and superintendents should be checking the work against their records and the contract documents to ensure that it is complete, accurate, and in full compliance with their contract obligations. This is a necessary function even in well-managed projects (and is best done on a continual basis throughout the project). It is more crucial toward completion, as there are numerous items (large, small, physical, administrative, documentation, verification, warranties, etc.) that could drop through the cracks and be overlooked. Yet these remain part of the obligations—they are part of the complete package the contractor is, by contract, to deliver to the owner.

As the project work winds down, the contractors demobilize the site, removing all office and storage trailers, excess materials, and temporary facilities. Most do this as their individual work is completed, and they will handle any needed work (see below) without a full crew and without the full array of equipment and plant. In most cases, some refurbishing of the site is required (e.g., cutting uncut grass, filling and minor grading, planting grass seed, removing temporary roads, and returning the unused portions of the site to its original condition prior to the start of project work).

SUBSTANTIAL COMPLETION AND FINAL INSPECTION

Often there is confusion, even among knowledgeable participants, over what constitutes Substantial Completion, and what must occur next. Substantial Completion is *not* Final Completion—it does not signal the end of contractual obligations or the walk-out-the-door finale of the work. Rather, it occurs roughly thirty days (no closer) *prior* to Final Completion, or more properly, thirty days prior to the date of completion listed in the Agreement (end of the Contract Time).

Substantial Completion (per AIA Document A201) is the "stage in the progress of the Work when the Work or designated portion thereof is sufficiently complete in accord with the Contract Documents so that the Owner can occupy or utilize the Work for its intended use."

It is important to note in this definition that while the owner *can* occupy or use, everything is not necessarily 100 percent complete; some inconvenience or disruptions may occur. It represents the point where the vast majority of the work is complete (except for minor adjustments, etc.), and the project is in such condition that the owner *could* take partial occupancy (for example, begin to move in, but not occupy or put into operation; or use certain portions of the project but without completion of all facilities or areas). It also is the point at which contractors should have reviewed and inspected their own work for both proper execution and completeness. Only then are they ready to present it for final inspection, approval, and acceptance.

THE "PUNCH LIST"

In a full-blown, scheduled event, the entire project is subject to final inspection by a party comprised of all discipline design professionals, the general contractor or construction manager, the owner, the various on-site representatives, and others that are pertinent to the task. The tour is a working activity in which every aspect of the work is inspected by the parties in keeping with their status and involvement on the project (see Figure 8-1).

In addition, the design professional (usually the architect) conducts an in-depth inspection. Visual and physical checking of virtually every item required by the contract documents occurs. Do lights light? Do receptacles deliver electricity? Do doors swing smoothly and latch? Are painted surfaces smooth and uniform? Does equipment function properly? Are joints neat, straight, and clean (or invisible, if that is the criterion)? Is concrete finished? and so forth. Each discipline has a complete list of specific items to check, as well as a general list and format to be

---

PUNCH LIST

Cross/Weymer—Architects

Date _____ Notes by:_____

PROJECT: NETTER DORMITORY COMPLEX—BUILDING NO. 2

> The following listed items were transcribed from a tape recording made as items were
> observed during the Final Inspection at the time of Substantial Completion.
> Listed items shall be corrected by the appropriate contractor.
> A request shall be made for another inspection upon completion of ALL items on this list.
>
> See Certificate of Substantial Completion for deadline for completion of this work.

First Floor

Bathroom/Administrative Area 101:
- Towel bar loose; tighten
- Clean and polish entire mirror
- Clean counter back and side splash trims
- Caulk between wall and splash trims
- Align ceiling air diffuser with ceiling grid

Administrative Area 102:
- Adjust door for positive latching upon closing
- Reattach floor base in right front corner [as you enter space]
- Caulk joints between countertop and walls

Figure 8-1 Example of a punch list, showing the type and detail of the information to be included. This is the result of the final review/inspection of the work and requires a close, meticulous, and highly detailed listing of work that is not fully compliant with the Contract Drawings. Nothing improper, no matter how small, can be overlooked, so a slow, careful, objective, knowledgeable, and sensitive eye is required for the inspection.

followed to ascertain and ensure that the work is what and where it should be, and is full accord with the contract documents.

Using pads and written notes or tape recorders (later transcribed and printed to be distributed to various parties for resolution), a list is compiled. This is commonly known as "the punch list". This list reflects both the quality of the work and the state of completeness. Quite often this list contains several hundred items (the number will vary with the size of the project, the complexity of the work, and the diligence of the contractors) that are not acceptable and are in need of repair, adjustment, tightening, redoing, recoating, removal and replacement, or perhaps initial installation (see Figure 8-2).

There is a need for understanding of this process. It is not a grade card for the contractors, but rather an assessment to ensure the owner that for every dollar paid, there is full and commensurate value received, as required by the contract documents. No one is perfect, and perfection is not the goal of the list—every human misses, overlooks, or ac-

CERTIFICATE OF SUBSTANTIAL COMPLETION

DATE OF ISSUANCE: _____

OWNER: _____

CONTRACTOR: _____

Contract: _____

Project: _____

OWNER's Project No. _____   A/E's Job No. _____

[ ]   This Certification of Substantial Completion applies to **all Work** required by the Contract Documents.

[ ]   This Certification of Substantial Completion is a**pplicable ONLY to the following specified portions** of the complete project or to listed parts of Contract Documents:

The Work to which this Certificate applies has been inspected by authorized representatives of the OWNER, CONTRACTOR, and ARCHITECT/ENGINEER, and found to be substantially complete.

The Work is hereby declared to be **substantially** complete within the requirements of the Contract Documents on:

_____
Date of Substantial Completion

*This Certification **does not constitute an acceptance of Work NOT** in accordance with the Contract Documents [see "Punch List" below] nor is it a release of Contractor's obligation to complete the Work in accordance with the Contract Documents.*

Date of this Certificate indicates the date of commencement of applicable warranties required by the Contract Documents (*except as attached).

[ ]   A "Punch-List" of items to be completed or corrected is attached hereto. This list may not be all-inclusive, and the failure to include an item on it does not alter the responsibility of the CONTRACTOR to complete all Work in accordance with the Contract Documents.

The items on the tentative list shall be completed or corrected by the CONTRACTOR within _____ days of the above date of Substantial Completion.

[ ] * A list of "excepted" Warranty items is attached hereto.

_____
Executed by ARCHITECT/ENGINEER   Date

_____
Accepted by CONTRACTOR   Date

_____
Accepted by OWNER   Date

Figure 8-2 Sample Certificate of Substantial Completion. Note the importance of the dates, the limits of the Certificate, and the note about the punch list

cepts conditions that are not as they should be. Perhaps one can cast this off as a difference of opinion, but really it is a matter of the persons responsible for the project (the design professionals) who acted as the owner's agents making sure that dollars and value match.

IMPACT OF SUBSTANTIAL COMPLETION

Another aspect of Substantial Completion that is misunderstood is that a single date is set out as the completion date, or the date when the Contract Time ends. Unfortunately, in most cases, every contractor is given the same date. This is a major fallacy. If everyone is given the same contract time, then there may be a false impression that all of the subcontractors can schedule their work up to the last minute, and all walk out the door at the very same time. There needs to be a coordinated schedule for the completion of work, and each subcontractor needs to be given a specific finish date. There are many examples where some work must follow other work: painting and finishing requires a decent level of temperature and humidity for the products to work (i.e., operational HVAC is required); movement of equipment and furnishings cannot be carried out after the painting if finalized, as minor touchup is almost always required (thus, the painter must be one of the last, if not the last discipline out the door).

The general contractor is charged with such coordination, but the situation needs to be openly discussed. Most certainly, subcontracts need to have modified timing to avoid a mass exodus on the day of Contract Time expiration.

Partial Use by Owner (No Occupancy)

Owner-supplied equipment, finishes, systems installed by other than project contractors: Once the punch list has been compiled, the project is in such condition that the owner can begin the process of moving in. While this does not entail actual occupancy and use of the facility, it is a time when the owner can take over certain finished areas for use as storage areas for the arrival of new equipment and furnishings. Also, quite often owners will have some work done by contractors other than those involved with the construction directly. For example, the supplying and laying of carpeting is one work item that can be done in this manner. Problems, though, can arise if the owner's contractors are not careful in their work, and damage or mar the work of the construction trades (who would still be active on the site to a reduced degree). Any such damage would have to be back-charged (billed separately) to the owner and/or the contractor, since the construction contract still prevails, and requires a proper level of completion and "like-new" condition of the work.

Care also must be taken in the instance of partial owner occupancy, to ensure that insurance coverage is such that both owner and construction contractors are protected in case of any incident. Basically this is maintaining the proper control over the job site, while both owner and contractors continue their work. It is to their mutual benefit, just as the coincident occupancy is.

In addition, there needs to be coordination between the efforts of the owner and their desired results, and the continuing efforts of the contractors to meet their deadlines, and the correct state of the project for final completion. Undoing work, changing work, or making new demands, on the part of the owner, is counterproductive. Stalling or causing delays or confusion, requiring extraordinary owner effort, on the part of the contractors, is similarly discouraged. After all, the owner is the sponsor and bill-payer and certainly has the right to use the building— it just should not be premature, nor in a manner that disrupts the final construction efforts.

FINALE

Resolving Punch List Items; Final Cleaning

The work of the punch list should be pursued in a line-by-line sequence—doing each item as listed, once and for the last time. Often these items are quite involved, even to the point of having to remove some work (involving other trades) to make the corrections. Also, late-arriving items must be installed, again involving other trade work (where proper accommodation has not been built into the original work). Still other items may involve discussion as to responsibility, who injured the work, or the contractor's opinion that the work is correct as done, and that the punch list is not in keeping with the contract.

In the main, this work proceeds along quite well. The on-site personnel, however, must understand that there has to be a sequence for this work. Quite often all contractors are given the same completion date for their work. This leads to confusion, as each then thinks he/she can work to the very end of the contract time. This can also cause anger, disruption, and delays in actual completion. Some finish trades (painting, for example) are required to provide a neat, finished, and unmarred set of surfaces. If other work is done behind them and there is some marring, then the painter is not finished, even though the painting was complete (and satisfactory) just prior to the other work being performed. Obviously, this can be a time of dispute and frustration, as the painter must, again, refinish already finished work.

The professionals must anticipate this, even to the point of requesting the general contractor to issue specific instructions for the punch list work sequence, or to give each contractor a different completion date, which allows for the sequence. Also, this sequence must be coordinated with the owner, who may have other workers coming onsite to perform separate work, or where moving and occupancy is eminent. Legally, when every contractor has the same completion date, they can work until that date. But everyone, by this time, is anxious to leave the project and move on to other ventures. Any added delay in completion is stressful, often nasty, and quite irritating. It is worth some extra effort to alleviate or eliminate the situation.

During this period, too, more and more demobilization will occur, as the contractors remove their resources and facilities in preparation to totally leave the site. One of the most contentious work items is final cleanup and removal of debris and excess materials. Good materials will be salvaged and removed by the contractors, but contractual care must be taken to ensure that cleanup of the project and project site is done, and done well. Often this chore is laid at the door of the general contractor, much to his/her chagrin. Other contractors will avoid the issue and merely do what they absolutely must do in this regard. It can be a very elaborate, time-consuming, and costly issue. Tons and truckloads of debris may have to be removed—but much depends on how vigorously and well this chore was accomplished continually during the progress of the work.

Certification for Occupancy Through Final Payment

A series of final inspections is required on most projects, prior to final completion. Some of these occur prior to Substantial Completion; others during the punch list period. Several will be governmental inspections by agencies that have taken permits on work in the project—building/structural, electrical, plumbing, et cetera. In many jurisdictions there is a requirement for the issuance of a Certificate of Occupancy. This document will be issued after notice from the contractor(s) that their work is ready for inspection, the final inspection, and approval of the work as satisfactory (meeting the minimum standards of the regulations).

Also, during the period between Substantial and Final Completion, the contractors will turn over manuals of operating instructions to the owner and will train the owners' personnel (where required) in the operation of the equipment and systems. This is a key interface, especially for very complex projects or where the equipment is very sophisticated or very new technology. Obviously, the best of systems is useless to the owners if their personnel cannot make the system do what it is supposed to do (unless there is a flaw in the contractor's work). In addition, these manuals provide information regarding maintenance, spare parts, warranties, and the proper continued use of the units.

The most important of the inspections is the final inspection of the design professional/owner team. Here the project is once again toured so the remedial work on the punch list items can be assessed, and hopefully found to be satisfactory and acceptable. Any discrepancies cycle back through the remedial work program until finally accepted. However, where the work is found to be contract-abiding, the project is deemed complete, and all parties demobilize and move to the last function: certification of the project work, and its completeness, and the final payment to the contractor(s). Checklists are available so each required contract item is checked and made right, if necessary, so the project certification can be made. Within the terms of the contract, the owner is then obligated to make final payment—at which point the project is hers/his, and becomes part of what is called "standing building stock"— an existing building. Now the owner is free to move in en masse, and to occupy, operate, and work the project as seen fit.

CHAPTER
9

COMPLETION AND OCCUPANCY

POSTSUBSTANTIAL COMPLETION

Turning the Building over to the Owner

When the last contractor has walked out the door and turned off the lights, the project belongs to the owner. From this point on, the owner will have to outfit, occupy, operate, and maintain the project, hopefully finding it in full accord with design concepts and programming—that is, the building or facility is what the owner desired in the beginning.

Sometimes this is merely an anticlimactic event, a murmur, unnoticed by most. The owner shows up one day, uses the new key, and finds no construction personnel on the site. The event and work of occupying is ready to start!

Other projects are much higher profile and culminate in formal ceremonies, turning over of the keys, flowery (and overly long) speeches, bands, parades, dedication, blessing, tours, and simple showing off. It is a grand day and time! In some cases, the owner will sponsor an event for the contractors (and their families, at times), where the workers can see and show the work they performed in its final form. At other times, the owner may sponsor a party—buffet, luncheon, or a more informal gathering—to salute the workers and to thank them.

In any event, the long-anticipated project is a reality, pristine (or as near as possible), ready for the life and function it was built to support. With the exception of a few (and very minor) glitches, the project is finished and ready for day-to-day operation.

Owner Occupancy (Partial or Full)

The owner/client becomes increasingly anxious about the project the closer it comes to completion. This is understandable, but can also be a situation where caution must be exercised.

Following the sequence of final inspection, punch list, remedial work to resolve the punch list, and acquisition of the certificate of occupancy from the governing regulatory agency, little is left but the final payment to the contractor. But as this sequence winds down, the owner will seek to start moving into the new facility, at least in the form of furnishings and equipment (not necessarily occupancy by staffers). Due care is required to ensure that no party to the construction contract is reduced or damaged in the process. It would be wonderfully simple if occupancy and use could be deferred in total until all construction work is complete and all construction workers are off the site. But that often is just not reality, so precaution is necessary.

The overriding issue is the condition of the project when owner occupancy occurs. There is a need for absolute unity of understanding of the condition, between owner and contractor, so any ensuing issues about damage, disruption, or other adversity is clearly set upon the proper responsible party.

There is an inherent risk in this in that any damage done during the move-in operations will become contentious if not carefully watched. For example, a university wishes to occupy a new dormitory as soon as possible, but has a separate contract (separate from the instruction contract) for the acquisition and installation of the carpeting. With full notice to and knowledge of the construction contractors, the carpet installation is performed over a weekend. On Monday, it is obvious that walls have been damaged or marred by the carpet installation (as the rolls of carpet were unrolled the edges made streak marks periodically along the walls of the corridors).

Now comes the problem—who is responsible for the repair of the wall finishes (paint, thankfully!) and who is to pay for the remedial work? This can become an issue until it is understood and resolved that the carpet installer is responsible and should make proper payment, but the painting work should be done by the painting subcontractor for the building construction. Understand—the building has *not* been turned over fully to the owner, so the contractors are still in control of it and responsible for its condition. By allowing the carpet installation as an extracurricular activity, the university and its carpet contractor are the responsible parties for the damage due to the carpet installation.

Another example is a motel that is in the finishing stages. The owner wants to partially occupy the building (the first two floors of a five-story building) and begin rental operations. Here, the government agency intervenes on safety issues (the fire alarm and exiting systems were not complete and could not be made so without finishing the upper floors). Arrangements are made whereby the owner pays for extra work to make the safety system operable on the first floors, and barricades the upper reaches of the building (including exit stairs, etc.), so occupants cannot mistakenly become trapped by trying to escape into unfinished areas.

A good axiom to remember is "No building is safer than at that moment just prior to occupancy—i.e., the entrance of the first human and the first box or piece of equipment." Once that situation occurs, the building almost literally begins to "die"—that is, to become abused, misused, and in many instances, dangerous.

Where owner occupancy is ongoing, that is, occurs throughout the construction sequence, the problems are different and often much more pervasive. The contractor(s) must take extraordinary measures to protect the owner's employees, equipment, and product; to provide a safe environment; and to provide proper egress and access to other facilities of the owner. Temporary partitions, barricades, equipment, and utility service connections may be required to avoid disruption of the operations, particularly on a sudden or emergency basis.

As the owner takes control of some finished areas within the construction areas, all of the considerations must be reevaluated and adjusted to continue correct and safe operations and other aspects of the owner's operations. In addition, it is often necessary to protect the construction areas from the employees, to prevent use, marring, or disruption of construction processes, applications, protections, curing, et cetera.

A mutual understanding is required, and often is executed in formal terms (written documentation), that once the owner takes occupancy, ownership, or responsibility for a specific area, any problems developed will not impact the construction personnel or firms. Hence, the need for inspection is crucial. Of course, in the United States there is a widely understood period of time that is generally accepted as a time for call-backs by the construction firms, to remedy problems within the construction that appear after final payment and occupancy. Usually this is set at one year, unless otherwise set by contract. Warranties and guarantees may be in place for longer periods of time if required by the construction documentation. These should be written to run from the date of substantial completion of the project, and not for some shorter period determined by the firm issuing the warranty or guarantee.

FINAL COMPLETION

There comes a point when there are no construction personnel on the job site; the equipment, tools, sheds, and temporary facilities are removed; and the project work is *finished*! If at all, there is but a moment of silence before the next array of activities and the new cast of personnel arrives and starts that precious and long-sought-after occupancy. Moving in, on the part of the client/owner is really a shifting of gears—a transition from a process that is quite mysterious and overwhelming (construction) to one of adjusting to the format and configuration envisioned those many weeks ago when the project was programmed. Remember, at that time, there was a postulation of how things were to function and relate, and how the new facility was to serve the new functions, personnel, and equipment.

Often client/owners are outright surprised at what is given over to them in the final project. Even large corporations with full-time project representation during construction find that what they expected and anticipated is not in place. The hope is that things are better, and a good, pleasant surprise, and not a serious shortcoming or imposition. In reality, this is the true goal of the project from day one, and is something all parties to the project must keep in mind throughout.

In the end, there is a need for consensus and agreement among the contractual parties that the project is, indeed, complete and acceptable to the owner, such that final payment to the contractor is due and appropriate. While there is a prevailing and generally court-accepted guarantee that call-backs for adjustments or repairs to project work items are in order for one year, the finale is necessarily definitive, final, and absolute.

10

POSTOCCUPANCY

AFTER FINAL COMPLETION

It is increasingly clear that the interest and the obligations of the design and construction professionals do not end at the moment the owner takes control of the project and occupies it.

It is commonly held that there is a one-year period after the final payment during which the various contractors are responsible to service the project, when something fails or becomes inoperable. In many instances, too, there are longer warranty and guarantee periods, twenty years for roofing systems, for an example, and in some cases, there is even a lifetime guarantee.

Circumstances do occur, and not unreasonably, in which a product fails to operate as required or workmanship proves inadequate. This is not necessarily an indication of substandard product or construction, but falls within the normal range of expectations when dealing with ordinary conditions.

Contractors and manufacturers understand this, in the main, and will service "call-backs" (calls requesting service and remedy of improper work). Indeed, they factored call-backs into their pricing. Not that they plan to fail, but they recognize that such occurrences do happen from time to time.

The design professionals may be asked to provide insight into such shortcomings, or to see that the proper company services the problem. That, too, is part of the contractual understanding. But in some circumstances, basic features of the project may prove to be problematic to the owner—some situations arise wherein the basic concept or design does not function as the owner feels it should, or understood that it would.

Again, this is within the normal range of human foibles, unless there is a major "glitch," disruption, or "miss" in the basic premise of the dens.

Professionals have come to the conclusion that it is to their benefit and to the benefit of their reputation to go back to finished projects some time after initial occupancy, to review the project with the owner, occupant, or user. There is always good in "learnings" that reveal what worked and perhaps more importantly, what did not. Either way, information gathered from a completed project can provide very valuable insight for future projects. Some of this information will prove to be procedural while most will be rather technical, regarding precise solutions and how they worked. To ignore this input really shuts down a resource that the office can build upon through changes in procedure, personnel, and approaches to projects and solutions. Of course, every project is different (even where prototypical projects are involved), since other clients and/or project conditions make for individualized decisions and solution.

Contractors, too, have an interest in after-completion evaluations, since they can also learn about shortcomings and other conditions. Their primary interest may be in retaining good relations with the client for future work assignments, but the work itself can provide more insight. While the solutions utilized may have come from the design professionals, the work itself holds some value to the contractor—the materials selected, the detailing, the connection to other work, the overall solution, et cetera, all are things of interest to the contractor. This even holds for similar work that may appear on other projects in the future, for other clients.

POSTOCCUPANCY EVLAUATION (POE)

Many professional offices have adopted some form of a formal program for after-completion service, review, and assessments. This is called postoccupancy evaluation (POE) (see Figure 10-1). The task is quite similar to the programming sequence at the inception of the project, but of course, in a different context—basically, "How are the things we designed, built, and incorporated working?"

Although this could be deemed to be a single task, it is one that can be and usually is repeated, and more than likely in modified forms. Each return to a project and review can be adjusted as necessary to assess different elements of the project; it does not have to be a full review of the entire project each time. The value of the POE programs is to focus attention on specific elements of the project to ascertain their function and their foibles.

Two primary areas of concern usually arise in the POE sequence. First are the shortcomings, if any, in the basic design concept and its execution. What was done that simply did not work out or has become a

Please write the number of your response in the box beside each item. If you disagree or strongly disagree, please write the item number on the last page and explain why you disagree.

	POSTOCCUPANCY EVALUATION					
Item Number	Building Features	Strongly Agree	Agree	Disagree	Strongly Disagree	No Opinion
		4	3	2	1	0
1	Front entrance of the building is easy to identify and access.					
2	Building is barrier free [handicapped accessible], both externally and internally.					
3	Entrances and exits are located to permit efficient student traffic flow.					
4	Number and size of restrooms is adequate throughout the building.					
5	Intercom system allows dependable two-way communication throughout the building.					
6	Floor coverings are appropriate to the room's/area's intended use.					
7	Building layout provides good separation for after-hours and weekend use.					
8	Building details, color schemes, material, and decor are aesthetically pleasing.					
9	Year-round comfortable temperature is provided throughout the building.					
10	Ventilation system provides adequate circulation of clean air.					
11	Mechanical systems operate quietly and don't disrupt learning areas.					
12	Building acoustics provide for appropriate ambient noise levels.					

(continued)

Figure 10-1 Example of a checklist for a postoccupancy evaluation of a project. Such lists can be standardized to a good degree, but often they need the addition of very specific points in keeping with the nuances of the project and its function(s).

Please write the number of your response in the box beside each item. If you disagree or strongly disagree, please write the item number on the last page and explain why you disagree.

Item Number	Building Features	Strongly Agree	Agree	Disagree	Strongly Disagree	No Opinion
	POSTOCCUPANCY EVALUATION					
		4	3	2	1	0
13	Areas are provided for student socialization.					
14	Quantity and quality of windows contribute to a pleasant environment.					
15	Corridor widths are adequate for student movement.					
16	Site and building are well landscaped.					
17	Finishes are of durable quality and easily maintained.					
	Safety and Security					
18	Access to the building is effectively controlled throughout the school day.					
19	Car, bus, and service vehicular traffic are separate.					
20	Pedestrian and vehicular traffic are separate, except in designated crosswalks.					
21	Sidewalks are designed and maintained for safety.					
22	Ample space is provided in corridors or protected areas for student safety in the event of natural disasters.					
23	Building has no "blind spots" that are difficult to monitor.					
24	Building has good sight lines in corridors and is easy to supervise.					
25	Site plantings do not allow for areas of concealment.					

Figure 10-1 (Continued).

Please write the number of your response in the box beside each item. If you disagree or strongly disagree, please write the item number on the last page and explain why you disagree.

Item Number	Building Features	Strongly Agree	Agree	Disagree	Strongly Disagree	No Opinion
	POSTOCCUPANCY EVALUATION					
		4	3	2	1	0
26	Stairwells are easy to supervise.					
27	Restrooms are easy to supervise.					

	The School Site					
28	Site is large enough to meet educational needs.					
29	Site is well landscaped.					
30	Pedestrian services include adequate sidewalks with designated crosswalks, curb cuts, and appropriate slopes.					
31	Sufficient on-site, solid surface parking is provided for daily use.					
32	Sufficient on-site, solid-surface parking is provided for evening/event use.					

	Educational Adequacy					
33	Rooms are adequately sound isolated.					
34	Lighting is sufficient for tasks.					
35	Light switching is conveniently located.					
36	Room lighting levels can be controlled for audio-visual presentations.					
37	Number of electrical outlets in teaching areas is sufficient.					
38	Size of academic learning areas meets desirable standards.					

(continued)

Figure 10-1 (Continued).

Please write the number of your response in the box beside each item. If you disagree or strongly disagree, please write the item number on the last page and explain why you disagree.

Item Number	Building Features	Strongly Agree	Agree	Disagree	Strongly Disagree	No Opinion
	POSTOCCUPANCY EVALUATION					
		4	3	2	1	0
39	Classroom space permits arrangements for small group activity.					
40	Location of academic learning areas is near related educational activities and away from disruptive noises.					
41	Personal space in the classroom away from group instruction allows privacy time for individual learning.					
42	Storage for student materials is adequate.					
43	Storage for teacher materials is adequate.					
44	Furniture and equipment are appropriate for instructional uses.					
45	The following teaching stations are designed and arranged to support the learning activities that need to occur:					
46	Core Academic Classroom					
47	Self-Contained Special Education Classroom					
48	Special Education Resource Classroom					
49	Visual Arts Classroom					
50	Music Room					
51	PE Multipurpose Room					

Figure 10-1 (Continued).

Please write the number of your response in the box beside each item. If you disagree or strongly disagree, please write the item number on the last page and explain why you disagree.

Item Number	Building Features	Strongly Agree	Agree	Disagree	Strongly Disagree	No Opinion
	POSTOCCUPANCY EVALUATION					
		4	3	2	1	0
	Supported Areas					
52	Teacher work areas are adequately sized and furnished.					
53	Media Center has adequate learning and support spaces.					
54	Student Dining Area is properly located and adequately sized.					
55	Administrative areas are in appropriate locations.					
56	Administrative personnel are provided sufficient workspace and privacy.					
57	Counselors' offices ensure privacy and sufficient storage.					
58	Health clinic is centrally located and equipped to meet requirements.					
59	Suitable reception space is available for students, teachers, and visitors.					
60	Custodial closets are conveniently located and sufficiently equipped.					
	Total					

Figure 10-1 (Continued).

problem in itself? The task is to go back and see how well the design is working. I don't mean just the opening night gala, but after the building's been in use for six months or a year. Don't just talk to management; talk to the designers and technicians who use the space. Find out what works and, more important, what doesn't.

A good portion of any project program is purely trying to guess what solution will work. Without the opportunity for trial and error (and subsequently changing the erroneous things), the conclusions are built into the project. It is occupancy that often uncovers situations that don't present the owner and users with what they thought was going to work.

This is not to say that the design professionals failed or that the owner was not candid and open, but rather that even working together, they simply did not envision the circumstances that now exist. The discovery of these items through the POE offers an opportunity to have them remedied (at an added cost, of course, outside the basic project cost) and provides the professionals with better insight and understanding of similar situations in the future—learnings, if you will.

Largely, these situations are not contentious, but they are points where mutual understanding and effort are required by all parties. They illustrate that even the best and most incisive efforts at programming often do not uncover each and every nuance surrounding a project.

This effort is separate and distinct from the owner's situation with the contractor. The latter is contract-based, in that the flawed work is fixed as part of the warranty system; it is based on equipment and workmanship and not on concept and design. The POE, on the other hand, is an effort to bring satisfaction and closure to both owner and design professional. It is an opportunity to air any irritation that is created by the owner's having to deal with physical conditions that were not anticipated or intended.

While perhaps not the goal of any architectural project, one by-product is the level of satisfaction that inures to each party, each participant, and each worker on all levels.

The completion of a project often results in a project party with all present to celebrate the effort and the finished project. Here the nuances, the irritations, and the frustrations of producing the project dissolve into respect for and admiration of the project—and collective effort.

In some cases, a more solemn occasion is held, where dignitaries gather to express their feelings and to enjoy the promise of the new project. Though far from the gold-painted shovels used to overturn the first soil or the project, this gathering is also a celebration, with satisfactory result and good wishes for successful function. A ribbon may be cut with ceremonial scissors to herald the opening of the project for both awe-inspired observation and the beginning of the work function for production of new services or products.

The most gruff trade worker takes pride and satisfaction in the effort given; the designer glories in the faithful achievement of the design concept, and the owner is heartened by the new opportunities and promises that the project offers.

Even the general community and public receives a gift—a new, well-executed project to enhance their community and take pride in.

Finally, the end of the progression!

TRADE ASSOCIATIONS STANDARDS-GENERATING ORGANIZATIONS GOVERNING AUTHORITIES

Because of the massive amount of information required for any project, design professionals often utilize technical information and reference standards contained in publications produced by various organizations. Trade associations, standards-generating organizations, and governing authorities are invaluable sources of technical information, literature, and audiovisual aids. Their documents are highly reliable, detailed, and wide-ranging. The information is product-specific, complete, and in-depth. It includes design, fabrication, processing, production, and installation data, along with pertinent (but general) details applicable to the products. There is no attempt to provide project-specific details, that being the task of the project personnel.

Usually, there is far more information than required, in that the testing and manufacturing procedures may be noted. Many items are provided gratis, but ask for catalog and applicable price list for available items and complete ordering information.

These documents are generally categorized as reference standards. The data are promotional in nature, not directed toward sales but toward understanding of the correct use and implementation of the products involved.

In lieu of repeating all of the necessary information on the drawings or in the specifications, professionals usually use a system of referring to the required materials, often using acronyms or abbreviations to represent the full names of the organizations involved. Following is a partial list of many such organizations; numerous other organizations exist that are not listed. The organizations are subject to change in name, address, telephone number, and Web addresses. Those listed below are believed to be accurate as of the date of production of this book. To verify or update information, readers are advised to consult one of the following sources:

Encyclopedia of Associations published by Gale Research Company

National Trade and Professional Associations of the United States published by Columbia Books, Washington, DC

ARCAT: The Product Directory for Architects published by The Architect's Catalog, Inc., Fairfield, CT

"Sources of Information" section of *The Directory*, published by the Sweet's Group of McGraw-Hill Construction Information Group

Architectural Graphics Standards, 11th edition published by John Wiley & Sons, Hoboken, NJ

Also, most large public libraries have a directory service that will locate addresses and telephone numbers in various cities.

AA	Aluminum Association, Inc. (The) www.aluminum.org	(202) 862-5100
AAADM	American Association of Automatic Door Manufacturers www.aaadm.com	(216) 241-7333
AAMA	American Architectural Manufacturers Association www.aamanet.org	(847) 303-5664
ABMA	American Bearing Manufacturers Association www.abma-dc.org	(202) 367-1155
ACI	American Concrete Institute www.aci-int.org	(248) 848-3700
ACPA	American Concrete Pipe Association www.concrete-pipe.org	(972) 506-7216
AEIC	Association of Edison Illuminating Companies, Inc. (The) www.aeic.org	(205) 257-2530
AF&PA	American Forest & Paper Association www.afandpa.org	(800) 878-8878 (202) 463-2700
AGC	Associated General Contractors of America (The) www.agc.org	(703) 548-3118
AHA	American Hardboard Association (Now part of CPA)	

AHAM	Association of Home Appliance Manufacturers www.aham.org	(202) 872-5955
AI	Asphalt Institute www.asphaltinstitute.org	(859) 288-4960
AIA	American Institute of Architects (The) www.aia.org	(800) 242-3837 (202) 626-7300
AISC	American Institute of Steel Construction www.aisc.org	(800) 644-2400 (312) 670-2400
AISI	American Iron and Steel Institute www.steel.org	(202) 452-7100
AITC	American Institute of Timber Construction www.aitc-glulam.org	(303) 792-9559
ALCA	Associated Landscape Contractors of America www.alca.org	(800) 395-2522 (703) 736-9666
ALSC	American Lumber Standard Committee, Inc. www.alsc.org	(301) 972-1700
AMCA	Air Movement and Control Association International, Inc. www.amca.org	(847) 394-0150
ANSI	American National Standards Institute www.ansi.org	(202) 293-8020
APA	APA—The Engineered Wood Association www.apawood.org	(253) 565-6600
APA	Architectural Precast Association www.archprecast.org	(239) 454-6989
API	American Petroleum Institute www.api.org	(202) 682-8000
ARI	Air-Conditioning & Refrigeration Institute www.ari.org	(703) 524-8800
ARMA	Asphalt Roofing Manufacturers Association www.asphaltroofing.org	(202) 207-0917
ASCE	American Society of Civil Engineers www.asce.org	(800) 548-2723 (703) 295-6300

ASHRAE	American Society of Heating, Refrigerating and Air-Conditioning Engineers www.ashrae.org	(800) 527-4723 (404) 636-8400
ASME	American Society of Mechanical Engineers www.asme.org	(800) 843-2763 (212) 591-7722
ASSE	American Society of Sanitary Engineering www.asse-plumbing.org	(440) 835-3040
ASTM	ASTM International (American Society for Testing and Materials International) www.astm.org	(610) 832-9585
AWCI	Association of the Wall and Ceiling Industry www.awci.org	(703) 534-8300
AWCMA	American Window Covering Manufacturers Association (Now WCSC)	
AWI	Architectural Woodwork Institute www.awinet.org	(800) 449-8811 (703) 733-0600
AWPA	American Wood-Preservers' Association www.awpa.com	(334) 874-9800
AWS	American Welding Society www.aws.org	(800) 443-9353 (305) 443-9353
AWWA	American Water Works Association www.awwa.org	(800) 926-7337 (303) 794-7711
BHMA	Builders Hardware Manufacturers Association www.buildershardware.com	(212) 297-2122
BIA	Brick Industry Association (The) www.bia.org	(703) 620-0010
BICSI	BICSI (Building Industry Consulting Service International, Inc.) www.bicsi.org	(813) 979-1991
BIFMA	BIFMA International (Business and Institutional Furniture Manufacturer's Association International) www.bifma.com	(616) 285-3963

CCC	Carpet Cushion Council	(203) 637-1312
	www.carpetcushion.org	
CDA	Copper Development Association Inc.	(800) 232-3282
	www.copper.org	(212) 251-7200
CEA	Canadian Electricity Association	(613) 230-9263
	www.canelect.ca/connections_ online/home.htm	
CFFA	Chemical Fabrics & Film Association, Inc.	(216) 241-7333
	www.chemicalfabricsandfilm.com	
CGSB	Canadian General Standards Board	(800) 665-2472
	w3.pwgsc.gc.ca/cgsb	(819) 956-0425
CIMA	Cellulose Insulation Manufacturers Association	(888) 881-2462 (937) 222-2462
	www.cellulose.org	
CISCA	Ceilings & Interior Systems Construction Association	(630) 584-1919
	www.cisca.org	
CISPI	Cast Iron Soil Pipe Institute	(423) 892-0137
	www.cispi.org	
CLFMI	Chain Link Fence Manufacturers Institute	(301) 596-2583
	www.chainlinkinfo.org	
CPA	Composite Panel Association	(301) 670-0604
	www.pbmdf.com	
CPPA	Corrugated Polyethylene Pipe Association	(800) 510-2772 (202) 462-9607
	www.cppa-info.org	
CRI	Carpet & Rug Institute (The)	(800) 882-8846
	www.carpet-rug.com	(706) 278-3176
CRSI	Concrete Reinforcing Steel Institute	(847) 517-1200
	www.crsi.org	
CSA	CSA International (Formerly IAS: International Approval Services)	(800) 463-6727 (416) 747-4000
	www.csa-international.org	
CSI	Cast Stone Institute	(770) 972-3011
	www.caststone.org	
CSI	Construction Specifications Institute (The)	(800) 689-2900 (703) 684-0300
	www.csinet.org	
CSSB	Cedar Shake & Shingle Bureau	(604) 820-7700
	www.cedarbureau.org	

CTI	Cooling Technology Institute (Formerly Cooling Tower Institute) www.cti.org	(281) 583-4087
DHI	Door and Hardware Institute www.dhi.org	(703) 222-2010
EIMA	EIFS Industry Members Association (Exterior Insulation and Finish Systems Industry Member Association) www.eima.com	(800) 294-3462 (770) 968-7945
EJCDC	Engineers Joint Contract Documents Committee www.asce.org	(800) 548-2723 (703) 295-6300
EJMA	Expansion Joint Manufacturers Association, Inc. www.ejma.org	(914) 332-0040
ESD	ESD Association (Electrostatic Discharge Association) www.esda.org	(315) 339-6937
FRSA	Florida Roofing, Sheet Metal & Air Conditioning Contractors Association, Inc. www.floridaroof.com	(407) 671-3772
FSA	Fluid Sealing Association www.fluidsealing.com	(610) 971-4850
FSC	Forest Stewardship Council www.fsc.org	(202) 342-0413
GA	Gypsum Association www.gypsum.org	(202) 289-5440
GANA	Glass Association of North America www.glasswebsite.com	(785) 271-0208
GS	Green Seal www.greenseal.org	(202) 872-6400
HI	Hydraulic Institute www.pumps.org	(888) 786-7744 (973) 267-9700
HI	Hydronics Institute www.gamanet.org	(908) 464-8200
HPVA	Hardwood Plywood & Veneer Association www.hpva.org	(703) 435-2900
IAS	International Approval Service (Now CSA)	

ICEA	Insulated Cable Engineers Association, Inc. www.icea.net	(770) 830-0369
ICRI	International Concrete Repair Institute, Inc. www.icri.org	(847) 827-0830
IEEE	Institute of Electrical and Electronics Engineers, Inc. (The) www.ieee.org	(212) 419-7900
IESNA	Illuminating Engineering Society of North America www.iesna.org	(212) 248-5000
IGCC	Insulating Glass Certification Council www.igcc.org	(315) 646-2234
IGMA	Insulating Glass Manufacturers Alliance (The) www.igmaonline.org	(613) 233-1510
ILI	Indiana Limestone Institute of America, Inc. www.iliai.com	(812) 275-4426
ISO	International Organization for Standardization www.iso.ch	41 22 749 01 11
ISSFA	International Solid Surface Fabricators Association www.issfa.net	(702) 567-8150
ITS	Intertek (Intertek Testing Services) www.intertek.com	(800) 345-3851 (607) 753-6711
ITU	International Telecommunication Union www.itu.int/home	41 22 730 51 11
KCMA	Kitchen Cabinet Manufacturers Association www.kcma.org	(703) 264-1690
LMA	Laminating Materials Association (Now part of CPA)	
LPI	Lightning Protection Institute www.lightning.org	(800) 488-6864 (847) 577-7200
MBMA	Metal Building Manufacturers Association www.mbma.com	(216) 241-7333

MFMA	Maple Flooring Manufacturers Association www.maplefloor.org	(847) 480-9138
MFMA	Metal Framing Manufacturers Association www.metalframingmfg.org	(312) 644-6610
MH	Material Handling (Now MHIA)	
MHIA	Material Handling Industry of America www.mhia.org	(800) 345-1815 (704) 676-1190
MIA	Marble Institute of America www.marble-institute.com	(440) 250-9222
MPI	Master Painters Institute www.paintinfo.com	(888) 674-8937
MSS	Manufacturers Standardization Society of the Valve and Fittings Industry Inc. www.mss-hq.com	(703) 281-6613
NAAMM	National Association of Architectural Metal Manufacturers www.naamm.org	(312) 332-0405
NACE	NACE International (National Association of Corrosion Engineers International) www.nace.org	(281) 228-6200
NAIMA	North American Insulation Manufacturers Association (The) www.naima.org	(703) 684-0084
NBGQA	National Building Granite Quarries Association, Inc. www.nbgqa.com	(800) 557-2848
NCAA	National Collegiate Athletic Association (The) www.ncaa.org	(317) 917-6222
NCMA	National Concrete Masonry Association www.ncma.org	(703) 713-1900
NCPI	National Clay Pipe Institute www.ncpi.org	(262) 248-9094
NCTA	National Cable & Telecommunications Association www.ncta.com	(202) 775-3550

NEBB	National Environmental Balancing Bureau www.nebb.org	(301) 977-3698
NECA	National Electrical Contractors Association www.necanet.org	(301) 657-3110
NeLMA	Northeastern Lumber Manufacturers' Association www.nelma.org	(207) 829-6901
NEMA	National Electrical Manufacturers Association www.nema.org	(703) 841-3200
NETA	InterNational Electrical Testing Association www.netaworld.org	(269) 488-6382
NFPA	NFPA International (National Fire Protection Association) www.nfpa.org	(800) 344-3555 (617) 770-3000
NFRC	National Fenestration Rating Council www.nfrc.org	(301) 589-1776
NGA	National Glass Association www.glass.org	(703) 442-4890
NHLA	National Hardwood Lumber Association www.natlhardwood.org	(800) 933-0318 (901) 377-1818
NLGA	National Lumber Grades Authority www.nlga.org	(604) 524-2393
NOFMA	National Oak Flooring Manufacturers Association www.nofma.org	(901) 526-5016
NRCA	National Roofing Contractors Association www.nrca.net	(800) 323-9545 (847) 299-9070
NRMCA	National Ready Mixed Concrete Association www.nrmca.org	(888) 846-7622 (301) 587-1400
NSSGA	National Stone, Sand & Gravel Association www.nssga.org	(800) 342-1415 (703) 525-8788
NTMA	National Terrazzo & Mosaic Association, Inc. www.ntma.com	(800) 323-9736 (540) 751-0930

NTRMA	National Tile Roofing Manufacturers Association (Now TRI)	
NWWDA	National Wood Window and Door Association (Now WDMA)	
PCI	Precast/Prestressed Concrete Institute0 www.pci.org	(312) 786-0300
PDCA	Painting & Decorating Contractors of America www.pdca.com	(800) 332-7322 (314) 514-7322
PDI	Plumbing & Drainage Institute www.pdionline.org	(800) 589-8956 (978) 557-0720
PTI	Post-Tensioning Institute www.post-tensioning.org	(602) 870-7540
RCSC	Research Council on Structural Connections www.boltcouncil.org	(800) 644-2400 (312) 670-2400
RFCI	Resilient Floor Covering Institute www.rfci.com	(301) 340-8580
RIS	Redwood Inspection Service www.calredwood.org	(888) 225-7339 (415) 382-0662
RTI	(Formerly NTRMA: National Tile Roofing Manufacturers Association) (Now TRI)	
SDI	Steel Deck Institute www.sdi.org	(847) 462-1930
SDI	Steel Door Institute www.steeldoor.org	(440) 899-0010
SEI	Structural Engineering Institute www.seinstitute.com	(800) 548-2723 (703) 295-6195
SGCC	Safety Glazing Certification Council www.sgcc.org	(315) 646-2234
SIA	Security Industry Association www.siaonline.org	(703) 683-2075
SIGMA	Sealed Insulating Glass Manufacturers Association (Now IGMA)	
SJI	Steel Joist Institute www.steeljoist.org	(843) 626-1995
SMA	Screen Manufacturers Association www.smacentral.org	(561) 533-0991
SMACNA	Sheet Metal and Air Conditioning Contractors' National Association www.smacna.org	(703) 803-2980

SPFA	Spray Polyurethane Foam Alliance (Formerly SPI/SPFD: The Society of the Plastics Industry, Inc.; Spray Polyurethane Foam Division) www.sprayfoam.org	(800) 523-6154
SPRI	SPRI (Single Ply Roofing Industry) www.spri.org	(781) 647-7026
SSINA	Specialty Steel Industry of North America www.ssina.com	(800) 982-0355 (202) 342-8630
SSPC	SSPC: The Society for Protective Coatings www.sspc.org	(877) 281-7772 (412) 281-2331
STI	Steel Tank Institute www.steeltank.com	(847) 438-8265
SWI	Steel Window Institute www.steelwindows.com	(216) 241-7333
SWRI	Sealant, Waterproofing, & Restoration Institute www.swrionline.org	(816) 472-7974
TCA	Tile Council of North America, Inc. www.tileusa.com	(864) 646-8453
TMS	The Masonry Society www.masonrysociety.org	(303) 939-9700
TPI	Truss Plate Institute, Inc. www.tpinst.org	(608) 833-5900
TPI	Turfgrass Producers International www.turfgrasssod.org	(800) 405-8873 (847) 705-9898
TRI	Tile Roofing Institute (Formerly RTI: Roof Tile Institute) www.tileroofing.org	(312) 670-4177
UL	Underwriters Laboratories Inc. www.ul.com	(800) 285-4476 (847) 272-8800
UNI	Uni-Bell PVC Pipe Association www.uni-bell.org	(972) 243-3902
USGBC	U.S. Green Building Council www.usgbc.org	(202) 828-7422
WASTEC	Waste Equipment Technology Association www.wastec.org	(800) 424-2869 (202) 244-4700
WCMA	Window Covering Manufacturers Association (Now WCSC)	

WCSC	Window Covering Safety Council (Formerly WCMA: Window Covering ManufacturersAssociation) www.windowcoverings.org	(800) 506-4636 (212) 661-4261
WDMA	Window & Door Manufacturers Association (Formerly NWWDA: National Wood Window and Door Association) www.wdma.com	(800) 223-2301 (847) 299-5200
WI	Woodwork Institute (Formerly WIC: Woodwork Institute of California) www.wicnet.org	(916) 372-9943
WMMPA	Wood Moulding & Millwork Producers Association www.wmmpa.com	(800) 550-7889 (530) 661-9591
WSRCA	Western States Roofing Contractors Association www.wsrca.com	(800) 725-0333 (650) 548-0112
WWPA	Western Wood Products Association www.wwpa.org	(503) 224-3930

Code Agencies

Often code-writing organizations are referred to by their acronyms in specifications and other construction documents. Following is a listing of such agencies.

BOCA	BOCA International, Inc. (See ICC)	
CABO	Council of American Building Officials (See ICC)	
IAPMO	International Association of Plumbing and Mechanical Officials www.iapmo.org	(909) 472-4100
ICBO	International Conference of Building Officials (See ICC)	
ICBO ES	ICBO Evaluation Service, Inc. (See ICC-ES)	
ICC	International Code Council (Formerly CABO: Council of American Building Officials) www.iccsafe.org	(703) 931-4533

ICC-ES	ICC Evaluation Service, Inc. www.icc-es.org	(800) 423-6587 (562) 699-0543
NES	National Evaluation Service (See ICC-ES)	
SBCCI	Southern Building Code Congress International, Inc. (See ICC)	

Federal Government Agencies

Often used as sources of information and standards, and referred to by acronym.

ADAAG	Accessibility Guidelines for Buildings and Facilities	(800) 872-2253
	Americans with Disabilities Act (ADA) Architectural Barriers Act (ABA) www.access-board.gov	(202) 272-0080
CE	Army Corps of Engineers www.usace.army.mil	
CFR	Code of Federal Regulations www.gpoaccess.gov/cfr/index.html	(888) 293-6498 (202) 512-1530
CPSC	Consumer Product Safety Commission www.cpsc.gov	(800) 638-2772 (301) 504-6816
CRD	Handbook for Concrete and Cement Concrete Research Division www.wes.army.mil	(601) 634-2355
DOD	Department of Defense www.dodssp.daps.mil	(215) 697-6257
EPA	Environmental Protection Agency www.epa.gov	(202) 272-0167
FAA	Federal Aviation Administration www.faa.gov	(202) 366-4000
FCC	Federal Communications Commission www.fcc.gov	(888) 225-5322
FDA	Food and Drug Administration www.fda.gov	(888) 463-6332
FS	Federal Specification Available from Department of Defense Single Stock Point www.dodssp.daps.mil	(215) 697-6257
	Available from General Services Administration www.fss.gsa.gov	(202) 501-1021

	Available from National Institute of Building Sciences www.nibs.org	(202) 289-7800
MIL SPEC	Military Specification and Standards Available from Department of Defense Single Stock Point www.dodssp.daps.mil	(215) 697-6257
OSHA	Occupational Safety & Health Administration www.osha.gov	(800) 321-6742 (202) 693-1999
PHS	Office of Public Health and Science www.osophs.dhhs.gov	(202) 690-7694
SD	State Department www.state.gov	(202) 647-4000
TRB	Transportation Research Board www.nas.edu/trb	(202) 334-2934
UFAS	Uniform Federal Accessibility Standards www.access-board.gov	(800) 872-2253 (202) 272-0080
USDA	Department of Agriculture www.usda.gov	(202) 720-2791

GLOSSARY

Knowledge of correct terminology is critical in the production of contract documents and in the general communications during design and construction.

As a tool of communication, it is important to use terms that are widely used and commonly understood, within the mainstream construction lexicon. This glossary lists commonly used terms.

For a more comprehensive listing of terminology, including materials, methods, and procedures, visit this book's companion Web site at **www.wiley.com/go/constructionofarchitecture**

The following is a short list of resources and references. The current edition should be verified with the publisher:

BUILDING NEWS CONSTRUCTION DICTIONARY ILLUSTRATED,
2000 ed.
ISBN 1557013268
Published by ENR/BNI Books

THE CONSTRUCTION DICTIONARY, 9th ed.
Greater Phoenix Chapter
National Association of Women in Construction
P.O. Box 6142
Phoenix, AZ 85005

CONSTRUCTION GLOSSARY, 2d ed.
by J. S. Stein
ISBN 047156933X
Published by John Wiley & Sons, Inc.

DICTIONARY OF ARCHITECTURE AND CONSTRUCTION, 4th ed.
by Cyril M. Harris
ISBN 0071452370
Published by McGraw-Hill Book Company

MEANS ILLUSTRATED CONSTRUCTION DICTIONARY, 3rd ed.
ISBN 0876295383
Published by R.S. Means Co., Inc.

A VISUAL DICTIONARY OF ARCHITECTURE
By Francis D. K. Ching
ISBN 0471288217
Published by John Wiley & Sons, Inc.

Also, many publications of the trade and professional organizations listed in the appendix provide definitions and descriptions specific to their products or services.

A/E   Architect/Engineer; the design professional hired by the owner to provide design and design-related services; a firm with personnel and expertise in both professions.

Activity   (1) A scheduling term; (2) the smallest work unit within a project; the basic building block of a project (see Project).

Addendum (pl. addenda)   Generally issued by the owner to the contractor during the bidding process and intended to become part of the contract documents when the construction contract is executed; written information (with drawings if necessary) adding to, clarifying, or modifying bidding documents.

Additional services   Services provided over and above those designated as basic services in owner agreements with A/Es and CMs.

Agency CM (ACM)   (CM without risk). A contractual form of the CM system exclusively performed in an agency relationship between the construction manager and owner. ACM is the form from which other CM forms and variations are derived.

Agent   Design professional, or other person authorized by a client (principal) to transact or manage some business in his/her behalf and owes the client a "fiduciary duty." Architects act in this manner by virtue of contract with owner/client; could also be construction manager under some project contracts.

Allowance   Sum of money set aside in a construction contract for items that have not yet been selected but are specified in the contract documents, e.g., face brick.

Alterations   (1) Remodeling or renovations involving partial construction work performed within an existing structure; (2) remodeling without a building addition.

Alternate bid   Amount stated in the bid to be added or deducted from the base bid amount proposed for alternate materials and/or methods of construction.

Apparent low bidder   The bidder who has submitted the lowest competitive proposal as determined by a cursory examination of the bids submitted.

Application for Payment   Contractor's written request for payment for completed portions of the work and/or for materials delivered or stored and properly labeled for the respective project.

Apprentice   Person training at the side of an experienced or highly qualified worker; helper, novice, or one requiring additional training for full qualification.

Approved   Term used to indicate acceptance of condition, material, system, or other work or procedure; reflects action by design professional or other authorized party, but does not relieve basic responsibility of party seeking such approval, as written in other binding documents and provisions.

Approved bidders list   List of contractors that have survived prequalification tests.

Approved changes   Changes of any nature in contract requirements that have been agreed upon through a change approval process and approved by the owner.

Arbitration   A procedure of explanation and negotiation used to settle differences or disputes between two parties through an impartial third party, who is trained to evaluate circumstances and propose suitable solutions; used in lieu of litigation.

Architect   Person trained in design and construction and registered by the state, who prepares architectural designs and associated construction documents to meet the owner's requirements, and observes construction of various types of building projects.

Architect/Engineer (A/E)   An individual or firm offering professional services as both architect and engineer.

Architectural design   Process of assembling and developing stated project requirements, regulatory concerns, and conceptual design principles into a coordinated program with associated sketches and drawings that depict the proposed project.

Architectural drawing   Part of a set (series) of drawings created and compiled to depict the desired design configuration and details for the general construction of a project (does not address structural or building service systems); singly, a line drawing of plan and/or elevation views of a proposed building for the purpose of showing the overall appearance of the building.

As-built drawings Set of contract drawings marked up and noted during the construction process or after construction that show the exact location, geometry, and dimensions of the constructed project; include field modifications, change orders, and similar documents. (As-built drawings are not the same as record drawings.)

Assemblies Portions of a building in combination (for example, a roof/ceiling assembly or a ceiling/floor assembly), where different materials are combined, installed, and interfaced to form protectives, and other aspects of construction for an entire building.

Attorney-in-fact A person who is given written authority (power of attorney) by another person to sign documents on his or her behalf.

Back charge Billing for work performed by one party in place of another who was responsible for the work; charge is to the responsible party.

Beneficial occupancy The point of project completion when the owner can use the constructed facility in whole or in part for its intended purpose, even though final completion may not yet be achieved.

Bid A binding offer, usually expressed in dollars, to provide specific services within clearly stated requirements; a formal, written offer or proposal from a contractor stating a price for the construction of a specific project or work, in accord with contract drawings and specifications.

Bid bond A written form of security executed by the bidder as principal and by a surety for the purpose of guaranteeing that the bidder will sign the contract, if awarded it, for the stated bid amount (to ensure performance in accordance with the bid).

Bid depository A physical location where trade contractor proposals are filed the day before general contractor bids are to be received by an owner, for pickup, opening, and acceptance or rejection by general contractors bidding the owner's project.

Bid division A portion of the total project reserved for contractors for bidding and performance purposes, i.e., division of work or work scope.

Bid division description A narrative description of the concise work scope to be bid and performed by a contractor; division of work description or work-scope description.

Bid documents The documents (drawings, details, and specifications for a particular project) distributed to contractors by the owner for bidding purposes. Also include published advertisement or written invitation to bid, instructions to bidders, form of contract, general and supplementary conditions, proposal forms, and other information including addenda.

Bid form   A standard written form furnished to all bidders for the purpose of obtaining the requested information and required signatures from the authorized bidding representatives.

Bid opening   The actual process of opening and tabulating bids submitted within the prescribed bid date/time and conforming with the bid procedures. A bid opening can be open (where the bidders are permitted to attend) or closed (where the bidders are not permitted to attend).

Bid shopper   A contractor, construction manager, buyer, or client who seeks to play one proposed supplier or subcontractor against another for the purpose of reducing a purchase price.

Bid shopping   Negotiations to obtain lower costs and prices; common practice among contractors to obtain the lowest possible price for subcontracted work; done both before the bid is entered, and often after (usually measures are taken to preserve the prices contained in the bid and forestall shopping).

Bid time   The date and time set by the owner, architect, or engineer for receiving bids.

Bidding   Process of compiling and submitting cost estimates/proposals for a project from various contractors and/or subcontractors; response to a request to bid or offer a price for executing the work of the project.

Bidding period   The calendar period allowed from issuance of bidding requirements and contract documents to the prescribed bid date/time.

Bidding requirements   The written minimum acceptable requirements, procedures, and conditions set out for the uniform submittal of bids, set forth by the owner to the contractor during the bidding process. The owner usually reserves the right to reject a bid if the bidding requirements are not met; includes advertisement for bids, notice to bidders, instructions to bidders, invitation to bid, and sample bid forms.

Bond   (1) Form of insurance issued by surety companies to insure proper execution of bid, work, performance, etc.; if contractor defaults, surety is responsible for completing the bonded activities. (see Bid bond, Contract bond, Contract payment bond, Contract performance bond, Labor and material payment bond, Performance bond, and Subcontractor bond) (2) The fusing of materials through chemical action.

Bonding company   A properly licensed firm or corporation willing to execute a surety bond or bonds, payable to the owner, securing the performance on a contract either in whole or in part, or securing payment for labor and materials.

Budget estimate   An estimate of cost based on rough or incomplete information, with a stated degree of accuracy. Loosely called a ball-park estimate.

Buildability   Extent to which a design facilitates the construction of a building in accord with overall requirements for the project; a collection of techniques and methods to ease construction.

Building   (1) To form by combining materials or parts; (2) a structure enclosed within a roof and exterior walls for the housing, shelter, enclosure, business, and support of individuals, animals, their activities, or property of any kind.

Building code official   Department head or chief of building regulations department; often a registered design professional, and also certified as code official by state or code organizations (see Building inspector).

Building codes   Laws, ordinances, regulations, and other legal requirements adopted by local governing jurisdictions to establish minimum acceptable safety standards for all types of construction and to set safe building practices and procedures. The codes generally encompass structural, electrical, plumbing, and mechanical remodeling and new construction.

Building inspector   A qualified government representative authorized to inspect construction in progress for compliance with applicable building codes, regulations, and ordinances; works for the building code official; often certified by state or code organizations.

Building line   Lines established and marked off by a surveyor denoting the exterior faces of a proposed building based on plans, specifications and official records; lines are generally extended and marked on batter boards placed about 6 feet outside the corners/lines of the building excavation and are used by trade workers as guidelines.

Building permit   A written document issued by the appropriate governmental agency to owner or contractor, prior to the start of construction on a specific project in accordance with drawings and specifications approved by the governmental authority, indicating proper review for compliance with various regulations (must be kept posted in a conspicuous place on the site until job is completed and passed by the building inspector).

Building process   All steps of a construction project from its conception to final acceptance and occupancy.

Building restriction [setback] lines   Lines imposed on property to define the area in which building may occur (lines denote inner limit of required yard or setback distances from property lines where construction is prohibited, usually set by zoning regulations).

Bulletin A delineation, narrative, or both describing a proposed change, for pricing by a contractor and for consideration as a change by the owner.

Callout A note on a drawing with a leader line to the feature, location, material, or work item involved.

Certificate of Occupancy (CO) Document issued by building code department stating that the project has been inspected and found to be built in compliance with local building code and other applicable regulations, and therefore may be occupied and used.

Change Order A written document signed by the owner and the contractor authorizing a change in the work or an adjustment in the contract sum or the contract time. (The contract sum and/or the contract time are changed only by Change Order.) A Change Order may be in the form of additional compensation or time or less compensation or time, known as a deduction (from the contract amount) (see Field instructions).

Change Order Request A written document issued by the owner, architect, or owner's representative, requesting an adjustment to the contract sum or an extension of the contract time.

Changed conditions Conditions or circumstances, physical or otherwise, that surface after a contract has been signed and alter the circumstances or conditions on which the contract is based (i.e., concealed conditions or latent conditions).

Claim A formal notice sent by a contractor to an owner asserting that the terms of the contract have been breached and compensation is being sought by the contractor from the owner.

Clerk-of-the-work An individual employed by an owner to represent him on a project at the site of the work. The clerk-of-the-work's abilities, credentials, and responsibilities vary at the discretion of the owner.

Client Person or organization who hires the design professionals and the contractors to build a project; most often the owner, but also can be the user or occupant of the finished facility.

Closed bid A bid in which only invited bidders or estimators are given access to the prescribed project information; usually the owner provides a designed list of invitees.

CM Abbreviation for construction management or construction manager (a firm that provides CM services or persons who work for a CM firm).

CM partnering A contractual commitment by the owner, A/E, and CM to achieve a common goal without a stakeholder's exposure to a potential for conflict of interest in pursuit of that goal.

CM services The scope of services provided by a construction manager and available to owners in whole or in part. (CM services are not consistent in scope or performance from one CM firm to another, nor with the those of the design professional.)

Code enforcement officer Local official authorized to administer building code; responsible for approval or denial of building permits, code inspections, and issuance of certificates of occupancy; in a given jurisdiction, may be one person or a department of several people, including field inspectors.

Commissioning The process at or near completion when a facility is put into use to see if it functions as designed; usually applied to manufacturing-type projects, and similar to beneficial occupancy in the commercial sector.

Completion schedule A schedule of the activities and events required to effect occupancy or the use of a facility for its intended purpose; used to determine if construction progress will meet the occupancy date.

Conditions of the Contract The General Conditions and the Supplementary and Special Conditions of the contract for construction.

Construct To assemble and combine construction materials and methods to make a structure.

Constructibility The optimizing of cost, time, and quality factors with the material, equipment, construction means, methods, and techniques used on a project; accomplished by matching owner values with available construction industry practices.

Construction budget The target cost figure covering the construction phase of a project, including the cost of contracts with trade contractors: construction support items; other purchased labor, material and equipment; and the construction manager's cost—but not the cost of land, A/E fees, or consultants' fees.

Construction Contract A legal document that specifies the what, when, where, how, how much, and by whom in a construction project.

Construction coordination The positive orchestration, cooperation, inner working, or interfacing of performing contractors on-site.

Construction cost (1) The direct contractor costs for labor, material, equipment, and services; contractor's overhead and profit; and other direct construction costs attributable to the project. (Construction cost does not include the compensation paid to the architect, engineer, and consultants, the cost of the land or rights-of-way, or other costs which are defined in the contract documents as being the responsibility of the owner.)

Construction document review The owner's review of the borrower's construction documents (plans and specifications), list of materials, and cost breakdowns for the purpose of confirming that these documents and estimates are feasible and are in accordance with the proposed loan or project appraisal; there is also a review by the building code agency to ascertain code compliance.

Construction documents Complete array of all drawings, specifications, addenda, change orders, field instructions, bulletins, and directives associated with a specific construction project. These documents delineate and graphically represent the physical construction requirements established by the A/E (see Contract documents).

Construction inspector A qualified individual authorized by the owner to assist in the inspection of the construction project to ensure compliance with the contract documents and/or a specific construction contract.

Construction management (CM) A project delivery system that uses a construction manager to facilitate the design and construction of a project by organizing and directing men, materials, and equipment to accomplish the purpose of the designer. A professional service or party concerned with organizing and directing personnel, constructibility, pricing, alternative construction methods, etc.; service that applies effective management techniques to the planning, design, and construction of a project from inception to completion for the purpose of controlling time, cost, and quality, as defined by the Construction Management Association of America (CMAA).

Construction Management Contract A written agreement wherein responsibilities for coordination and accomplishment of overall project planning, design, and construction are given to a construction management firm.

Construction manager (CM) Experienced person or firm hired by an owner/client to provide added construction insight, and oversight over design, scheduling, construction methods, and actual construction; can have either a contracting or design professional background.

Construction phase The fifth and final phase of the architect's basic services, which includes the architect's general administration (G&A) of the construction contract.

Construction schedule A graphic, tabular, or narrative representation or depiction of the construction portion of the project-delivery process, showing activities and duration in sequential order.

Construction support items Purchases, services, or materials required to facilitate construction at the site. (As part of the construction budget, these are financial obligations of the owner and the logistic responsibility of the CM.)

Construction team The designated responsible project management of each trade contractor, plus the level 2 and level 3 managers of the owner, A/E, and CM (i.e., the project team).

Constructor-XCM A variation of the extended services form of CM, in which the construction manager self-performs some of the construction on the project.

Consultant Professional firm and/or individual hired by the owner or client to provide narrow-scope professional advice, information, designs, and other allied services.

Contingencies Line-item amounts in the project budget, dedicated to specific cost areas where oversight is an inherent problem in project delivery.

Contract (1) An agreement between two or more parties, especially one that is written and enforceable by law; (2) the writing or document containing such an agreement.

Contract administration The contractual duties and responsibilities of the A/E, contractor, or CM during the construction phase of a specific project, for generally overseeing the actual construction and servicing the interactive provisions in the contract for construction.

Contract bond A written form of security from a surety company on behalf of an acceptable prime or main contractor or subcontractor, guaranteeing complete execution of the contract and all supplemental agreements pertaining thereto and guaranteeing the payment of all legal debts pertaining to the construction of the project.

Contract date Usually on the front page of the agreement; may also be the date opposite the signatures when the agreement was actually signed, or the date when it was recorded, or the date when the agreement was actually awarded to the contractor. Also known as date of the agreement.

Contract document phase The third phase of the architect's basic services, in which the architect prepares working drawings, specifications, and bidding information; phase of design for an architectural project in which documents for construction are completed and bidding documents formulated.

Contract document review A review of bid and/or contract documents on a continuing basis or at short intervals during the preconstruction phase, to preclude errors, ambiguities, and omissions.

Contract documents All executed agreements between the owner and contractor which collectively form the contract between the contractor and the owner: any general, supplementary, or other contract conditions; the drawings and specifications; all bidding documents less bidding information; preaward addenda issued prior to execution of the contract; postaward Change Orders; and any other items specifically stipulated as being included in the contract documents.

Contract overrun   A cost deficit after determining the difference between the original contract price and the final completed cost, including all adjustments by approved Change Order.

Contract payment bond   A written form of security from a surety company to the owner, on behalf of an acceptable prime or main contractor or subcontractor, guaranteeing payment to all persons providing labor, materials, equipment, or services in accordance with the contract.

Contract performance bond   A written form of security from a surety company to the owner, on behalf of an acceptable prime or main contractor or subcontractor, guaranteeing the completion of the work in accordance with the terms of the contract.

Contract sum   The total agreeable amount payable by the owner to the contractor for the performance of the work under the contract documents; total cost of the project; may be adjusted by a Change Order.

Contract time   Period of time set out in the contract for completion of the project; usually stated in working days or calendar days; may be adjusted via Change Order.

Contract underrun   The cost savings after determining the difference between the original contract price and the final completed cost, including all adjustments by approved Change Order.

Contractibility   The optimizing of cost, time, and quality factors with the contracting structures and techniques used on a project; accomplished by matching owner contracting requirements with available construction industry practices.

Contracting officer   An official representative of the owner with specific authority to act in his behalf in connection with a specific project.

Contractor   A properly licensed individual or company that contracts to perform a defined scope of work on a construction project and agrees to furnish labor, materials, equipment, and associated services to perform the work as specified for a specified price (various types of contractors include general, remodeling, and subcontractor).

Contractor's option   A written provision in the contract documents giving the contractor the option of selecting certain specified materials, methods, or systems without changing the contract sum.

Contractor's qualification statement   A written statement of the contractor's experience and qualifications submitted to the owner during the contractor selection process. (The American Institute of Architects publishes a standard contractor's qualification statement form for this purpose.)

Contractual liability   The liability assumed by a party under a contract.

Control CM   A person designated by the CM firm to interface with the owner's and A/E's representatives on the project team at the second management level.

Coordination meeting   Meeting held in the field to review project status and coordinate scheduled activities.

Coordinator   A person designated to assist a control CM, project manager, or level 2 manager in executing the CM format.

Cost breakdown   (1) A breakdown of all the anticipated costs on a construction or renovation project; (2) a financial statement furnished by the contractor to the architect or engineer delineating the portions of the contract sum allotted for the various parts of the work, used as the basis for reviewing the contractor's applications for progress payments.

Cost codes   A numbering system given to specific kinds of work for the purpose of organizing the cost control process of a specific project.

Cost control/management   Deliberations, actions, and reactions to project cost fluctuations during a project to maintain the project cost within the project budget.

Cost of construction   The target cost figure covering the construction phase of a project, which includes the cost of contracts with trade contractors; construction support items; other purchased labor, material, and equipment; and the construction manager's cost—but not the cost of land, A/E fees, or consultant fees.

Cost of work   All costs incurred by the contractor in the proper performance of the work required by the plans and specifications for a specific project.

Cost plus contract   A form of contract usually between an owner and contractor, A/E, design professional, or CM, under which the contractor, A/E or CM is reimbursed for his/her direct and indirect costs and, in addition, is paid a fee for his/her services. The fee is usually stated as a stipulated sum or as a percentage of cost.

Covenants   Rules usually developed by a builder or developer regarding the physical appearance of buildings in a particular geographic area. Typical covenants address building height, appropriate fencing and landscaping, and the type of exterior material (stucco, brick, stone, siding, etc.) that may be used.

Critical date schedule   A schedule of milestones from the start of construction to occupancy, used as the main measure of progress to keep the project on schedule.

Critical path   The continuous chain of activities from project start to project finish, whose durations cannot be exceeded if the project is to be completed on the project-finish date; a sequence of activities that collectively require the longest duration to complete (the duration of the sequence is the shortest possible time from the start event to the finish event). Activities on the critical path have no slack time.

Critical path method (CPM)   A planning, scheduling, and control line-and-symbol diagram drawn to show the respective tasks and activities involved in constructing a specific project.

Critical path schedule   A schedule that utilizes the critical path scheduling technique, using either the arrow or precedence diagramming method.

CSI master format   A uniform system of numbers and titles for organizing construction information into a regular, standard order or sequence; promotes standardization and thereby facilitates the retrieval of information and improves construction communication.

Daily Construction Report   A written document and record that has two main purposes: (1) to furnish information to off-site persons who need and have a right to know important details of events as they occur daily and hourly; and (2) to furnish historical documentation that might later have a legal bearing in cases of disputes. (Daily reports should be factual and impersonal. Each report should be numbered.)

Date of commencement of the work   The date established in a written notice to proceed, from the owner to the contractor.

Date of substantial completion   The date certified by the architect when the work or a designated portion thereof is sufficiently complete, in accordance with the contract documents, so the owner may occupy the work or designated portion thereof for the use for which it is intended.

Design   (1) The overall concept and configuration of a project developed to meet stated needs, desires, and goals of the client; drawn showing the plans, elevations, sections, details, and other features necessary for the construction of a new structure (as used by the architect, the term "plan" denotes a horizontal projection; "elevation" applies to vertical exterior views; (2) a graphical representation consisting of plan views, interior and exterior elevations, sections, and other drawings and details to depict the goal or purpose for a building or other structure.

Designability   A pragmatic, value-based assessment of the design in comparison with the stated physical and aesthetic needs of the owner.

Design/bid/build   Traditional and currently the most widely used project delivery system; owner has separate contracts with a design organization and with a contracting organization.

Design/build   A project delivery system whereby a single entity is responsible for both design and construction of the project (owners like the single point of responsibility).

Design development phase   The term used on architectural projects to describe the transitional phase from the schematic phase to the contract document during design; the second phase of the architect's basic services wherein the architect prepares drawings and other presentation documents to fix and describe the size and character of the entire project as to architectural, structural, mechanical and electrical systems, materials and other essentials as may be appropriate, and prepares a statement of probable construction cost.

Design-development phase—design-XCM   A variation of the extended services form of CM, in which the A/E also provides the CM function.

Design professional   Term applied to one responsible for creation of a design scheme or concept for a portion of a building project; in particular, a properly registered architect or engineer.

Detail   (1) An individual part or item; (2) a graphical scale representation, e.g., a drawing at a larger scale, of construction parts or items showing materials, composition, and dimensions in a limited area of the project construction; type of sectional drawing showing special, in-depth information about a particular portion of the construction; usually drawn at larger scale than other views to show all construction required.

Detailed construction schedule   A graphic, tabular, or narrative representation or depiction of the construction portion of the project-delivery process, showing individual activities and durations or activities in sequential order at the lowest level of detail (level 3 schedule).

Direct costs   The costs directly attributed to a work scope, such as labor, material, equipment, and subcontracts, but not the cost of operations overhead and the labor, material, equipment, and subcontracts expended in support of the undertaking. Direct costs, hard costs, and construction costs are synonymous.

Drawing detail   A drawing done at a large scale, which shows a limited area of work—the fit of a door frame jamb into the adjacent wall, for example; numerous views that provide increased amounts of information, relationships and construction items that cannot be easily shown on other types of drawings.

Drawings   (1) The portion of the contract documents that graphically illustrates the design, location, geometry, and dimensions of the components and elements contained in a specific project in sufficient detail to facilitate construction; (2) (sing.) a line drawing.

Dual services   The providing of more than one principal service under a single contract or multiple contracts.

Easement   Designated and legally documented area of property where a right or privilege is granted by the property owner to another party, entitling the user to a specific, exclusive, but limited use of the property noted (for example, running of a utility line).

Elevation   (1) A side of a building; (2) building drawing that shows vertical dimensions; (3) also the height of a point in reference to sea level; sometimes called "grade elevation."

Engineer   Person trained and registered (by the state) to professionally engage in work in one of the areas of the engineering disciplines; e.g., civil, structural, electrical, mechanical (HVAC, plumbing); also referred to as a "design professional." (Many types of engineers are not construction-related.)

Erect   To raise or construct a building frame; generally applied to prefabricated materials, such as structural steel, as they are installed on the job site.

Erector   The subcontractor who raises, connects, and accurately sets (plumb and level) a building frame from fabricated steel or precast concrete members.

Estimate of construction cost   A calculation of costs prepared on the basis of a detailed analysis of materials and labor for all items of work, as contrasted with an estimate based on current area, volume, or similar unit costs.

Estimated cost to complete   An estimate of the cost still to be expended on a work scope in order to complete it. The difference between the cost to date and the estimated final cost.

Estimated final cost   An estimate of the final cost of a work item based on its cost to date and the estimated cost to complete it (sum of the cost to date and the estimated cost to complete).

Estimating   A process of compiling and calculating the amount of material, labor, and equipment required for a given project and the overall cost and/or time necessary to complete the work as specified.

Ethics   Principles, rules, or standards of performance for professionals set by the organization or association to which the professional belongs or is associated by the public trust; guidelines for performance of professional services and duties.

Extras   Common term for additional work requested of a contractor that was not included in the original contract; billed separately; may or may not impact time of completion of project.

Fabricator   Company that prepares, fashions, or adapts standard materials or members (such as structural steel) for erection and installation to specific project conditions by cutting, fitting, punching, coping, and otherwise making them ready for specific installations.

Fast-track construction   The process of designing portions of a project while portions already designed are under construction. A method of project management that involves a continuous design-construction operation, where project work is carried on while drawings are being finished; as drawings are finalized they are incrementally released for construction (construction lags drawing production); overall program reduces total time for design/construction sequence.

Feasibility phase   The conceptual phase of a project preceding the design phase, used to determine from various perspectives whether a project should be constructed or not.

Fee enhancement   The awarding of an additional fee over and above the basic fee for services, based on the performance quality of the party providing the basic service.

Field construction manager   A person designated by the CM firm to interface with the owner's and A/E's representatives on the project team at the third management level. A person located at the site and charged to administer the procedures established by the team's level 2 manager for the construction of the project.

Field instruction (FI)   Formal, written instructions from design professional for changes in the work/project that do not impact project cost or time for completion (compare with Change Order).

Field management   The coordination and management of owner-contracted resources on-site during construction.

Field measure   Taking actual dimensions and sizes during the construction work to ensure correct spacing or sizing.

Field Order (FO)   A written order issued to a contractor by the owner, or owner's representative (i.e., A/E design professional), effecting a minor change or clarification with instructions to perform work not included in the contract for construction. The work will eventually become a Change Order. A Field Order is an expedient process used in an emergency or situation that in many cases does not involve an adjustment to the contract sum or an extension of the contract time.

Field Report   A written document and record that has two main purposes: (1) to furnish information to off-site persons who need and have a right to know important details of events as they occur daily and hourly; and (2) to furnish historical documentation that might later have a legal bearing in cases of disputes. (Reports should be factual and impersonal, numbered to correspond with the working days, stating "no work today" due to rain, strike, or other causes.)

Field schedule A graphic, tabular, or narrative representation or depiction of the construction portion of the project-delivery process, showing field activities and durations in sequential order. A short-interval, field-based schedule that plans contractor and subcontractor activities on a month-to-month, week-to-week, or day-to-day basis from the project milestone schedule.

Field Work Order (FWO) A written request to a subcontractor or vendor, usually from the general or main contractor, for services or materials.

Field-based CM field organization A project organization structure that bases the CM's second-level representative and certain resource persons in the field rather than in the office.

Final acceptance The action of the owner accepting the work from the contractor, when the owner deems the work completed in accordance with the contract requirements. Final acceptance is confirmed by the owner when making the final payment to the contractor.

Final completion The point at which both parties to a contract declare the other has satisfactorily completed its responsibilities under the contract.

Final design phase The designation used by design professionals for the last portion of the design process prior to the full production of contract (working) documents; the phase that produces the design concept, approved by the client/owner.

Final inspection A final site review of the project by the contractor, owner, or owner's authorized representative prior to issuing the certificate for Substantial Completion.

Final payment The last payment from the owner to the contractor of the entire unpaid balance of the contract sum as adjusted by any approved Change Orders.

Financial and management control system A manual or computerized management control system used by the project team to guide the course of a project and record its status and progress.

Financial stakeholder A party involved by contract to perform a prescribed, definitive physical work-scope for a sum of money, who stands to lose or gain money from the eventual outcome of the project or how it is performed.

Finish Date The date that an activity or project is completed.

Finished (1) Completed; all required work finalized, in-place, with nothing else required; (2) material or equipment to which a material has been applied as a final decoration or protection (for example, a coat of paint, resilient flooring).

Fixed fee   A set contract amount for all labor, materials, equipment, services, and contractor's overhead, and profit for all work being performed for a specific scope of work.

Fixed limit of construction costs   A construction cost ceiling agreed to between the owner and architect/engineer for designing a specific project.

Fleet averaging   Using a point system to show compliance with energy building requirements by using average figures for all air-conditioning units in the same subdivision.

Float   A scheduling term indicating that an activity or a sequence of activities does not necessarily have to start or end on the scheduled date to maintain the schedule on the critical path; the difference between the early start and late finish of an activity, minus the activity's duration. Also referred to as slack time.

Floor plan   Horizontal sectional view, cut through a proposed building/structure at approximately 4 feet above floor line, showing the basic layout of building or addition, including placement of walls, windows, and doors, as well as dimensions; includes all features, layout, configuration, and details of the design and construction; most important source of information for other contract documents.

Furnish   To supply, and deliver to the job site, ready for unloading, unpacking, assembly, installation, and similar operations (see Install, and Provide).

General Condition items   Purchases, services, or materials required to facilitate construction at the site. As part of the construction budget, these are financial obligations of the owner and the logistic responsibility of the CM.

General Conditions of the Contract for Construction   Commonly called "General Conditions." The written portion of the contract that prescribes the rights, responsibilities, and relationships of the various parties signing the agreement and outlines the administration of the contract for construction (e.g., American Institute of Architects (AIA) Document A201); also sets general operating procedures and definitions related to project. General conditions are usually included in the book of specifications but are sometimes found in the architectural drawings.

General contracting   The traditional contracting method, in which a prime or main contractor bids the entire work after the final design, plans, and specifications are complete and have been approved by the owner; single overall "general" contractor performs some work using own forces, while hiring subcontractors to perform other special portions of work; single contractor responsible for coordinating the whole project.

General contracting system The traditional project-delivery system that utilizes the services of a general contractor; the GC assembles and submits a proposal for the work on a project and then contracts directly with the owner to construct the project as an independent contractor.

General contractor (GC) A contractor responsible for all facets of construction of a building or renovation; properly licensed individual or company having primary responsibility for the work. The general contractor contracts to build a building or a part of it for another party, and hires, oversees, and coordinates other contractors called subcontractors, who perform specific specialized work on projects. Also called "prime contractor."

Guarantee An agreement by which a party accepts responsibility for fulfilling an obligation.

Guaranteed maximum price construction management (GMP-CM) A form of the CM system where the construction manager, in addition to providing ACM services, guarantees a ceiling price to the owner for the cost of construction.

Hard costs All items of expense directly incurred by or attributable to a specific project, assignment, or task. Direct costs, hard costs, and construction costs are synonymous.

Hazard insurance Insurance for a building while it is under construction.

Improvements Alterations and additions to property that tend to increase value; buildings, utilities, streets, etc., in wood, glass, masonry, plaster, drywall, tile, brick, concrete, metal and other materials, and various types and configurations of construction; can be in the form of new construction or remodel work.

Indemnification clause Provision in a contract in which one party agrees to be financially responsible for specified types of damages, claims, or losses.

Independent contractor One free from the influence, guidance, or control of another, who does not owe a fiduciary duty (e.g., an architect, engineer, prime or main contractor, construction manager at-risk).

Indicated Graphic representations, notes, or schedules on the drawings, or paragraphs and schedules in the specifications; used to help locate references and information. Similar to "shown," "noted," "scheduled," and "specified."

Indirect costs Costs for items and activities other than those directly incorporated into the building or structure but necessary to complete the project. A contractor's or consultant's overhead expense; expenses indirectly incurred and not chargeable to a specific project or task. The terms "indirect costs" and "soft costs" are synonymous.

In-house resources   Resources physical, monetary, or human, available within an organization for providing contracted services.

Inspection   (1) The act of inspecting (viewing, observing, or monitoring in a critical manner); (2) an official examination or review of the work completed or in progress to determine its compliance with contract requirements.

Inspection list   A list prepared by the owner or his/her authorized representative of items of work requiring immediate corrective or completion action by the contractor (also called an inspection report).

Install   On-site operations of unloading, unpacking, assembling, erection, placing, locating, anchoring, applying, working to dimension, connecting, testing, finishing, curing, protecting, cleaning, and similar activities for proper and complete use/operation of area, equipment, appliance, surface, or item.

Job description   A broad-scope explanation of a position's requirements, indicating the duties for the position and the expertise and capabilities required of a person to adequately perform in that position.

Joint venture   Temporary arrangement of firms of similar disciplines, combining work forces to provide greater financial strength, improved services or more acceptable performance qualifications as a combined organization to design and/or construct a specific project.

Labor and material payment bond   A written form of security from a surety (bonding) company to the owner, on behalf of an acceptable prime or main contractor or subcontractor, (1) guaranteeing payment to the owner in the event the contractor fails to pay for all labor, materials, equipment, or services in accordance with the contract; and (2) guaranteeing payment of any claims against the owner from contractors and suppliers who have not been paid for labor, material, and equipment incorporated into the project.

Letter of intent   A notice from an owner to a contractor stating that a contract will be awarded to the contractor providing certain events occur or specific conditions are met by the contractor. The letter will usually serve a formal notice to proceed on the project.

Lien, mechanic's or material   The right to take and hold or sell an owner's property to satisfy unpaid debts to a qualified contractor for labor, materials, equipment, or services to improve the property.

Lien release   A written document from the contractor to the owner that releases a lien following its satisfaction.

Lien waiver   A written document from a contractor, subcontractor, material supplier, or other construction professional having lien rights against an owner's property, relinquishing all or part of those rights.

Life-cycle cost   The cost of purchasing, installing, owning, operating, and maintaining a construction element over the life of the facility.

"Like new"   Term applied to remedial work of modification or repair of existing work; replacement not required but care is required to make condition as noted.

Liquidated damages   A monetary amount agreed upon by two parties to a contract prior to performance under the contract, specifying what either party owes the other if that party defaults under the contract.

Load   Weight imposed on buildings and structures by various elements, both natural and man-made; weight that must be properly and adequately supported by the building frame to prevent collapse or other failure.

Long-lead items   Material and equipment required for construction that have delivery dates too far in the future to be included in a contractor's contract at bid time. They are usually prepurchased directly by the owner to fit their delivery into the project schedule in a timely manner.

Lot   A parcel of land with boundaries determined by the county or other local jurisdiction; part of the metes and bounds and other land-identification systems.

Lump sum agreement   A written agreement in which a specific amount is set forth as the total payment for completing the contract.

Lump sum bid   A single entry amount to cover all labor, equipment, materials, services, and overhead and profit for completing the construction of a variety of unspecified items of work without the benefit of a cost breakdown.

Management information and control system   A manual or computerized system used by the project team to guide the course of a project and record its status and progress.

Manufacturer's instructions   The written installation and/or maintenance instructions developed by the manufacturer of a product, which provide useful information about a product, its handling, and its installation; very important for proper use and installation and may have to be followed in order to maintain the product warranty; often used to supplement and substitute for extensive specifications text.

Master schedule   A schedule that spans from the start of design to occupancy; includes the signal activities that control the progress of the project from start to finish; level 1 schedule.

Meeting attendance form   A form consisting of three columns (individual's name, individual's title, and company the individual represents). Each person attending the meeting fills in his or her respective information. The date of the meeting should be included for reference.

Meeting notes   A written report consisting of a project number, project name, meeting date and time, meeting place, meeting subject, list of persons attending, and list of actions taken and/or discussed during the meeting; generally distributed to all persons attending the meeting and any other person having an interest in the meeting.

Milestone schedule   A schedule of milestones spanning from the start of construction to occupancy, used as the main measure of progress to keep the project on schedule.

Millwork   General term for interior woodwork and trim, made of finished wood machined to profile, size, and finish; manufactured in millwork plants and planing mills; includes such items as inside and outside doors, window and door frames, blinds, porch work, mantels, paneling, stairways, moldings, and interior trim.

Multiple bidding   Soliciting and receiving bids from trade or work-scope contractors when using a multiple contracting format.

Multiple contracting   A contracting format that separates the project's single work scope into a number of interfacing smaller work scopes, to be individually and competitively bid or negotiated.

New   Unused condition, fresh from manufacture, production, or fabrication (unless specifically noted otherwise) of all materials, devices, equipment, units and systems for a project; this meets owner's expectations and payment is based on this principle.

Nonconforming   Most often a zoning consideration where a building, use, occupancy, or improvement is dissimilar to surrounding properties in age, size, use, or style, and does not meet current zoning requirements; a land use or building that existed prior to enactment of current regulations and does not now comply. (For example, a small retail store in an area now zoned for single-family housing.)

Notice of Award   A letter from an owner to a contractor stating that a contract has been awarded to the contractor and a contract will be forthcoming, which usually functions as a Notice to Proceed.

Notice to Proceed   A notice from an owner directing a contractor to begin work on a contract, subject to specific stated conditions.

Occupancy phase   A stipulated length of time following the construction phase, during which contractors are bonded to ensure that materials, equipment, and workmanship meet the requirements of their contracts, and that supplier- and manufacturer-provided warranties and guarantees remain in force.

Occupancy schedule   A schedule of the activities and events required to effect occupancy or the use of a facility for its intended purpose. It is used to determine if construction progress will meet the occupancy date.

On-site supervision Site-based personnel with supervisory responsibilities.

Open bid A bid in which any qualified bidder or estimator is given access to the prescribed project information; project information is not private.

Owner An individual, association, firm, organization, corporation, or other entity that owns real property, needs the project, and will pay for it (also called "client") is party to both design and construction contracts.

Owner-architect agreement A written form of contract between architect and client for professional architectural services.

Owner-builder An owner who takes on the responsibilities of the general contractor to build a specific project.

Owner-CM agreement Contract between construction manager and client for professional services.

Owner-construction agreement Contract between owner and contractor for a construction project.

Performance and payment bond Guarantee by a surety company that if a contractor fails to perform under a contract, the surety company will complete the work.

Performance bond Usually a written form of security from a surety (bonding) company to the owner, on behalf of an acceptable prime or main contractor or subcontractor, guaranteeing payment to the owner in the event the contractor fails to supply all labor, materials, equipment, or services in accordance with the contract.

Performance specifications The written material containing the minimum acceptable standards and actions necessary to complete a project, including the minimum acceptable quality standards and aesthetic values expected upon completion of the project.

Permit A governmental/municipal authorization to perform a building process.

PERT An abbreviation for Program Evaluating and Review Technique.

PERT schedule A diagram that illustrates, charts, and reports a project's estimated start and completion times, and work in progress.

Phased construction A unitized approach to constructing a facility by designing and constructing separate project elements; each element is a complete project in itself.

Phased or stage bidding The process of receiving proposals from contractors on projects that are constructed as more than one total work scope.

Plan A line drawing (by floor), representing the horizontal geometrical section of the walls of a building. The section (a horizontal plane) is taken at an elevation to include the relative positions of the walls, partitions, windows, doors, chimneys, columns, pilasters, etc. A plan can be thought of as cutting a horizontal section through a building at an eye-level elevation.

Plan reviewer (checker)   A building department official who examines the building permit documents to assess compliance.

Plan submittal   Submission of construction plans to the city or county in order to obtain a building permit.

Plans   A set of all drawings including sections, details, and any supplemental drawings for complete execution of a specific project, showing the location, geometry, and dimensions of a project or its elements in sufficient detail to facilitate construction.

Plat   Drawing of a parcel or parcels of land based on and giving its legal description and other survey data indicating the block numbers; the location, boundary lines, dimensions and number of each lot; and the location and names of existing and planned streets; may be filed as an official record of the land via map of a geographical area as recorded by the county.

Plot   Lot, parcel, or other piece of land (real estate) with specific dimensions; potential building/construction site.

Postbid shopping   Negotiations between prime contractors (buyers) and trade contractors (sellers) to obtain lower prices after signing a prime contract with an owner.

Prebid shopping   Negotiations between prime contractors (buyers) and trade contractors (sellers) to obtain lower prices prior to submitting prime contract proposals to owners.

Preconstruction meeting   Meeting convened to bring all parties to a project together to discuss mutual and project-related topics, prior to actual start of construction; valuable to creating a good project atmosphere and commonality of understanding on all aspects of the project.

Preconstruction phase   All required phases prior to the start of construction.

Preconstruction planning   A team-building process used for the purpose of establishing below-market-dollar budget, overall project scheduling, and design criteria; also identification and selection of the most feasible planning, design, and construction team.

Predecessor   An activity that must be completed before another activity can begin.

Predesign phase   The phase prior to the start of design where feasibility studies are done and conceptual project cost estimates are prepared.

Preliminary design phase   Applies to engineering projects; the initial design effort following signing of the owner-engineer agreement, followed by the final design phase.

Preliminary drawings   The drawings that precede the final approved drawings. Usually these drawings are stamped or titled "Preliminary" or "Preliminary/Not for Construction"; and the "Preliminary" is removed from the drawings after review and approval by the architect and/or owner.

Preliminary lien notice   A written notice given to the owner of a specific project by the subcontractors and any person or company furnishing services, equipment, or materials to that project. The notice states that if bills are not paid in full for the labor, services, equipment, or materials furnished or to be furnished, a mechanic's lien leading to the loss, through court foreclosure proceedings, of all or part of the property being so improved may be placed against the property, even though the owner has paid the prime contractor in full.

Prequalification   A screening process of prospective bidders in which the owner or his/her appointed representative gathers background information from a contractor or construction professional for selection purposes. Qualifying considerations include competence, integrity, dependability, responsiveness, bonding rate, bonding capacity, work on hand, similar project experience, and other specific owner requirements.

Prime contract   (1) A contract held by an owner; (2) a written contract directly between a prime or main contractor or subcontractor for work on a specific project.

Prime contractor   (1) Any contractor having a contract directly with the owner; (2) usually the main (general) contractor for a specific project.

Private sector   The domain where projects are funded with capital other than from taxes.

Product data   Detailed information provided by material and equipment suppliers demonstrating that the item provided meets the requirements of the contract documents.

Professional engineer   A professional firm and/or individual who is professionally trained and engaged in an engineering discipline.

Professional liability insurance   Insurance provided for design professionals and construction managers that protects the owner against the financial results and liability of negligent acts by the insured; usually referred to as errors and omissions (E&O) insurance.

Professional services   Services provided by a professional, in the legal sense of the word, or by an individual or firm whose competence can be measured against an established standard of care.

Professionalism   Considerate, courteous, ethical behavior when dealing or communicating with others on a construction project.

Program (1) Written list of needs, requirements, and regulatory obligations, set out by the owner (and the law) for a specific project; (2) an ordered list of events to take place or procedures to be followed for a specific project.

Program management Services provided to an owner who has more than one construction project, for the purposes of providing standardized technical and management expertise on all projects, as defined by the Construction Management Association of America (CMAA).

Program schedule A schedule that spans from the start of design to occupancy; includes the signal activities that control the progress of the project from start to finish.

Program team The project team, usually consisting of the owner, A/E design professional, and CM represented by their level 1, 2, and 3 persons.

Progress meeting A meeting dedicated to contractor progress during the construction phase.

Progress payment Partial payments on a contractor's contract amount, periodically paid by the owner for work accomplished by the contractor to date; determined by calculating the difference between the completed work and materials stored and a predetermined schedule of values or unit costs.

Progress schedule A line diagram showing proposed and actual starting and completion times for the respective project activities.

Project The overall scope of work being performed to complete a specific construction job.

Project budget The target cost of the project established by the owner and agreed to be achievable by the team; usually includes the cost of construction and the CM fee, plus any other line-item costs (land, legal fees, interest, design fees, CM fees, etc.) that the owner wishes to have included in the budget.

Project cost All costs for a specific project including costs for land, professionals, construction, furnishings, fixtures, equipment, financing, and any other project-related costs; costs expended on a project, which debit the line items that comprise the project budget.

Project delivery system A variety of contractual arrangements open to choice of owners, which create differing arrangements for the project team, set specific responsibilities, and form a general pattern for the conduct of the project.

Project directory A written list of all parties connected with a specific project, which usually includes a classification or description of the party (i.e., owner, architect, attorney, general contractor, civil engineer, structural engineer, etc.), with name, address, telephone, and fax numbers opposite their respective classifications or description. (It is particularly important that emergency or after-hour telephone numbers are included. These numbers should be kept confidential if requested by the respective parties.)

Project manager A qualified individual or firm authorized by the owner to be directly responsible for day-to-day management and administration, and for coordinating time, equipment, money, tasks, and people for all or specified portions of a specific project.

Project Manual An organized book setting forth the bidding requirements, conditions of the contract, and the technical work specifications for a specific project that documents and augments the drawings; it contains the General Conditions, Supplementary and Special Conditions, the Form of Contract, Addenda, Change Orders, Bidding Information and Proposal Forms as appropriate, and the Technical Specifications.

Project meeting A meeting dedicated essentially to contractor performance and progress payments, involving supervisors from contractor home offices and the team's level 2 and 3 managers.

Project representative A qualified person authorized by the owner and assigned to the project (part- or full-time) to assist in administration of contract(s) to protect the owner's interest; may be owner's employee or duly authorized employee of design professional or both.

Project site Specific tract of land, lot, or portion thereof that is dedicated to the project and its construction; the physical location where a structure or group of structures was or is to be located, i.e., a construction site.

Project team A team consisting of the architect/engineer, construction manager, and owner, represented by their level 1, 2, and 3 persons, plus the designated leaders of contracted constructors.

Proposal A written offer from a bidder to the owner, preferably on a prescribed proposal form, to perform the work and to furnish all labor, materials, equipment, and/or services for the prices and terms quoted by the bidder.

Proposal Form A standard written form furnished to all bidders for the purpose of obtaining the requested information and required signatures from the authorized bidding representatives.

Public sector The domain where owners fund projects with monies that come in whole or in part from taxes.

Punch List The document resulting from the process of inspecting and listing completed work, to determine where there is need for correcting deficiencies and making minor adjustments at the end of the job; prepared by the owner or his/her authorized representative of items of work requiring immediate corrective or completion action by the contractor.

Pure CM   A contractual form of the CM system exclusively performed in an agency relationship between the construction manager and owner (CM without risk). ACM is the form from which other CM forms and variations are derived.

Qualified   An individual or firm with a recognized credential, degree, certificate, or professional standing; or who by extensive knowledge, training, and experience has successfully demonstrated the ability to identify and solve or resolve problems associated with a specific subject matter or project type.

Quality   The value levels of material and equipment selected by the A/E. Conformance to the technical specifications during construction.

Quality assurance (QA)   The procedure established by the project team to inject and extract the level of quality designated by the owner.

Quality Control (QC)   That part of the quality assurance procedure that determines if specified quality is attained.

Quality Engineering   That part of the quality assurance procedure where the required level of quality is accurately inserted into the construction documents by the A/E.

Quotes   Foreshortened or slang term for quotations, which cite firm prices for work or material given by contractors and suppliers for labor and materials.

Record drawings   A set of contract document drawings, marked up as construction proceeds to reflect changes made during the construction process, showing the exact location, geometry, and dimensions of all elements of the constructed project as installed. (It is good practice to make as-built drawings by marking the changes on reproducible drawings such as mylar, vellum, or sepias for duplication purposes later.)

Reimbursable expense   Charges to the owner covering costs for services that could not or intentionally were not quantified at the time the fee arrangement was made.

Reimbursable expenses (or costs)   Amounts expended for or on account of the project which, in accordance with the terms of the appropriate agreement, are to be reimbursed by the owner.

Release of lien   A written action properly executed by an individual or firm supplying labor, materials, or professional services on a project that releases his mechanic's lien against the project property.

Resident architect   An architect permanently assigned at a job site who observes the construction work for the purpose of protecting the owner's interests during construction; also called project representative.

Resident engineer (RE) (inspector) An individual permanently assigned at a job site for the purpose of representing the owner's interests during the construction phase, i.e., owner's representative.

RFI (1) Abbreviation for "request for interpretation"; (2) a written request from a contractor to the owner or architect for clarification or information about the contract documents following contract award.

RFP Abbreviation for "Request for Proposal"; the second request for uniform detailed information from prospective CM practitioners being screened for a project.

Roll-out A loose term used to describe the rapid succession (completion) of similar projects over a given time period.

Safety Report A report prepared following a regularly scheduled safety inspection of the project. The Occupational Safety and Health Act (OSHA) of 1970 clearly states the common goal of safe and healthful working conditions.

Samples Limited-size physical pieces, examples or prototypes, and detailed information provided by material and equipment suppliers, demonstrating that the item provided meets the requirements of the contract documents.

Schedule (1) A time-related plan for performing work or achieving an objective; (2) written/graphic listing of various units of construction (doors, windows, toilet accessories, finish hardware, soil borings, room finishes, lintels, kitchen equipment, etc.); (3) activity to plan sequence of work, assignment of contractors, delivery of materials, etc., to meet stated completion date for project.

Schematic A preliminary sketch or diagram representing the proposed intent of the designer.

Schematic design phase The initial design phase on an architectural project; the first phase of the A/E design professional's basic services in which he/she consults with the owner to ascertain the requirements of the project, prepares schematic design studies consisting of drawings and other documents showing the scale and project components, and delineates the owner's needs in a general way for the owner's approval.

Scheme (1) A chart, diagram, or outline of a system being proposed; (2) an orderly combination of related construction systems and components for a specific project or purpose.

Scope of work (SOW) A written range of view or action; outlook; hence, room for the exercise of faculties or function; capacity for achievement; all in connection with a designated project.

Set (1) The change in concrete and mortar from a plastic (semiliquid) to a solid (hardened) state; (2) assemblage of drawings created and compiled to depict a complete construction project.

Setback A required minimum distance from the property line to the line/point where construction may begin; open area also called a "required yard," where no constructed features may occur; applied to each section of a property line; usually required by zoning regulations.

Shop drawings Drawings produced by manufacturers or fabricators that show exactly how items or equipment will be constructed to meet the requirements of the contract drawings; instructions to the "shop" for production of the item; used as submittals to the design professional as verification of how work will be accomplished.

Site The land area or real estate location where a structure or group of structures was or is to be placed, i.e., a construction, project, or job site.

Site-cast (cast-in-place) concrete Concrete placed and cured in its final position in a building.

Site conditions A term used to describe the attributes of a construction site, for example, level, sloping, rocky, wet, etc.

Site-constructed Built on the job or project location.

Site plan The drawing that shows the boundaries of the property, existing features (natural and man-made), the layout of the proposed building, its location, site utilities and other proposed improvements. Also called a site improvement or plot plan.

Site work The preparation of a site for building construction (clearing, grading, excavating, trenching, installing utility service lines).

Slab-on-grade (1) A concrete floor slab or surface lying upon, and supported directly by, the ground beneath; (2) a type of construction in which wall footings are needed but little or no foundation wall is poured, and the floor slab floats inside the foundation (not supported on the walls).

Soft costs Cost items in addition to the direct construction cost. Soft costs generally include architectural and engineering, legal, permits and fees, financing fees, construction interest and operating expenses, leasing and real estate commissions, advertising and promotion, and supervision.

Special Conditions (1) Amendments to the General Conditions that change standard requirements to unique requirements appropriate for a specific project; (2) a section of the conditions of the contract, other than the General Conditions and Supplementary Conditions, which may be prepared for a particular project; (3) specific clauses setting forth conditions or requirements peculiar to the project under consideration, and covering work or materials involved in the proposal and estimate, but not satisfactorily covered by the General Conditions.

Special consultants   Experts in highly specialized fields not inherent to an owner, A/E, or CM.

Specifications   A detailed, exact statement of particulars, especially statements prescribing the kinds and attributes of materials and methods, and quantitative and qualitative information pertaining to material, products, and equipment to be incorporated into a specific project. Detailed written instructions which, when clear and concise, explain each phase of work to be done, quality and level of workmanship required, and the general methods of installing and erecting the work; these serve to complement, explain, and augment graphic information of working drawings. The most common arrangement for specifications substantially parallels the Construction Specification Institute (CSI) format.

Standard details   A detail drawing or illustration sufficiently complete and detailed, and generic enough for reuse on other projects with minimum or no changes.

Standard dimension   A measurement unique to a specific manufactured item.

Standards of professional practice   A listing of minimum acceptable ethical principles and practices adopted by qualified and recognized professional organizations to guide their members in the conduct of specific professional practice.

Start-up   The period prior to owner occupancy when mechanical, electrical, and other systems are activated and the owner's operating and maintenance staff are instructed in their use.

Static decisions   Decisions that are made or can be made under the full influence of the project team's checks and balances.

Statute of limitations   The period of time in which legal action must be brought for an alleged damage or injury. The period commences with the discovery of the alleged damage or injury, or in construction industry cases, with completion of the work or services performed. Legal advice should be obtained.

Stipulated Sum Agreement   A written agreement in which a specific amount is set forth as the total payment for completing the contract.

Study and report phase   Principally applicable to engineering projects. Includes the investigation and determination of specific conditions and/or areas, activities, or phases of the project, and provides recommendations of design solutions to the owner's needs.

Subcontract   A written form of agreement between the prime or main contractor and another contractor or supplier for the satisfactory performance of services or delivery or material as set forth in the plans and specifications for a specific project (also known as Sub).

Subcontractor A qualified subordinate contractor (individual or firm) who has a contract with the prime or main contractor. The subcontractor usually specializes in and agrees to do certain specific trade or skilled work on a building. Tile work, waterproofing plumbing, heating, electrical work, and other limited portions of construction work are sublet and performed by subcontractors.

Subcontractor bond A written document from a subcontractor given to the prime or main contractor by the subcontractor guaranteeing performance of his/her contract and payment of all labor, materials, equipment, and service bills associated with the subcontract agreement.

Sublet To subcontract all or a portion of a contracted amount.

Submittal(s) Documents required, by project specifications, to be returned to the design professionals and contractors, by manufacturers, suppliers, and subcontractors, showing and explaining, in precise terms, how fabrication and preparation of materials and systems will be done for the specific project; includes shop drawings, product data, samples, certifications, etc. Professionals and contractors check and approve these documents when in accord with general design concept.

Substantial completion The stage in the progress of the work when the work, or designated portion of the work, is sufficiently complete in accordance with the contract documents so that the owner can occupy or utilize the work for its intended use.

Substantial completion date The date on which a contractor reaches a point of completion, when subsequent interfacing contractors can productively begin work or the owner can occupy the project, in whole or in part, without undue interference.

Substitution A proposed replacement or alternate offered in lieu of and represented as being equivalent to a specified material or process; must be fully equivalent to that specified.

Sub-subcontractor An individual or contractor who has a written contract with a subcontractor to perform a portion of the work, for example, a carpet-laying service hired by a carpet supplier.

Superintendent A job title usually reserved for the administrative-level person who supervises the work of an on-site contractor.

Supervision (1) The act, process, or function of supervising construction materials, methods, and processes for a specific project; (2) hands-on field direction of the contracted work by a qualified individual of the contractor.

Supplemental Conditions Supplements or modifies the standard clauses of the general conditions to accommodate specific project requirements (synonymous with Supplementary Conditions).

Surety company or **surety**   A properly licensed firm or corporation willing to execute a surety bond, or bonds, payable to the owner, securing the performance on a contract either in whole or in part, or securing payment for labor and materials.

Survey   (1) A procedure that examines and investigates the attributes of land areas; reviews legal descriptions, records, utility services, topography, physical features (natural and man-made), and overall state of the land area; (2) drawing produced to depict investigation of documents and field observations; made to scale, by a registered land surveyor, showing the lengths and directions of the boundary lines of the lot; the surrounding lots and streets; the position of the house and all exterior improvements such as walkways, driveways, decks, and porticos within the lot; and any existing encroachments.

T&M   (1) An abbreviation for a contracting method called time and materials; (2) a written agreement between the owner and the contractor wherein payment is based on the contractor's actual cost for labor, equipment, materials, and services plus a fixed add-on amount to cover the contractor's overhead and profit.

Take-off   Process of measuring and otherwise ascertaining quantities of various materials for estimating purposes; associated more with materials than with labor.

Team   The designated responsible project management of each trade contractor, plus the level 2 and level 3 managers of the owner, A/E, and CM (i.e., project team).

Technical inspection   Matching technical specification criteria with visual or mechanical tests on the project site or in a remote location or laboratory, to ascertain conformance.

Technical review   The critique of design solutions, or criteria used for design solutions, by a party other than the one providing the solutions or criteria, to determine adequacy and suitability of purpose.

Technical specifications   Written criteria augmenting the drawings pertaining to the technical construction of the project that cannot be conveniently included on the plans.

Tenant's rentable square feet   Usable square feet plus a percentage (the core factor) of the common areas on the floor, including hallways, bathrooms, telephone closets, and some main lobbies. Rentable square footage is the number on which a tenant's rent can be based.

Tenant's usable square feet   The square footage contained within the demising walls.

Tenure   The duration, term, or length of time required by agreement or precedent for performance of services.

Testing agency   An entity, separate from any of the contractual parties on a project, engaged to perform inspections, tests, and analysis either at the site, in a laboratory, or elsewhere; reports results to proper project party and interprets results if required; may function to meet specifications, or to investigate problems that arise. Building codes list some such agencies that are approved and acceptable due to impartiality, reliability, and past performance.

Tilt-up construction   A method of constructing walls and sometimes floors, by pouring concrete or putting wooden walls together in flat panels. When complete, they are moved to the building site where they are tilted into permanent place; units can also be site-built and then raised (tilted) into place.

"Time is of the essence."   A provision in a construction contract by the owner that punctual completion within the time limits or periods in the contract is a vital part of the contract performance and that failure to perform on time is a breach and the injured party is entitled to damages in the amount of loss sustained (e.g., "time is of the essence in the completion of the construction contract").

Time of completion   The date or number of calendar or working days stated in the contract to substantially complete the work for a specific project.

Timely completion   Completing the work of the contract before the date required.

TI's (tenant improvements)   The interior improvements of the project after the building envelope is complete. TI's usually include finish floor coverings; ceilings; partitions; doors, frames, and hardware; fire protection; HVAC consisting of branch distribution duct work, control boxes, and registers; electrical consisting of lighting, switches, power outlets, phone/data outlets, exit and energy lighting; window coverings; general conditions; and the general contractor's fee. The cost of tenant improvements is generally borne by the tenant; the costs of tenant improvements will vary with every building and with tenant requirements.

Trade contractor   A contractor specialized in providing/installing specific elements of the overall construction requirements of a project.

Transit   A surveyor's instrument used by builders to establish points and elevations both vertically and horizontally. It can be used to line up stakes or to plumb walls, or the angle of elevation from a horizontal plane can be measured.

Transmittal   A written document used to identify information being sent to a receiving party. The transmittal is usually the cover sheet for the information being sent and includes the name, telephone/fax number, and address of the sending and receiving parties. The sender may include a message or instructions in the transmittal. It is also important to include on the transmittal form the names of other parties the information is being sent to.

Travel time   Wages paid to workmen under certain union contracts and under certain job conditions for the time spent in traveling from their place of residence to and from the job.

Truss   Structural member formed with several smaller structural steel or wood members fastened together to make a lattice-like framework that will span long distances; utilizes principle of rigid triangular panels; designed to act as a beam of long span, while each member is usually subjected to longitudinal stress only, either tension or compression.

Uniform system   The CSI Master Format is a "uniform system" of numbers and titles for organizing construction information into a regular, standard order or sequence. By establishing a master list of titles and numbers, Master Format promotes standardization and thereby facilitates the retrieval of information and improves construction communication. It provides a uniform system for organizing information in project manuals, for organizing project cost data, and for filing product information and other technical data.

Unit price contract   A written contract wherein the owner agrees to pay the contractor a specified amount of money for each unit of work successfully completed as set forth in the contract.

Up-front services   Free or reduced-rate services provided to prospective clients in the interest of obtaining a contract. Often rationalized as part of a firm's selling or public relations program.

Value engineering   A technical review process; the close matching of engineering design to the value an owner derives from the design.

Value management   The matching of project decisions and directions with the expressed requirements of the owner, from an owner value-derived perspective.

Value manager   A person qualified to perform value management services for a client.

Vendor   Supplier who provides manufactured products or units; one that sells materials or equipment not fabricated to a special design.

Verbal quotation   A written document used by the contractor to receive a subcontract or material cost proposal over the telephone prior to the subcontractor or supplier sending their written proposal via mail or facsimile.

Warranty   Assurance by a providing party that the work, material, and equipment under warranty will perform as promised or as required by contract.

Warranty phase   The phase of a project in which a party accepts responsibility for fulfilling an obligation and warrants that the work under warranty meets its intended use for a specifically established timeframe.

Work   The total of tasks, construction, installation, etc., that must occur to build, finish, and produce the project anticipated and under contract; comprises the complete scheme of construction required by the contract documents including all labor, material, systems, tests, ratings, devices, apparatus, equipment, supplies, tools, adjustments, repairs, expendables, aids, temporary work and/or equipment, superintendence, inspection/approvals, plant, release, and permissions required to perform and complete the contract in an expeditious and orderly manner. The successful performance of the entire scope of the project.

Work[ing] day   Usually same as weekday [Monday through Friday]; excludes weekends and holidays; describes the number of hours when work is performed during each calendar day.

Working drawing   A drawing sufficiently complete with plan and section views, dimensions, details, and notes so that whatever is shown can be constructed and/or replicated without instructions but subject to clarifications.

Work letter   A written statement (often called Exhibit B to a lease or rental agreement) of the specific materials and quantities the owner will provide at his own expense. The work letter defines the building standards, including the type of ceiling, the type and number of light fixtures, the size and construction of the suite-entry and interior doors. Building standards define the quality of tenant spaces. Generally, a work letter is associated with the leasing or renting of office space by a tenant within a building envelope.

Work order (WO)   A written order, signed by the owner or his representative, of a contractual status requiring performance by the contractor without negotiation of any sort.

Work-scope description   A narrative description of the concise scope-of-work to be bid and performed by a specific contractor, subcontractor, etc.

XCM   An abbreviation for "extended services—CM"; a form of construction management (CM) where other services such as design, construction, and contracting are included, with additional construction management (ACM) services provided by the construction manager.

Yard   (1) Commonly, that area of a lot from the building to the property lines; (2) in zoning, redefined as that minimum prescribed distance and open area back from the property lines where building cannot occur (also called setbacks, or required yards).

Zoning   (1) Restrictions of areas or regions of land within specific geographical areas based on permitted building size, character, and uses as established by governing urban authorities; (2) local government regulations that control the use of land so adjacent uses are similar, compatible, and not intrusive upon each other; also regulate access, open areas, setbacks; intended to create a positive, unintrusive general atmosphere or environment in neighborhoods; prohibits nuisance and undesirable uses from locating in areas devoted to less objectionable uses; (3) creating separate sections of a building to be served by different systems or portions of system of mechanical services (for example, separate supply ducts carrying air-conditioned air to different areas of building).

Zoning certificate   Document issued by government zoning agency indicating acceptance or giving approval for proposed land use or project; used in association with (and usually in addition to) building permits.

INDEX

Accessories, installation of, 212–214
Accreditation of architecture schools, 135
ACM (agency CM), 252
Activity, 252
"Actual cost of the project" bidding, 167
Addenda, 157–158, 252
Additional services, 252
A/E, *see* Architect/Engineer
Agency CM (ACM), 252
Agents, 252
    CM as, 76, 145
    designers as, 18
    design professional as, 48
Agreement for Construction, *see* Construction Contract/Agreement
Air handling system, 205
Alarm systems, 183, 205
Allen, Edward, 172
Allowance, 252
Alterations, 253
Alternate bids, 253
Apparent low bidder, 253
Application for Payment, 253
Apprentices, 148, 253
Approved, defined, 253
Approved bidders list, 253
Approved changes, 253
Arbitration, 253
Architects, 35–36
    defined, 253
    hiring, 41–45
Architect/Engineer (A/E), 252, 253
Architectural design, defined, 253. *See also* Design
Architectural drawings, defined, 253–254. *See also* Drawings
Architectural practice, changes in, 5–8

Architecture:
    aspects of, 12–13
    defined, 2
    elements of, 3–4
    fundamental axiom defining, 10–12
    genesis of, 16–17
    paper, 2
    relationship of construction and, 1, 2
    rhetorical, 2
    utilitarian, 3
    variety of projects/styles in, 8–10
    virtual, 2–3
As-built drawings, 254
Assemblies, 254
Associates, 37
Attorneys:
    in contract award, 167–168
    in team selection, 41
Attorney-in-fact, 254
Award of contracts, 167–168

Back charge, 220, 254
Bankers, 33–34
Basis of Design, 215
Bearing wall systems, 187, 193
Beneficial occupancy, 254
Bids:
    "actual cost of the project," 167
    defined, 254
    "lowest and best bid," 166–167
    receipt of, 158–161
    review and analysis of, 166–167
    submittal of, 161–163
Bid bonds, 254
Bid depository, 254
Bidding:
    "actual cost of the project," 167
    assistance in, 156–158
    bid review and analysis, 166–167
    defined, 255

errors in, 167
    guidelines for, 158–161
    preparation for, 155–156
    process for, 163–166
    receipt of bids, 158–161
    submittal of bids, 161–163
Bidding documents, 124
Bidding period:
    construction team formulation during, 142
    defined, 255
Bidding requirements, 158
    defined, 255
    in Project Manual, 123–124
Bid division, 254
Bid division description, 254
Bid documents, 156, 158, 254–255
Bid forms, 162–163, 255
Bid opening, 255
Bid price, 49
Bid review and analysis, 157, 166–167
Bid shopper, 255
Bid shopping, 157, 255
Bid time, 255
Blind work, 84
Blueprints, *see* Drawings
BOCA (Building Officials and Code Administrators), 138
Bonds, 255
Bonding company, 255–256
Branch systems, connecting to mechanical equipment, 209–211
Bridge projects, 175
Budget estimate, 256
Buildability, 83, 256. *See also* Constructibility
Buildable area, 53, 60
Buildings:
    defined, 256
    as goal of design, xiii–xiv

Building codes, 138–139
  defined, 256
  International Building Code, 138
Building code officials, 256
Building envelope ("skin") systems,
      185–192
  cast-in-place or precast concrete,
    187, 192
  installation of, 199–204
  lightweight framing, 185, 188–189
  masonry, 185, 186
  structural framing with subsystem,
    187, 190–191
Building inspectors, 256
Building layout, 173–174
Building line, 256
Building Officials and Code
      Administrators (BOCA), 138
Building permits, 32, 256
Building process, 256
Building restriction (setback) lines,
    256–257. *See also* Setbacks
Building sections—cross and
    longitudinal, 96, 98–99
Building the Empire State (Carol
    Willis and Donald Friedman),
    25
Built-ins, installation of, 212–214
Bulletin, 257
Buy-in, by contractors, 4–5, 22

CAD drafting, 81
CAD operator/technician, 39, 81
Call-backs, 227, 229
Callouts, 257
Cast-in-place concrete:
  building envelope systems, 187, 192
  framing systems, 196–197
Caudill, William W., xiii–xiv
CCDs (Construction Change
    Directives), 129
Certificate of Need, 30
Certificate of Occupancy (CO),
    222–223, 257
Certificate of Substantial
    Completion, 218
Changed conditions, 257
Change Orders (COs), 129, 169–170,
    257
Change Order Request, 257
Cladding construction, *see* Building
    envelope ("skin") systems
Claims, 257
Clearing and grubbing process,
    172–173
Clerk-of-the-work, 154–155, 257

Clients, 32. *See also* Owners
  defined, 257
  in design effort, 11
  drawing information from, 67–68
  relationship with design
      professional, 46–50
Closed bid, 257
CM, *see* Construction management
CMs, *see* Construction managers
CM partnering, 257
CM services, 258
CO, *see* Certificate of Occupancy
COs, *see* Change Orders
Codes, building, 138–139
Code compliance, 138–140
  programming for, 68
  responsibility for, 139–140
Code enforcement officer, 258
Code-writing organizations, 248–249
Cofferdams, 176
Commissioning, 215–216, 258
Commissioning Plan, 216
Communications systems, 183, 205
Completion date, 221, 222
Completion schedule, 258
Concrete:
  building envelope systems, 187,
    192
  framing systems, 196–197
Conditions of the Contract, 258
Consideration, 130
Construct, defined, 258
Constructibility, 83–84, 258
Construction:
  blending of design, management,
    and, 17–19
  common goal of design and,
    xiv–xv
  defined, 1–2
  functional knowledge for, 12–13
  imperfection in, 115–116
  relationship of architecture and, 1,
    2
  as team activity, 14–16, 19–20
Construction budget, 258
Construction Change Directives
    (CCDs), 129
Construction Contract/Agreement,
    85, 258
Construction coordination, 258
Construction cost, 258
Construction document review,
    258–259
Construction (contract) documents,
    85–86, 124–125, 259
Construction inspector, 259

Construction management (CM), 59
  defined, 259
  forms of, 145
Construction Management Contract,
    259
Construction managers (CMs),
    145–147
  constructibility review by, 83–84
  defined, 259
  degree of involvement for, 146
  in design phase, 75–76
  input from, 49
  professionals demeaned/
    discredited by, 49, 50
Construction notes, 88
Construction phase, 171–214
  building "skin" installation,
    199–204
  connecting branch systems to
    mechanical equipment,
    209–211
  defined, 259
  earthwork, grading, excavation,
    180–181
  extension of utility lines and
    systems, 199
  finishes, installation/application
    of, 211–213
  initial on-site operations, 173–174
  initiation of material and systems
    purchases, 178–180
  installation of specialties, built-ins,
    furnishings, and accessories,
    212–214
  interior walls and partitions,
    206–209
  mechanical systems installation,
    204–207
  mobilization, 174–177
  on-site mobilization and staging,
    174–176
  project progress meetings,
    177–178
  project schedule, 178
  raw (undeveloped) site, 172–173
  renovations, mobilizing for,
    176–177
  roof and floor framing system
    installation, 197–199
  roof system installation, 204
  substructure (foundation) system
    installation, 182–186
  superstructure (structural system)
    erection, 185–197
  underground utilities installation,
    183

Construction (project) schedule, 171, 172, 178, 259
Construction Specifications Institute (CSI), 125, 137–138
Construction support items, 259
Construction team, 260
Construction Users Roundtable (CURT), 16
Constructors, 141–142. *See also* Contractors
  distrust between designers and, 18–19
  responsibilities of design professionals vs., 142
Consultants, 45–46, 260
Contingencies, 260
Contracts. *See also* Construction Contract/Agreement
  award of, 167–168
  defined, 130, 260
  function of and necessity for, 130–131
  standard forms for, 168
Contract administration, 260
Contract administrator, 40–41
Contract bond, 260
Contract date, 260
Contract documents, 124. *See also specific documents, e.g.:* Specifications
  Change Orders, as part of, 169–170
  defined, 260–261
  PDS effect on, 58
  production of, *see* Document production phase
  relationships among, 132–136
  review of, 139
Contract document phase, 260
Contract document review, 260
Contract drawings, *see* Working drawings
Contract for Construction, *see* Construction Contract/Agreement
Contract forms and conditions, in Project Manual, 123–124
Contractibility, 261
Contractibility manager, 38–39
Contracting officer, 261
Contract modifications, as contract documents, 124
Contractors, 141. *See also specific types of contractors*
  apprentices, 148
  buy-in of, 4–5, 22
  and code compliance, 140

completion dates for, 221, 222
construction managers, 145–147
constructors, 141–142
defined, 141, 261
distrust between designers and, 18–19
friction with design professionals, 49
general contractors, 141, 142
journeymen, 148
legal responsibilities of, 130–131
as part of construction team, 20
postoccupancy evaluations by, 230
in progression of project, 23
progress meetings for, 177–178
selection of, 166
sensitivity to owner's situation, 31
subcontractors, 142, 147
tradespersons, 147–155
workers, 147
Contractor's option, 261
Contractor's qualification statement, 261
Contract overruns, 261
Contract payment bonds, 261
Contract performance bonds, 261
Contract specifications, *see* Specifications
Contract sum, 261
Contract time, 220, 221, 261
Contractual liability, 262
Contract underruns, 261
Control CM, 262
Conversion of preliminary/conceptual design information, 84–85
Cooperative (co-op) students, 39, 148
Coordination meeting, 262
Coordinator, 262
Cost breakdown, 262
Cost codes, 262
Cost control/management, 262
Cost of construction, 262
Cost of work, 262
Cost plus contract, 262
Covenants, 262
CPM (critical path method), 263
Critical date schedule, 262
Critical path, 262–263
Critical path method (CPM), 263
Critical path schedule, 263
CSI MasterFormat, 263
CSI, *see* Construction Specifications Institute
CURT (Construction Users Roundtable), 16
Curtain-walls, 203

Daily Construction Report, 263
Damage, during move-in, 226
Dam projects, 175
Date of commencement of the work, 263
Date of substantial completion, 220, 263
D/B, *see* Design/build
D/B/B, *see* Design/bid/build
Demobilization, 216, 222
Demolition notes, 88
Design:
  blending of construction, management, and, 17–19
  buildings as goal of, xiii–xiv
  contractor's buy-in into, 4–5, 22
  defined, 263
  evolution of, 70, 71
  as one aspect of architecture, 12, 13
Designability, 263
Design approval, 76–77
Design/bid/build (D/B/B):
  contractor buy-in with, 22
  defined, 263
Design/build (D/B), 264
Design concept, 73
  approval of, 76
  conversion of, 84–85
  evolution of, 75
  expansion/detailing of, 80
  finished product vs., 111
Design development phase, 80–82, 264
Design-development phase—design-XCM, 264
Designers. *See also* Design professionals
  distrust between constructors and, 18–19
  use of term, 38
Design phase, 70–80
  design development, 80–82
  project design, 70–73
  revisions, changes, and additions, 75–76
  schematic design development, 73–77
  subsurface investigation, 77–80
Design professionals:
  compliance responsibilities of, 140
  defined, 264
  hiring, 41–45
  as part of construction team, 19, 20
  postcompletion evaluations by, 230–236

Design professionals (*cont'd*)
  in progression of project, 23
  qualifications of, 35
  relationship with owner, 46–50
  responsibilities of constructors vs.,
      142
  selection of, 35, 41–45
  sensitivity to owner's situation, 31
Design team, 45–46
Details:
  defined, 112, 264
  and finished construction, 115–116
  and long-term product, 114–116
  wall, 100–101
  Frank Lloyd Wright's attention to,
      117
Detailed construction schedule,
      264
Detailing, 111–121
  attitudes toward, 113–114
  college course in, 119
  defined, 112
  flawed, 117, 118
  and legal liability, 120–121
  perspective for process of, 119–120
  and quality of product, 114–116
  value of, 120
Developers, 32–33
Direct costs, 264
Discipline lead, 38
Documentation. *See also*
      Specifications
  adversariality in, 21
  for bidding, 124, 156, 158
  CM's role in, 146
  construction documents, 124–125
  contract documents, 124
  design concept approval, 77
  in design development phase, 80
  function of and necessity for
      contracts, 130–131
  land records, 51
  program, 68–70
  Project Manual, 123–124
  responsibilities for, 123
Document production phase, 85–121
  building sections—cross and
      longitudinal, 98–99
  challenge involved in, 109–111
  construction (contract)
      documents, 85–86
  detailing and details, 111–121
  door and window schedules,
      106–108
  drawing requirements, 90
  drawings by content, 87–90

exterior elevations, 96–98
  floor plans, 93–96
  foundation plan, 102–103
  framing plans—floors and roofs,
      103–104
  interrelation, cross-referencing,
      and coordination of, 108–109
  room finish schedule, 105–106
  schedules, 105
  site improvement (site, plot) plan,
      91–93
  size of, 109
  and specifications, 109
  wall sections and details, 100–101
  working (contract) drawings,
      86–87
Doors:
  on floor plans, 96
  framing for, 209
Door schedule, 106–108
Drawings:
  coordination of, 205
  defined, 264
  level of quality set by, 116
  need for specifications with, 21
  pairing specifications and, 86
  preliminary, 77
  relationship of specifications to,
      132–133
  shop, 179
Drawings by content, 87–90
Drawing details, 264. *See also*
      Details
Drawing requirements, 90
Dual services, 265

Earthwork, 174–175, 180–181
Easements, 53, 55, 265
EIFS, 202–203
Electrical system, 183, 205
Elevations, 96–98, 265
Empire State Building, 7, 24–25
Engineers:
  defined, 265
  professional, 36
  value, 144
Engineering, as one aspect of
      architecture, 12, 13
Erect, defined, 265
Erector, 265
Estimated cost to complete, 265
Estimated final cost, 265
Estimate of construction cost, 265
Estimating, 265
Estimators, 144–145
Ethics, 265

Excavation, 180–181
Expediters, 145
Exterior elevations, 96–98
Extras, 265

F. W. Dodge, Inc., 156
Fabricators, 265–266
Fast-track construction, 266
Feasibility phase, 266
Feasibility study, 50–51, 53, 57
Federal government agencies,
      249–250
Fee enhancement, 266
FI (field instruction), 266
Field-based CM field organization,
      267
Field construction manager, 266
Field instruction (FI), 266
Field management, 266
Field measure, 266
Field Order (FO), 266
Field Report, 266
Field schedule, 267
Field superintendent, 24
Field Work Order (FWO), 267
Final acceptance, 267
Final cleaning, 221–222
Final completion, 222, 228, 267
Final design phase, 267
Final inspection, 217–218, 223, 267
Final payment, 267
Financial and management control
      system, 267
Financial institutions, 33–34
Financial stakeholder, 267
Financiers, 33–34
Finishes, installation/application of,
      211–213
Finish Date, 267
Finished, defined, 267
Fire protection system, 183, 205
Fixed fee, 268
Fixed limit of construction costs,
      268
Fleet averaging, 268
Float, 268
Floors:
  framing plans, 103–104
  framing system installation,
      197–199
Floor plans, 93–96, 268
FO (Field Order), 266
Footings, 181, 183–186
Forepersons, 144
Foundation plan, 102–103
Foundation systems, 183–186

deep, 181, 182
excavation for, 180, 181
installation of, 182–185
shallow, 182
Framing, interior, 198, 207, 208
Framing plans—floors and roofs, 103–104
Framing systems, 187
bearing wall, 187, 193
cast-in-place concrete, 196–197
for larger/heavier buildings, 195
precast concrete, 197
roof and floor, 197–199
skeletal grids, 195–196
structural steel, 196
types of, 187
Friedman, Donald, 25
Fundamentals of Building Construction (Edward Allen), 172
Furnish, defined, 268
Furnishings, installation of, 212–214
FWO (Field Work Order), 267

Galileo, 72
GCs, *see* General contractors
General Condition items, 268
General Conditions of the Contract for Construction (AIA Document A201), 48, 128, 268
General contracting, 268
General contracting system, 269
General contractors (GCs), 141, 142
bids submitted by, 157
defined, 269
in design phase, 76
scheduling responsibility of, 178
General notes, 88
GMP-CM (guaranteed maximum price construction management), 269
Governing authorities, 237
Grading, 180
Guarantees, 227, 229, 269
Guaranteed maximum price construction management (GMP-CM), 269

Hard costs, 269
Hazard insurance, 269
Hunt, William Dudley, Jr., 15

IBC (International Building Code), 138
ICBO (International Conference of Building Officials), 138

IDP (Intern Development Program), 135
Improvements, 269
Indemnification clause, 269
Independent contractors, 269
Indicated, defined, 269
Indirect costs, 269
In-house resources, 270
Inner-city projects, 175–176
Inspections:
defined, 270
final, 217–218, 223
Inspection list, 270
Install, defined, 270
Installers, 154
Insurance companies, 33–34
Interior walls, construction of, 206–209
International Building Code (IBC), 138
International Conference of Building Officials (ICBO), 138
Intern Development Program (IDP), 135
Investigative survey, 51–55

Job captain, 38
Job clerks, 154
Job description, 270
Joint venture, 270
Journeymen, 148
Junior partners, 37

Kick-off meeting, 168–169

Labor and material payment bond, 270
Lambert Field (St. Louis, Missouri), 197
Land configuration, matching project to, 55–57
Land developer, 32–33
Land records, 51, 52
Landscape notes, 88
Land surveyor, 41
Lenders, 33–34
Lessees, 33
Lessors, 33
Letter of intent, 270
Lien, mechanic's or material, 270
Lien release, 270
Lien waiver, 270
Life-cycle cost, 270–271
Lightweight framing building envelopes, 185, 188–189
"Like-new" condition, 221, 271
Line survey, 51–55

Liquidated damages, 271
Load, 183, 271
Long-lead items, 271
Lots, 271
"Lowest and best bid," 166–167
Lump sum agreements, 271
Lump sum bids, 271

Management, blending of construction, design, and, 17–19
Management information and control system, 271
Manufacturers, shop drawings for, 179
Manufacturer's instructions, 271
Masonry building envelopes, 185, 186, 202–203
MasterFormat, 125, 126
Master schedule, 271
Materials:
for building skin, 201–202
initiating purchase of, 178–180
matching finishes to, 212
Mechanical systems:
connecting branch systems to equipment, 209–211
installation of, 204–207
Meeting attendance form, 271
Meeting notes, 272
"Mile High" Illinois Tower, 13
Milestone schedule, 272
Millwork, 272
Mobilization, 174–177
on-site, 174–176
for renovations, 176–177
Mortgage companies, 33–34
Multiple bidding, 272
Multiple contracting, 272

National Architectural Accrediting Board (NAAB), 135
National Council of Architectural Registration Boards (NCARB), 135
Natural gas system, 183
Navigational lock projects, 175
NCARB (National Council of Architectural Registration Boards), 135
New, defined, 272
Nonconforming, 272
Notes (on drawings), 88
Notice of Award, 168, 272
Notice to Proceed, 168, 178, 272
Numbering drawings, 89

Occupancy, 226–227
   Certificate of, 222–223, 257
   partial, 227
   throughout project, 227
Occupancy phase, 272
Occupancy schedule, 272
Occupants, 33
Olin's Construction (H. Leslie
      Simmons), 171
On-site operations:
   initial, 173–174
   mobilization and staging, 174–176
On-site supervision, 273
Open bids, 164, 273
Ouellette, Dan, 109–120
Owners, 32. *See also* Clients
   agents of, 145
   defined, 273
   design approval by, 76–77
   in hiring process, 41–45
   legal responsibilities of, 130
   PDS decisions by, 57–58
   in progression of project, 23
   project inception/initiation by,
      30–31, 34–35
   relationship with design
      professional, 11, 46–50
   as responsible for code
      compliance, 140
   turning building over to, 225
Owner-Architect/Engineer
      Agreement/Contract, 46, 47,
      273
Owner-builder, 273
Owner-CM agreement, 273
Owner-construction agreement, 273
Owner-design professional
      relationships, 46–50
Owner's representative, 34

Panel-walls, 203
Paper architecture, 1
Partial occupancy, 227
Partial use by owner (no occupancy),
      220–221
Partitions, interior, 206–209
Partners, 37
PDS, *see* Project delivery system
Pena, William, 65
Perfection of building, 114–116
Performance and payment bond,
      273
Performance bond, 273
Performance specifications, 273
Permits:
   building, 32, 256

defined, 273
   requirements for, 68
PERT, defined, 273
PERT schedule, 273
Phased bidding, 273
Phased construction, 273
Plans:
   defined, 273–274
   floor, 93–96
   foundation, 102–103
   framing—floors and roofs, 103–104
   site improvement, 54, 62, 91–93,
      280
Plan notes, 88
Plan reviewer (checker), 274
Plan rooms, 156
Plan submittal, 274
Plat, 274
Plot, 62, 274. *See also* Site
      improvement plan
Plumbing, 205
POE, *see* Postoccupancy evaluation
Postbid shopping, 274
Postoccupancy, 229–236
   call-backs, 229
   postoccupancy evaluation,
      230–236
Postoccupancy evaluation (POE),
      230–236
   areas of concern in, 230, 235
   form for, 231–235
   purpose of, 236
Postsubstantial completion, 225–227
Prebid meeting, 157
Prebid shopping, 274
Precast concrete:
   building envelope systems, 187,
      192
   framing systems, 197
Preconstruction meeting, 168–169,
      274
Preconstruction phase, 274
Preconstruction planning, 274
Predecessor, 274
Predesign phase, 65–67, 274
Preliminary design, conversion of,
      84–85
Preliminary design phase, 73–75, 274
Preliminary drawings, 275
Preliminary lien notice, 275
Prequalification:
   defined, 275
   for private project bids, 164
Prime contract, 275
Prime contractor, 275
Principals, 36–37

Private sector:
   bidding process in, 164
   defined, 275
   receipt of bids in, 158
Problem-seeking, 65, 66
Process piping, 205
Procurement, 178–180
Product data, 275
Product data sheets, 179–180
Professional engineers, 36, 275
Professionalism, 275
Professional liability insurance, 275
Professional services, 275
Program, 65–70
   defined, 276
   importance of document, 68–70
   needs met by, 67–68
   predesign phase, 65–67
   in preliminary design, 74–75
Program management, 276
Program schedule, 276
Program team, 276
Progression, 22–28
   defined, 22
   flexibility in, 27–28
   phases of, 23–24
   and planning out of work tasks,
      24–25
   understanding, 25–27
Progress meetings, 177–178, 276
Progress payment, 276
Progress schedule, 276
Project, defined, 276
Project architect (engineer), 38
Project budget, 276
Project costs:
   defined, 276
   programming to reduce, 68
   and specifications, 129–130
   for surveys, 60
   for wooded sites, 56
Project delivery system (PDS), 57–59,
      276
Project development phase, 5
Project directory, 276–277
Project inception/initiation, 29–35
   owner as impetus for, 30–31, 34–35
   and people involved in projects,
      32–34, 36–41
   reasons for, 29–30
Project managers, 143, 277
Project manuals, 123–125
   bid forms in, 162
   contents of, 127
   defined, 277
   specifications in, 135

Project meeting, 277
Project representative, 40–41, 277
Project schedule, 171, 172, 178
Project site, 277. *See also* Site
Project specifications, *see*
    Specifications
Project team, 277
Proposal, 277
Proposal Form, 277
Public sector:
    bidding process in, 163–164
    defined, 277
    "lowest and best bid" for, 166–167
    receipt of bids in, 158
Punch list, 217, 219–220
    defined, 277–278
    resolving items, 221–222
Pure CM, 278

QA (quality assurance), 278
QC (Quality Control), 278
Qualified, defined, 278
Quality:
    and attention to details/detailing,
        114–116
    attitude toward, 115
    defined, 278
    of Frank Lloyd Wright's work, 117
Quality assurance (QA), 278
Quality Control (QC), 278
Quality Engineering, 278
Quotes, 278

Rand, J. Patrick, 14
Raw (undeveloped) site, 172–173
Record drawings, 278
Reference standards, 237
Registered Land Certificate, 60
Regulatory agencies, 138, 139
Reimbursable expenses (or costs),
    278
Release of lien, 278
Renovations, mobilizing for, 176–177
Renters, 33
Resident architect, 278
Respect, for work of others, 20–21
RFI, 279
RFP, 279
Rhetorical architecture, 2
Roll-out, 279
Roofs/roof systems:
    on exterior elevations, 97
    framing plans, 103–104
    framing system installation,
        197–199
    installation of, 193–195, 204

Room finish schedule, 105–106
Rough grading, 180

Safety Report, 279
Samples, 279
SBCCI (Southern Building Code
    Congress International), 138
Schedules, 105
    construction (project), 171, 172,
        178, 259
    defined, 279
    door, 106–108
    room finish, 105–106
    window, 106–108
Scheduling techniques, 178
Schematics, 279
Schematic design phase, 73–75, 279
Scheme, 279
Science, as one aspect of
    architecture, 12, 13
Scope of work (SOW), 279
Seal laws, 43
Sections:
    cross and longitudinal, 96, 98–99
    wall, 100–101
Security systems, 183, 205
"Selling Stone Products to
    Architects" (Dan Ouellette),
    109–120
Set, 279
Setbacks, 53, 280
Sewer system, 183
Shop drawings:
    defined, 280
    production of, 179
Signature architects, 6
Simmons, H. Leslie, 171
Site:
    defined, 280
    initial layout for, 173
    raw (undeveloped), 172–173
    topographical survey of, 59–63
Site-cast concrete, 280. *See also* Cast-
    in-place concrete
Site conditions, 55, 56
    defined, 280
    subsurface investigation, 77–80
    surveying, 52–53
Site-constructed, defined, 280
Site improvement (site, plot) plan,
    54, 62, 91–93, 280
Site secretaries, 154
Site selection, 50–55
Site work, 280
Skeletal grids, 195–196
Slab-on-grade, 280

Soft costs, 280
Soil borings, 78–79
Soil conditions, subsurface, 77–80
Sole proprietors, 37–38
Southern Building Code Congress
    International (SBCCI), 138
SOW (scope of work), 279
Special Conditions, 280
Special consultants, 281
Specialties, installation of, 212–214
Specifications, 125–138
    concept, 127
    Construction Specifications
        Institute, 137
    context, 126–127
    as contracts, 130–131
    defined, 133, 281
    in design concept, 77
    evolution of, 136
    function of, 127–128
    and impact of project cost,
        129–130
    legal function of, 128, 135–136
    need for, 21, 109
    production of, 85
    and relationships among contract
        documents, 132–136
Specifications manual, 86
Specifications writers, 39–40, 50,
    135
Stage bidding, 273
Staging, on-site, 174–176
Standards:
    reference, 237
    for working drawings, 87–90
Standards-generating organizations,
    237
Standards of professional practice,
    281
Standard details, 281
Standard dimension, 281
Starchitects, 6
Start-up, 281
Static decisions, 281
Statute of limitations, 281
Steam system, 183
Steel lumber, 199
Stipulated Sum Agreement, 281
Structural framing with subsystem
    building envelopes, 187,
    190–191
Structural steel framing systems, 196
Structural system erection, *see*
    Superstructure erection
Study and report phase, 281
Subcontracts, 281

Subcontractors, 142, 147
defined, 282
GC's work with, 142
list of, provided with bid, 157
in progression of project, 23
sub-bids from, 165–166
Subcontractor bond, 282
Sublet, 282
Submittals, 282
Substantial Completion, 217–218
defined, 282
impact of, 220–221
Substantial completion date, 282
Substitution, 282
Substructure system installation,
182–186
Sub-subcontractors, 282
Subsurface investigation, 77–80
Superintendent, 143–144, 282
Superstructure (structural system)
erection, 185–197
bearing wall systems, 187, 193
framing systems, 187, 193,
195–196
roof structure installation,
193–195
types of systems, 185–192
Supervision, 282
Supplemental Conditions, 282
Surety/surety company, 283
Surveys, 51–55
checklist for, 61
defined, 283
topographical, 59–63
Surveyor, 41
Swiss Re building (London), 8
Systems, initiating purchases of,
178–180

Take-off, 165, 283
Teams:
construction, 142
defined, 283
design, 45–46
as fundamental concept, 14–16
as necessary construction concept,
19–20
in programming, 66
respect for work of others on,
20–21
selection of, 41
site selection, 50
of trade workers, 153
Technical inspection, 283
Technical review, 283

Technical specifications:
defined, 283
in Project Manual, 123–124
Technicians, 153–154
Technology, as one aspect of
architecture, 12, 13
Telephone system, 183
Temporary construction facilities:
on-site, 173, 175
for renovations, 177
Tenant improvements (TIs), 284
Tenant's rentable square feet, 283
Tenant's usable square feet, 283
Tenure, 283
Testing agency, 284
Tilt-up construction, 284
"Time is of the essence," 284
Timely completion, 284
Time of completion, 284
TIs (tenant improvements), 284
T&M, 283
Topographical survey, 51, 59–63
Trade associations, 172, 237
Trade contractors, 284
Tradespersons, 147–155
Trade workers:
flawed detailing and work of,
118
motivation for quality from, 115
providing useful data for, 120
types of, 147–155
Transit, 284
Transmittal, 284–285
Travel time, 285
Trusses, 285

Underground utilities installation,
183
Uniform systems, 285
Unions, 148, 149
Unit price contracts, 285
Up-front services, 285
Users, 33
Utilitarian architecture, 3
Utilities, 55
excavation for, 180
extension of lines/systems, 199
underground, installation of, 183

Vacuum systems, 205
Value engineering, 285
Value engineers, 144
Value management, 285
Value managers, 285
Vendors, 285

Verbal quotations, 285
Virtual architecture, 2–3

Walls:
on exterior elevations, 97
on floor plans, 95
interior, construction of, 206–209
Wall sections and details, 100–101
Warranties, 227, 229, 285
Warranty phase, 286
Water system, 183
Weisbach, Gerald G., 14
White, Edward T., 65
Willis, Carol, 25
Windows, on floor plans, 96
Window schedule, 106–108
Window-walls, 203
WO (work order), 286
Work:
checking, 216
defined, 286
planning tasks of, 24–25
Work(ing) day, 286
Workers, 147. *See also* Trade workers
Working (contract) drawings, 85–87
defined, 286
details on, 112
numbering, 89
standards for, 87–90
Work letter, 286
Work order (WO), 286
Work-scope description, 286
World Trade Center towers, 13, 14
Wrap up, close out phase, 215–223
certification for occupancy
through final payment,
222–223
finale, 221–222
impact of substantial completion,
220–221
partial use by owner (no
occupancy), 220–221
punch list, 217, 219–220
resolving punch list items; final
cleaning, 221–222
substantial completion and final
inspection, 217–218
Wright, Frank Lloyd, 13, 117, 118

XCM, 286

Yard, 286

Zoning, 53, 287
Zoning certificate, 287